THE LONG SHADOW

THE LONG SHADOW

FAMILY BACKGROUND, DISADVANTAGED URBAN YOUTH, AND THE TRANSITION TO ADULTHOOD

KARL ALEXANDER, DORIS ENTWISLE,
AND LINDA OLSON

A Volume in the American Sociological Association's
Rose Series in Sociology

Russell Sage Foundation • New York

Library of Congress Cataloging-in-Publication Data

Alexander, Karl L.
  The long shadow : family background, disadvantaged urban youth, and the transition to adulthood / Karl Alexander, Doris Entwisle, and Linda Olson.
    pages cm. — (American Sociological Association's Rose series in sociology)
  Includes bibliographical references and index.
  ISBN 978-0-87154-033-1 (pbk. : alk. paper) — ISBN 978-1-61044-823-9 (ebook)
  1. Youth with social disabilities—Maryland—Baltimore. 2. Youth with social disabilities—Education—Maryland—Baltimore. 3. Poor youth—Maryland—Baltimore—Social conditions. 4. Poor families—Social aspects—Maryland—Baltimore. I. Entwisle, Doris R. II. Olson, Linda Steffel. III. Title.
  HV1437.B35A44 2014
  362.740835'097526—dc23

2013041429

The paper used in this publication meets the minimum requirements of American National Standard for Information Sciences—Permanence of Paper for Printed Library Materials. ANSI Z39.48-1992.

Text design by Suzanne Nichols.

RUSSELL SAGE FOUNDATION
112 East 64th Street, New York, New York 10065
10 9 8 7 6 5 4 3 2 1

The Russell Sage Foundation

The Russell Sage Foundation, one of the oldest of America's general purpose foundations, was established in 1907 by Mrs. Margaret Olivia Sage for
"the improvement of social and living conditions in the United States." The
Foundation seeks to fulfill this mandate by fostering the development and dissemination of knowledge about the country's political, social, and economic
problems. While the Foundation endeavors to assure the accuracy and objectiv-
ity of each book it publishes, the conclusions and interpretations in Russell Sage
Foundation publications are those of the authors and not of the Foundation,
its Trustees, or its staff. Publication by Russell Sage, therefore, does not imply
Foundation endorsement.

Previous Volumes
in the Series

American Memories: Atrocities and the Law
Joachim J. Savelsberg and Ryan D. King

America's Newcomers and the Dynamics of Diversity
Frank D. Bean and Gillian Stevens

Beyond the Boycott: Labor Rights, Human Rights,
and Transnational Activism
Gay W. Seidman

Beyond College For All: Career Paths for the Forgotten Half
James E. Rosenbaum

Changing Rhythms of the American Family
Suzanne M. Bianchi, John Robinson, and Melissa Milkie

Counted Out: Same-Sex Relations and Americans' Definitions of Family
Brian Powell, Lala Carr Steelman, Catherine Bolzendahl,
and Claudi Giest

Divergent Social Worlds: Neighborhood Crime and the Racial-Spatial Divide
Ruth D. Peterson and Lauren J. Krivo

Egalitarian Capitalism: Jobs, Incomes, and Growth in Affluent Countries
Lane Kenworthy

Ethnic Origins: History, Politics, Culture, and the Adaptation of Cambodian
and Hmong Refugees in Four American Cities
Jeremy Hein

Family Consequences of Children's Disabilities
Denis Hogan

Good Jobs, Bad Jobs: The Rise of Polarized and Precarious
Employment Systems in the United States, 1970s to 2000s
Arne L. Kalleberg

Making Hate a Crime: From Social Movement to Law Enforcement
Valerie Jenness and Ryken Grattet

Market Friendly or Family Friendly? The State and Gender Inequality
in Old Age
Madonna Harrington Meyer and Pamela Herd

Nurturing Dads: Social Initiatives for Contemporary Fatherhood
William Marsiglio and Kevin Roy

*Passing the Torch: Does Higher Education for the Disadvantaged
Pay Off Across the Generations?*
Paul Attewell and David Lavin

Pension Puzzles: Social Security and the Great Debate
Melissa Hardy and Lawrence Hazelrigg

*Social Movements in the World-System: The Politics of Crisis
and Transformation*
Dawn Wiest and Jackie Smith

*They Say Cut Back, We Say Fight Back! Welfare Activism In an Era
of Retrenchment*
Ellen Reese

Trust in Schools: A Core Resource for Improvement
Anthony S. Bryk and Barbara Schneider

Forthcoming Titles

*Embedded Dependency: Minority Set-Asides, Black Entrepreneurs,
and the White Construction Monopoly*
Deirdre Royster

Family Relationships Across the Generations
Judith A. Seltzer and Suzanne M. Bianchi

Global Order and the Historical Structures of Daral-Islam
Mohammed A. Bamyeh

Interracial Romance and Friendship in Adolescence and Adulthood
Grace Kao, Kara Joyner, and Kelly Stamper Balistreri

The Logic of Terrorism: A Comparative Study
Jeff Goodwin

A Pound of Flesh: Criminal Debt as a Permanent Punishment for Poor People
Alexes Harris

*Urbanization's Changing Nature: Industrial Hazards, Systemic Risk,
and the Remaking of American Cities*
Scott Frickel and James Elliott

The Rose Series in Sociology

THE AMERICAN Sociological Association's Rose Series in Sociology publishes books that integrate knowledge and address controversies from a sociological perspective. Books in the Rose Series are at the forefront of sociological knowledge. They are lively and often involve timely and fundamental issues on significant social concerns. The series is intended for broad dissemination throughout sociology, across social science and other professional communities, and to policy audiences. The series was established in 1967 by a bequest to ASA from Arnold and Caroline Rose to support innovations in scholarly publishing.

LEE CLARKE
JUDITH GERSON
LAUREN KRIVO
PAUL MCLEAN
PATRICIA ROOS

EDITORS

In Memoriam

Our dear friend and collaborator of more than thirty years, Doris Entwisle, passed away while *The Long Shadow* was in final production. Doris inspired us with her intellect and drew us to her with her warmth and compassion. She was not one to dwell on misfortune, at least not her own—Doris was remarkably strong. For that reason, we use this dedication to celebrate her life, not mourn her passing. Doris left us knowing the volume was complete; it brought a smile to her face.

Contents

List of Illustrations xii

About the Authors xiv

Preface xv

Acknowledgments xix

CHAPTER 1 *The Long Shadow* and Urban Disadvantage 1

CHAPTER 2 The Baltimore Backdrop 21

CHAPTER 3 Family Disadvantage 32

CHAPTER 4 Neighborhood and School 50

CHAPTER 5 Transitioning to Adulthood 75

CHAPTER 6 Socioeconomic Destinations 91

CHAPTER 7 Origins to Destinations Across Generations 121

CHAPTER 8 Stratification by Race and Gender 157

CHAPTER 9 Life-Course Perspective of Urban Disadvantage 173

Appendix A 189

Appendix B 195

Notes 213

References 233

Index 257

= List of Illustrations =

Box 3.1	Neighborhoods Apart: Natural and Man-Made Boundaries	41
Box 3.2	White Working-Class Family Support	44
Box 4.1	Loss of Community: Social Capital in Baltimore's Poor Black Communities	64
Box 5.1	Transitioning to Adulthood the Old-Fashioned Way	80
Box 5.2	Done All, the Back Story	82
Box 6.1	Three Community College Enrollment Spells Without a Degree	102
Box 8.1	Making It in the New Economy the Old-Fashioned Way: Two Tales	164
Figure 7.1	Origins to Destinations in Life-Course Perspective	129
Figure 7.2	Problem Behaviors in Adulthood	151
Photo 2.1	Bethlehem Steel Plant at Sparrows Point	22
Photo 2.2	Baltimore's Downtown Inner Harbor	25
Photo 2.3	Classic Baltimore Working-Class Row Homes	27
Photo 2.4	Distressed Row Homes	27
Table 1.1	The Corner in 2000 Census Data	5
Table 1.2	The Corner in 1980 Census Data	8
Table 3.1	Family Socioeconomics and Demographics of Birth Families	35
Table 4.1	Neighborhood Conditions, Circa 1980	54
Table 4.2	Crime Exposure, Neighborhood Rates/100,000, 1980–1982 Averaged	57
Table 4.3	Neighborhood Quality Through Resident Surveys, 1980	60
Table 4.4	Racial and Income Composition of Baltimore Elementary Schools, 1982	66
Table 4.5	Academic Profile for the Schools	70

Table 4.6	School Resources: Staffing and Infrastructure for the Schools	72
Table 5.1	Transitioning to Adulthood, Milestones Passed	78
Table 5.2	Milestones to Adulthood: High-Prevalence Configurations	78
Table 5.3	Women's Priorities Across Social Lines	87
Table 6.1	Percent Months Employed and Percent Months in School	93
Table 6.2	Highest Levels of Educational Enrollment and Completion at Age Twenty-Eight	97
Table 6.3	Most Recent Full-Time Job	105
Table 6.4	Representative Occupations at Age Twenty-Eight	107
Table 6.5	Schooling, Earnings, and Occupational Status	108
Table 6.6	Women's Personal and Family Earnings	113
Table 6.7	Employment History and Marital-Partnership Status	115
Table 6.8	SES Destinations: Lower, Middle, and Higher, by Race-Gender	117
Table 7.1	Intergenerational Mobility	124
Table 7.2	Origins to Destinations: Individual Socioeconomic Status (Standardized Regression Coefficients)	134
Table 7.3	Origins to Destinations: Family Socioeconomic Status (Standardized Regression Coefficients)	137
Table 7.4	Origins to Destinations: Years of Education (Standardized Regression Coefficients)	138
Table 7.5	Origins to Destinations: Occupational Status (Standardized Regression Coefficients)	139
Table 7.6	Origins to Destinations: Individual Earnings (Standardized Regression Coefficients)	140
Table 7.7	Origins to Destinations: Family Earnings (Standardized Regression Coefficients)	141
Table 8.1	Earnings, Personal and Family (Standardized Regression Coefficients)	159
Table 8.2	Working-Class Families and Social Capital: Help Finding Work at Age Twenty-Two	162
Table 8.3	Vocational Development of Noncollege Men	163
Table 9.1	Reflections on Life's Trajectory	174
Table 9.2	Occupational Status and Earnings	180
Table B.1	Attrition Analysis	198
Table B.2	Panel Attrition	201
Table B.3	Years of Education Completed	204

About the Authors

Karl Alexander is John Dewey Professor and chair of the Department of Sociology at the Johns Hopkins University.

Doris Entwisle was Research Professor of Sociology at the Johns Hopkins University.

Linda Olson is an associate research scientist with the Baltimore Education Research Consortium (BERC) and the Center for Social Organization of Schools at the Johns Hopkins University.

═ Preface ═

T HE PURPOSE of this book is to improve our understanding of how social contexts—especially those of family, neighborhood, and school—bear on the long-term well-being of disadvantaged urban youth. Well-being, for our purposes, is captured not only in objective measures such as educational level, occupation, earnings, family formation, and avoidance of problem behaviors (substance use, brushes with the law), but also in self-perceptions of well-being and life satisfaction. In counterpoint to the more typical view of urban disadvantage that dwells on misfortune and failure, we give equal attention to the means by which urban youth advance their status and improve their life experience.

To accomplish this goal we draw heavily on the life experience of the Baltimore Beginning School Study Youth Panel (BSSYP, or Youth Panel), a probability sample of just under eight hundred urban youth who began school in Baltimore, Maryland, in 1982 and came into maturity during the latter decades of the twentieth century and the first decade of the twenty-first. Through repeated surveys of them, their parents, and their teachers, we monitored the group's progress beginning in first grade and continuing through age twenty-eight or twenty-nine, watching on as they forged lives for themselves during a time and in a place that promised to pose great challenge for many. *The Long Shadow* is about the Youth Panel's social mobility, from origins to destinations, and focuses on those who began life in families of low socioeconomic standing—half the panel.

The Back Story

In 1982, when we launched this project, few sociological studies addressed the experience of children below high school age or linked early experience to later life outcomes. However, we were mindful of Glen Elder's (1974) research on children of the Great Depression and Sheppard Kellam and colleagues' (1975) Chicago-based Woodlawn project with first

graders. These established the life-long importance of children's formative experience in the social contexts that frame their development.

What motivated the study initially was our desire to understand the
repercussions of children's adjustment to formal schooling—the first
grade transition from home child to school child. At the time, the period
of early schooling had been virtually unexplored from a sociological perspective and though developmental psychologists were studying young
children, they had little to say about social context beyond that provided
by mothers. Socioeconomic status (SES) as a construct in developmental models was still over a decade away. Additionally, the search for
continuities in attitudes and behaviors, or from childhood to adulthood,
proved frustrating because the technology for penetrating large data sets
was not up to the task.

Sociologists were attentive to social context, but among older youth.
Most research on stratification processes across generations took high
schoolers as the starting point, mainly males, as in the line of research
on status attainment introduced by William Sewell and his colleagues
(Sewell, Haller, and Portes 1969; Sewell, Haller, and Ohlendorf 1970).
As for data sources, national longitudinal studies focused on chil-
dren's early schooling were still a decade or more off, for example, the
ECLS-K:1999 and ECLS-K:2011 projects (National Center for Education
Statistics 1999, 2011).

It was in this general climate that the Youth Panel was launched
with what was, in those days, a large probability sample. The intent
was to look closely at the course of development among a mostly disadvantaged panel of children, black and white, at the point of school
entry. The purpose was to observe many outcomes—not just failures
and problem behaviors, but evidence of satisfactory school performance
and personal well-being. The family's economic status and parents' SES
as well as parents' expectations and attitudes toward their children from
early in first grade were included. Children's status was mapped repeat-
edly over short intervals. Schools were conceptualized as complex social
structures that could contribute to children's development in many ways
besides cognitive growth. Retention and other administrative groupings
of children were analyzed as potential causes of disorderly or delayed
development.

The project continued almost a quarter century, monitoring the sample's life progress up to a decade after high school. *The Long Shadow*
takes advantage of the long duration and broad sweep of the project's
fieldwork to examine the unfolding script of the children's lives starting
at age six, through elementary school, middle school, and high school,
and continuing far into their third decade. It identifies resources that
matter for adult well-being, as well as how they overlap and cumulate

across the life course. We see both consistency and change. Some patterns evident early in life persist, but others are replaced or modified, always against the changing backdrop of conditions in Baltimore—deindustrialization, population loss, and, for many, impoverishment.

Some of the findings reported in this volume will be familiar, but novel details also appear. Some of the latter involve the situation of poor whites in the sample, and by implication in other places like Baltimore. They are a group seldom visible in research on the urban disadvantaged, but the contrast between their life experience and that of African Americans is striking. Status attainment through school (which we probe in detail) helps perpetuate the advantage of higher-SES youth over lower, but it is access to good paying work that perpetuates the privilege of working-class white men over working-class black men. By partnering with these men, white working-class women share in that privilege. African Americans who begin life in similar circumstances as their white counterparts realize neither advantage—they lack access to well-paid jobs and, as young adults, black women are much more likely to be without husbands and partners, which sets them back financially.

Acknowledgments

I N THE FALL of 1982, we set out with graduate students and a small staff recruited for a project intended to last three years but that stretched over many. Children and their parents were interviewed individually, teachers responded to self-administered questionnaires, and school record data were transcribed by hand on-site until we purchased a portable photocopier to carry from school to school (when school system records later were centralized and computerized, we began receiving school record data electronically).

Over the history of the study, project staffing expanded and contracted on an as-needed basis in what amounted to an in-house survey research center. We are grateful to the many students, employees, interns, and core staff who helped with interviewing, coding, data entry, tracking, project management, and IT. The tally includes forty-two graduate students, eighty-eight Johns Hopkins University undergraduates, and a dozen student interns from other schools. It is impractical to acknowledge each personally; instead, as a gesture of our gratitude, a sampling of their names appear as pseudonyms throughout this volume.

Some names do require mention though. Very special thanks are due to Sona Armenian (data research assistant), Pat Gucer (project manager), Gail Fennessey (data manager), Heidi Slagle (administrative secretary), Anna Stoll (research project coordinator), Jane Sundius (data analyst), Mary Ann Zeller (project secretary), and Gloria Zepp (project secretary), also Binnie Bailey, Mary Ann Zeller (in a different capacity), and Terri Thomas, administrative managers for the Department of Sociology. Joanne Fennessey deserves special mention. Jo was with the project almost two decades, providing service in a variety of capacities. She maintained the project's network of computers, managed our ever expanding database, prepared data and documentation for deposit with Harvard University's Murray Research Center (where all Youth Panel data are available for secondary analysis), helped program the computerized administration of our age twenty-eight Mature Adult Survey, and, for the *The Long Shadow* specifically, interrogated a set of qualitative interviews for the quotes and biographical sketches sprinkled throughout this volume. Tami Hildebrant, administrative secretary and Jo's daughter, also deserves special mention. Tami did the heavy lifting involved in preparing this manuscript.

We also are indebted to many in the Baltimore City schools for their enthusiastic cooperation, including the superintendent of research, the 130 or so principals who welcomed us into their schools, and every teacher with a student in the study (at least five hundred). They tolerated our innumerable interruptions and welcomed our presence. The BSSYP could not have been done without their help.

The same holds for the children of the Youth Panel and their parents. Working with them has been a great privilege. They reaped no great personal rewards from their participation, yet were extraordinarily generous in revealing themselves to us, and we are indebted to them. In first grade, we sat on little chairs at little tables to solicit the children's thinking about school; twenty-five years later, many had little ones of their own. Sadly, some who were with us at the journey's start are with us no longer, victims of urban disadvantage at its worst. *The Long Shadow* looms large.

Many struggled in ways documented in these pages, while others overcame obstacles to achieve a fulfilling quality of life—to be happy, to be alive, to establish solid families, and to attain a comfortable standard of living even without the benefit of a college degree. We applaud their successes and are saddened by their setbacks. The BSSYP is not an intervention project—we have done little to help those who have struggled. Our responsibility, rather, is to make good use of the opportunity they have afforded us. We hope *The Long Shadow*, which we dedicate to them, lives up to that obligation.

Awards from the National Institute for Child Health and Development (NICHD) and the Foundation for Child Development launched the BSSYP and were followed by a succession of overlapping three- to five-year grants from the Department of Education's Office for Educational Research and Improvement, continuing support from the NICHD, the National Institute for Mental Health, and three funders who stood with us for a decade or more, an uncommon public–private partnership: the Sociology Program of the National Science Foundation (Pat White), the Spencer Foundation (John Rury and Lauren Young), and the William T. Grant Foundation (Bob Granger and Ed Seidman). The names in parentheses are not anonymous program officers. We count ourselves fortunate to have found our way to such strong advocates who shared our sense of the value of the enterprise and trusted in us to see it through at a high level.

Thanks are also due to our many collaborators and colleagues for their contributions to the project over the years and to this volume. Within the BSSYP, they include Aaron Pallas, Doris (Cadigan) Lefkowitz, Karen Ross, Robert Bozick, Jane Sundius, Jennifer Johnson, Susan Dauber,

Maxine Thompson, Sam Bedinger, Rebecca Herman, Nader Kabbani, Carrie Horsey, Peter Weinstein, and Kerri Kerr. As regards *The Long Shadow,* we thank the seminar participants at the Russell Sage Foundation and the Johns Hopkins University Department of Sociology who heard us present an early version of *The Long Shadow.* That first effort is barely recognizable in this volume thanks to their good counsel. Andy Cherlin, Dee Royster, and Barbara Entwisle deserve special commendation for helping inform the revisions.

Last, but hardly least, we thank Suzanne Nichols, director of Publications at the Russell Sage Foundation, and the editorial committees of the American Sociological Association's Rose Series in Sociology—first at Stony Brook and more recently at Rutgers—for their patience and support over the years it took to see this project through to completion. A special word of appreciation is due to Pat Roos of the Rutgers team for her close reading of what we thought was our final submission. She turned it around quickly and identified numerous problems, mostly small but all useful and several quite important.

Chapter 1

The Long Shadow and Urban Disadvantage

T HIS VOLUME is an account of the developmental foundation that connects children's socioeconomic well-being as young adults to family conditions growing up. It is set in Baltimore, Maryland, during the last two decades of the twentieth century into the first decade of the twenty-first, years that were not kind to the deindustrializing cities of the East Coast and Midwest. As these cities suffered economic decline, their residents suffered economic hardship.

For children, family is the launching pad and the focus of this volume. A family's resources and the doors they open cast a long shadow over children's life trajectories—personal and academic at the start, and extending later to prospects for achieving success in adulthood. This view is at odds with the popular ethos that we are makers of our own fortune. Such self-serving mythology is not easily shaken, but according to the Nobel Laureate economist Joseph Stiglitz ("Equal Opportunity, Our National Myth," *New York Times Opinionator*, February 16, 2013), the rhetoric of equal opportunity rests on particularly shaky grounds: "the life prospects of an American is more dependent on the income and education of his parents than in almost any other advanced industrial country."

That long shadow is the organizing theme of this book and is focused on those we call the urban disadvantaged: Baltimore's children whose parents rank low by conventional markers of socioeconomic standing (level of education, occupation, and income). In classic sociological terms, it is an inquiry into intergenerational social mobility, origins to destination, but here embedded in a life-course developmental framework that extends from early childhood into young adulthood.

Baltimore as Context

Baltimore's decades-long economic decline was well under way in the early 1980s when the children at issue in this volume set out on their journey through the city's public schools. Beginning in 1970, and continuing

1

through the five years they were in elementary school (1982–1987), half the city's jobs in primary metals, shipbuilding repair, and transportation assembly disappeared (Levine 1987, 107). The historic core of Baltimore's industrial might had relocated offshore, to the region's rapidly expanding suburbs and low-wage parts of the country, or simply faded away in favor of the new postindustrial economy. This new economy provides lucrative careers for workers in high-end technology and the so-called FIRE industries—finance, insurance, and real estate—but mainly low-wage, low-benefit jobs for those in the expanding service sector (for example, Olson 1997). Ranked eighty-seventh among the nation's hundred largest cities in median income, by 2000 Baltimore had become a poor city in the country's wealthiest state (Walters and Miserendino 2008, 3).

Poor, yes, but not uniformly so. Baltimore in fact had become, and is today, "two cities—a city of developers, suburban professionals, and 'back-to-the-city' gentry . . . and a city of impoverished blacks and displaced manufacturing workers, who continue to suffer from shrinking economic opportunities, declining public services, and neighborhood distress" (Levine 1987, 103). This book is about the children of the second Baltimore, the one largely untouched by the much-touted renaissance redevelopment of the city's Inner Harbor port area away from shipping and manufacturing in favor of tourism and white-collar employment (Levine 1987; Ann LoLordo, "A Smaller, Poorer City in the Future," *Baltimore Sun,* January 18, 1987, p. 1E). They are the urban disadvantaged, as explained in the sections that follow.

The Urban Disadvantaged: Who Are They, Who Are They Not?

Who are these children? Disadvantaged families live in the poorest parts of the city. Often these are areas of concentrated poverty, where 20 percent, 40 percent, or more of the residents are poor or jobless or both. In the worst of these, when children leave home they find themselves in the midst of poverty, crime, and urban decay, and see boarded-up houses and empty businesses lining their streets. Consider Mae's (a pseudonym) account of the West Baltimore neighborhood—low income, African American—where she grew up:

> I was living . . . near like the Pratt Street area, Pratt and Baltimore Street, in between. It was bad, it was real bad. Drug, very hard drug area. Actually, I seen, like, right in my street where I lived at, I seen somebody die there. . . . That's how it was for me, you know.

Middle-class children might catch a glimpse of this world on the way downtown for a ballgame or to visit a museum, but it is at a far remove, in kind if not distance, from what they experience when out and about. Inviting playgrounds and parks dot their world, with ample green space and the latest equipment, and the daily rhythm to life has people doing ordinary things—going off to work in the morning, or out to shop, or into the yard to garden.

But the ordinary in one setting can be quite extraordinary in another. Adults are visible throughout the day in high-poverty neighborhoods too, but often just hanging out, sometimes sipping from bottles in brown paper bags. Gangs, public drug-dealing, and prostitution can make the playgrounds not all that inviting. Often they are covered with concrete, not grass, with broken bottles and used needles strewn about. William Julius Wilson (1978) tells us that life in low-income urban America was not always this way, but the exodus of jobs, the middle class (whites initially, later followed by African Americans), and stabilizing institutions has left many of them bereft of employment opportunities and good role models for children.

Despite a large scholarly literature on these "ghetto poor," to use Wilson's now preferred characterization (2006), in the popular mind they are still the urban underclass, pejorative connotations and all. Consider Myron Magnet's (1987) characterization from around the time at issue: "What primarily defines them is not so much their poverty or race as their behavior—their chronic lawlessness, drug use, out-of-wedlock births, non-work, welfare dependency and school failure. 'Underclass' describes a state of mind and a way of life."[1]

We think we know who these people are: angry black men caught up in the swirl of crime and drugs and poorly educated young black women with babies out of wedlock, images that dominate media portrayals of communities like Mae's. The area of West Baltimore where Mae grew up achieved unwelcome notoriety in the book *The Corner* (Simon and Burns 1997) and then, in 2000, a made-for-television movie based on it.[2] A look at the urban underclass as portrayed in *The Corner* will prove instructive, as its geographic focus and time frame take in some of the children whose lives are chronicled in this volume. Instructive as a negative example, it advances a view of the urban disadvantaged that is widely held, but badly mistaken.

The Face of Urban Disadvantage in The Corner

Subtitled *A Year in the Life of an Inner-City Neighborhood, The Corner* is a journalistic account of two neighborhoods on Baltimore's west side brought down by an open-air drug market. It is a truly horrific portrayal of life on the mean streets of the city, a tale of families decimated and lives destroyed by drugs and the drug trade. The publisher, Random House, tells us online that *The Corner* "examines the sinister realities of inner cities across the country."[3] No doubt it does, but the "realities" it portrays are one-sided and incomplete. Two other urban ethnographies from around the same time, Elijah Anderson's *Code of the Street* (2000) in Philadelphia and Mary Pattillo-McCoy's *Black Picket Fences* (2000) in Chicago, provide a stark contrast.

All three books have much to say about the tangled web of drugs, crime, and urban decay, but *The Corner* offers little more: in a book of 535 pages, one is hard pressed to find more than a handful of sympathetic characters. In its rendering of life in the big city, there are no caring teachers or social workers or ministers or store owners or cops or parents or neighbors. The ties that bind, rather, are utterly and unremittingly destructive.

Missed in their account is that these communities are not just drug dens; they also are home to many "decent folk" (Anderson 2000), the poor, near-poor, and nonpoor who struggle mightily to forge respectable lives free of fear. *The Long Shadow* also is about those living in "inner cities across the country," but our experience offers a different view of these neighborhoods. To correct the distortions perpetrated in popular accounts like *The Corner*, we turn to two sources: census data on the section of Baltimore profiled in *The Corner* and our own sampling of children who grew up there.

A Census Profile of The Corner

The Corner is a real place—a map in the front of the book locates it at the intersection of West Fayette and North Monroe Streets in West Baltimore. This intersection straddles two of the 266 Baltimore Neighborhood Statistical Areas developed by the City Housing Authority from census blocks to approximate authentic neighborhoods, which census tracts do not quite do because their boundaries can be quite arbitrary. They are Penrose-Fayette Street Outreach (PF) on the west side of North Monroe (3,810 residents in 2000) and Franklin Square (FS) on the east side (3,550 residents). Most of *The Corner*'s drama takes place in Franklin Square, the more economically depressed of the two. So who lives in these two neighborhoods, and is *The Corner*'s rendering faithful to their reality?

Using the 2000 Census because it is closest in time to the book's 1997 publication, we find that both neighborhoods are racially segregated and include many female-headed, single-parent households. Against Baltimore City overall and relative to Penrose-Fayette, conditions in Franklin Square are much harsher. Franklin Square has the kind of neighborhood profile one might expect from *The Corner*, but even that neighborhood defies simple characterization as an underclass ghetto.

Table 1.1   The Corner in 2000 Census Data

Census Characteristics	Franklin Square	Penrose-Fayette	Baltimore City
Number of residents	3,550	3,810	651,154
Black residents	95.9	97.8	64.3
Poverty rate			
All families	33.7	12.5	18.8
Families, children under eighteen	40.2	20.5	26.2
Female-headed households, children under eighteen	44.6	30.4	38.3
Households with married couples	14.7	23.0	26.7
Households female headed, children under eighteen	23.0	17.2	13.3
Households, householder living alone	34.2	24.5	34.9
Residents twenty-five and over with:			
No high school diploma	44.4	42.7	31.6
High school graduate	35.8	30.5	28.2
Some college and above	19.8	26.9	40.2
Bachelor's and above	3.6	5.6	19.1
In labor force	52.4	45.7	56.5
Employed	42.8	37.9	50.4
Unemployed	9.2	7.9	6.0
Income below $10,000	36.4	13.5	18.7
Income $25,000 and above	41.7	55.8	57.2
Income $35,000 and above	25.4	38.7	43.4

Source: Authors' compilation based on data from the 2000 Census for Baltimore (U.S. Bureau of the Census 2000).
Note: All numbers except total residents in percentages.

In it, as well as in Penrose-Fayette, the vast majority of residents are not poor, nor are they unmarried mothers with dependent children (see table 1.1).

These neighborhoods are diverse in other respects as well. In both PF and FS, many residents age twenty-five and older do not have high school degrees, but the majority do—some by way of the general educational development certificate (GED)—and many attended college: 20 percent in FS and 26.9 percent PF, of whom 3.6 percent and 5.6 percent, respectively, completed a bachelor's degree.

As would be expected, unemployment rates in these communities are high, but roughly half their residents are in the labor force.[4] Most are employed, and in a perhaps surprising array of jobs. In Franklin Square in 2000, 15 percent are in management and professional positions and another 25 percent in sales and office occupations, categories of employment outside the service sector and laborer categories (not reported in table 1.1, but from the same source). Additionally, Franklin Square is not unusual in that these two occupational sectors account for 47 percent of all jobs in Penrose-Fayette.

In 2000, the poverty cutoff nationally for a family of four was $17,050. Many residents of FS and PF had incomes that low or lower, but 42 percent of FS households had incomes over $25,000 and 25 percent were over $35,000; PF incomes were higher still, 56 percent over $25,000 and 39 percent over $35,000. So while these two communities indeed are home to many poor and near-poor residents, the people who live there are not all destitute. Some are in fact comfortably well off.

Too often, journalistic accounts of the urban poor portray them in stereotyped, monolithic terms, and this is especially true of the black poor. The problems in these communities are real and severe and *The Corner* no doubt faithfully captures one facet of life in them. But one facet is not the whole.

The Corner Through the Lived Experience of Its Children

We now consider these two communities from a rather different vantage point. For almost twenty-five years, we tracked the life progress of 790 children who began first grade in the fall of 1982 in twenty Baltimore public elementary schools. This book is about their journey from childhood into young adulthood. It happens that one of these schools, the poorest of the twenty, is located in a neighborhood that borders the two depicted in *The Corner*. To characterize that school as high need would be an understatement—90 percent of its children received reduced price or free meals at school, marking them low income.[5] Our random sample of first graders from that school includes twenty-two African American males, almost all of whom as first graders lived in Franklin Square. We last spoke with eighteen of the twenty-two in 2005. Their average age at the time was twenty-eight—first graders no longer. Though but a small sampling of the area's residents, their numbers are ample to establish that not all *The Corner's* children follow the path anticipated for them in that volume. By extension, the same can be said of children in Baltimore's other low-income communities.

Seven of the eighteen interviews were conducted in lockups and seventeen of the eighteen had been arrested at some point in their lives, all but one leading to a conviction. Their arrests mostly were drug related (using and distributing), often paired with other offenses, including possession of a firearm, assault, domestic violence, and attempted murder. Fifteen of the eighteen acknowledged using drugs, mainly marijuana, but cocaine as well in one instance and in two others another substance not identified.[6] Ten told of other users in the family, six mentioning their fathers, three their mothers, and two each brothers and sisters.[7]

The book seems a lot like *The Corner* to this point, but the young people whose lives are chronicled in *The Corner* blur together. They are individuals, of course, but in matters of consequence, the unfolding scripts of their lives are much the same. Not so for the youth in *The Long Shadow.* Seven had dropped out of high school (one later completed the GED). The rest graduated and six went on to obtain postsecondary certification: one an associate's degree, one a bachelor's degree, and four technical school certificates. That kind of educational distribution might not be expected of young people growing up in the shadow of *The Corner's* drug markets and drug culture.

Their work histories also are instructive. When interviewed at age twenty-eight, of the eleven not incarcerated, nine were employed full time, mostly in the construction trades, but one was a barber and one a correctional officer. Over the longer term, five of the eighteen were employed full time for the entire preceding twenty-four months and two worked full time more than 90 percent of the time since high school. Their earnings on the whole were modest, but the exceptions are noteworthy: two earned above $50,000, and five others between $25,000 and $35,000. These are young black men from The Corner working steadily and drawing a decent paycheck.

Here is how one young man who survived The Corner reflects on his experience as a young adult. When we spoke with him, Floyd was employed, and though he had attended community college for two years, family obligations kept him from finishing:

It was a lot of drugs, drug activity, lot of, you know, shooting and homicide, stuff like that going on. I made up my mind, though, that I wasn't going to let myself be subjected to, you know, all the negativity around me. You know, I felt for myself, you know, I had things in mind. I became a father at a young age, so that helped me to, you know, want more for myself, to try to do better.

I mean, to me, success coming out of the neighborhood that I came out of, and doing what I'm doing, I think I've succeeded in what I wanted to do. To not become a statistic. To not be on a corner selling drugs, not be out there getting high. To be able to live, say that I have things that are mine. I think I will be completely successful, like I said, . . . once I become comfortable with living.

This reflection on the meaning of *success* is not an account one likely would hear from someone a half dozen years out of college who grew

Table 1.2   The Corner in 1980 Census Data

	Black in Neighborhood	Below 75% Poverty Level	Below Poverty Level	Below 200% Poverty Level	Women Head with Child in Poverty
Four black neighborhoods	96.9	28.0	40.2	67.9	60.8
Two white neighborhoods	12.3	28.3	39.9	67.3	74.0
Baltimore City	55.6	17.0	22.9	45.9	49.7

Source: Baltimore City Department of Planning 1983.
Note: All numbers except median family income in percentages.
[a]Equivalent to $28,271 in 2013 dollars.
[b]Equivalent to $26,010 in 2013 dollars.
[c]Equivalent to $44,386 in 2013 dollars.

up in one of the city's wealthier neighborhoods, or from one of The Corner's urban underclass, for that matter. This young man never did drugs growing up. Although he did have a problem encounter with the law, he was not convicted and never served time. His story has no high-paying job or fancy car; his standard of success is more substantial.

Floyd's account is one departure from *The Corner's* negative portrayal of the urban disadvantaged. Another is that they are not all African American. This particular school drew from six surrounding neighborhoods. Two were low-income white, but apart from their racial makeup (95 percent and 80 percent white, according to the 1980 Census) are practically interchangeable with the five African American communities: for example, 40.2 percent poverty in the African American and 39.9 percent in the white, both well above the 22.9 percent citywide rate (table 1.2). In terms of deep poverty (below 75 percent of the poverty level) and near poverty (below 200 percent of the poverty level), the figures likewise are similar. Although occupational profiles in the white communities are somewhat more favorable, the picture in fact is mixed: white median family income is lower and the white poverty rate for children living in female-headed households is higher (see table 1.2).[8]

That poor whites live side by side with poor blacks in one of the most distressed sections of Baltimore would not be anticipated from *The Corner*, nor, for that matter, from most academic accounts of urban disadvantage (for example, Anderson 2008). Partly, it is because we tend to think of black and white poverty differently. Sandra Barnes (2005, 17), citing census data from 2000, notes that "75 percent of all impoverished are white," but also that (taken from Flanagan 1999): "poverty among

Women Head with Child	High School Graduate Age Twenty-Five Plus	Men Unemployed	Employed Professional and Management Occupations	Employed Laborer and Service Occupations	Median Family Income ($1,000s)
51.8	27.6	35.5	7.4	47.6	10.0[a]
37.8	26.5	30.4	15.6	33.5	9.2[b]
40.5	48.4	23.2	19.5	25.6	15.7[c]

whites appears to be less expected, less recognized, less stigmatized, and less often the focus of research and commentary." Andrew Hacker (1995, 100) adds that:

> Neither sociologists nor journalists have shown much interest in depicting poor whites as a "class." In large measure the reason is racial. For whites, poverty tends to be viewed as atypical or accidental. Among blacks, it comes close to being seen as a natural outgrowth of their history and culture.

Nationally in 2011, poor whites exceeded the poor African American total by roughly eight million: 19,171,000 versus 10,929,000. Because the white population base is so much larger, however, the African American poverty rate was and is vastly higher: 27.6 percent versus 9.8 percent (DeNavas-Walt, Proctor, and Smith 2012, 14). In 1982, the first grade year for members of the Beginning School Study Youth Panel (BSSYP, or Youth Panel), the nation's central cities were home to 6.8 million poor whites, 14.5 percent of the white population and an increase of 42 percent from the 1969 total (Wilson and Aponte 1985, 239).[9] In that light, it ought not to surprise that a sampling of schoolchildren from some of Baltimore's neediest neighborhoods would include low-income whites; the surprise is that the presence of whites in these kinds of communities has received so little attention.

When they were twenty-eight, we interviewed fourteen of the seventeen white men originally sampled as first graders. At the outset, their family background and neighborhood census profiles were barely distinguishable from those of their black classmates, but what of later? Six had dropped out of high school and eight had arrest records, four resulting in convictions. Most of their offenses were drug related, paired with auto theft, assault, robbery, and shoplifting. Eleven acknowledged drug use, including cocaine (six) and prescription drugs (three); half told of other users in the family. Among blacks, marijuana was the drug of choice; among whites, the list was more expansive. As regards schooling, here too the experience is fairly similar: three of the six dropouts had GEDs; four others had attended college—one had a bachelor's degree, one a master's degree, and the others had begun but did not finish associate's programs.

Differences do begin to show up in these young men's work experience: thirteen of the whites were working full time when we spoke with them, ten continuously over the preceding two years. Like their black counterparts, many were working in construction, but their number also included a graphic designer, a social science researcher, and a catering company manager. Two also reported earnings over $50,000, but the white earnings distribution was more favorable overall, nine earning between $25,000 and $40,000.

Such differences in the adult standing of whites and blacks who began life in similar distressed conditions are not peculiar to the children of Baltimore's high-poverty West Side, but how similar in fact were those conditions growing up? Viewed through the lens of census data on neighborhood poverty levels and the like, all these neighborhoods appear to be distressed, but impressions from the inside can be different. Consider Alice's fond reminiscence of her low-income white West Side neighborhood, a part of the city outsiders are advised to avoid:

> For me, back when I was growing up, it was fine. I mean, you had the fights and all, but what neighborhood doesn't? And, but, I mean, it was fine, I mean, we got along with everybody. We, like a lot of the neighbors would have like sometimes block parties, and stuff like that, and we just, the neighbors would get close, have cookouts, and stuff like that, and just have fun.

It is commonly thought that high-poverty neighborhoods are socially fragmented and suffer a weak sense of community, but that is mistaken (see, for example, Sampson, Morenoff, and Gannon-Rowley 2002). Apropos of the point, we see in chapter 3 that these segregated black and white high-poverty neighborhoods are quite different in other pertinent respects: crime rates in the white communities were much lower and their sense of neighborliness much higher.

When low-income whites and blacks live in close proximity, one might think race the great divide, but here too, impressions can be misleading. Consider Clyde's account:

> it ain't like I see on TV. It's a lotta different things like . . . like a lotta blacks live like in the inner city and the whites are like higher up and it's different. Down by us . . . down in the . . . uh . . . economically depressed area, it like we all together. That says we all live together. It ain't like a all-black neighborhood here and they don't like us cause we're a all-white neighborhood. Everybody . . . we all live together down there. It's more blacks around our way. But . . . everybody gets along with everybody.

Idealized perhaps, but from this young man's perspective, the big clash locally was with the "uppity class people" in a neighborhood some distance off—those he calls "the rock 'n roll type":

> it ain't like the black and white thing. It's like inner city. That's where we live at. And we used to fight them. Ain't like we fought em cause they're white. It just they used to act different. They used to sit and talk about us like we were stupid and everything like that. It's just they would talk about us, white and black and like Hispanic kids was down there. Cause, you know, it wasn't cause of the race. It was like cause they're different. Different . . . um . . . economic class.

Clyde is working-class white, a high school dropout who completed high school by way of the GED.

This excursion into the area of Baltimore made infamous in *The Corner* reminds us that no single template can do justice to life in the "inner cities across the country"; nor do all of the urban disadvantaged fit the underclass profile. The point of most immediate relevance is that urban disadvantaged and urban underclass are not the same. The underclass are, under most constructions of the term, a small minority of the nation's poor, and that includes the poor who reside in high-poverty communities (see Jencks 1991). Indeed, by some estimates they are a declining minority (see Jargowsky and Sawhill 2006), though whether that reversal still holds owing to the recent deep recession remains to be seen.

This book is not a journalist account of the urban underclass, but rather a social-scientific inquiry into the lives of the urban disadvantaged. *The Corner's* characterization of life on the "mean streets" of Baltimore is recognizable in some of the youth who are the focus of this volume, but *The Long Shadow* also tells of the successes of those who recover from a misstep along the way. Our goal is to present a picture of the whole range of urban disadvantage over a long enough time frame to gain perspective on some of the considerations that move them along different life paths. From this glimpse of inner-city children grown up, we have already learned that:

not all disadvantaged youth follow the same path;

many who slip along the way manage to recover;

urban disadvantage is not color coded as is commonly thought; and

neighborhoods that appear similar to the casual observer can be quite dissimilar in ways that bear on children's later life prospects.

Urban Disadvantage, Materially Construed

For us, and in this volume, the long shadow of family background is cast by material conditions of family life, along with opportunities stratified along lines of race and gender. Today's high technology, knowledge-based economy increasingly favors those with a college degree. In 2002, compared with men without a high school education, those age twenty-five to thirty-four with some college earned 20 percent more and those with bachelor's degrees earned 65 percent more, up from premiums of 5 percent and 19 percent, respectively, in 1980.[10] This is hardly a recent phenomenon. Smoothing over the ups and downs of the business cycle, the earnings premium that today attaches to a college degree appears to be an historic high.[11]

A shortfall of credentialed skills leaves many behind, and African American men are the hardest hit: among high school dropouts in the 2004–2005 school year, the earnings of black men ages twenty to twenty-eight averaged $2,038, against median earnings of $15,288 among Hispanics and $14,269 among non-Hispanic whites (Sum et al. 2007). Indeed, for men like these simply finding work is a challenge, and hanging onto it another. According to Andrew Sum and his colleagues (2007, 2–3), "only 1 of every 3 young black male high school dropouts was able to obtain any type of employment during the average month in 2005" and just 23 percent worked full time. That so few African American dropouts find any kind of work explains how their annual earnings can be so low—an excess of zero earnings drives down the average. Wilson (2008, 58, figure 4.1) adds that the black-white employment gap widens as one descends the education ladder, from 86 percent versus 88 percent among male college graduates in 2005, to 57 percent versus 73 percent among high school graduates, to 33 percent versus 54 percent among high school dropouts.[12]

The so-called feminization of poverty is gendered urban disadvantage in another guise. The phrase was coined by Diane Pearce (1978) to spotlight the doubling of poverty levels in female-headed households between 1950 and 1974. Pearce implicated escalating divorce rates, but those rates since have leveled, displaced by a rapid rise in out-of-wedlock and never-married childbearing as the driving forces behind increases in the feminization of poverty (Cherlin 2005, 36). In 1960, never-married mothers accounted for fewer than 5 percent of the children of single mothers; by 2006, they accounted for 43 percent (Thibos, Lavin-Loucks, and Martin 2007, 6). African American women find themselves especially challenged by the burdens associated with single parenting: today more than 70 percent of black children are born outside marriage, against 29 percent of non-Hispanic white births (Martin et al. 2012, 45).[13]

Many of these households are mired in poverty—for example, in 2007, compared with 8.5 percent of children in married couple households, 43 percent of children in female-headed households fell below the poverty line. Again, a bad situation overall is worse among African Americans: more than half the children in African American single-mother households live in poverty but only just under a third of white children do (Federal Interagency Forum on Child and Family Statistics 2009, 115; see also Thibos, Lavin-Loucks, and Martin 2007).

These figures establish what is well understood: family circumstances and a depressed economy in places like Baltimore put many children at risk, but at risk for what? That risk is best defined by the challenges they overcome: in the short term, to stay on a positive path—to stay in school, avoid trouble, and find work in a tough economy; in the longer term, to achieve upward mobility, financial stability, and a fulfilling personal life. As statistics like those recounted remind us, many of the urban disadvantaged—low-income, black and white, men and women—fall short. This book shows that it is wrong to generalize broadly from such statistical profiles.

Family conditions early in life cast a long shadow. That principle holds broadly, but with exceptions, and in this context they are numerous. The literature on so-called resilient youth shows that many who grow up in disadvantaged circumstances succeed in overcoming often daunting challenges (for example, Furstenberg, Brooks-Gunn, and Morgan 1987; Masten, Best, and Garmezy 1991; Haggerty et al. 1996). Perhaps, as Frank, a black male from a poor family with a high school diploma and a strong work history, told us, "It's not where you live, it's how you live, and the things you make up your mind to do."

Is it really that simple to will oneself to success? Frank's view that we create our destiny is widely shared. Certainly as a society we treasure rags to riches stories of individuals of great accomplishment who overcome humble origins to achieve The American Dream. They abound in industry, and even at the very highest levels of government. But for every Lee Iacocca or Barack Obama, we see a Henry Ford or a Jack Kennedy. Such great leaps are not the issue here. More relevant is that many of the urban disadvantaged succeed in overcoming the drag of conditions that hold others back. This volume aims to identify the resources and personal qualities that help disadvantaged youth, but also the barriers they face. It is a book about social stratification in the urban context, informed by the experience of the panel of Baltimore children whose life trajectories we tracked for nearly a quarter century from 1982 to 2006. They are an internally diverse group—black and white, mostly low income at the outset, but also some who began life in more favorable circumstances. The next section provides background on the project. The chapter concludes with an overview of the book.

The Beginning School Study Youth Panel

The Youth Panel commenced in the fall of 1982, when the youth profiled in this volume began first grade in twenty Baltimore public elementary schools. For us, the transition into first grade represents a singular life-course transition (see, for example, Entwisle and Alexander 1989, 1993), which accounts for the "beginning school study" moniker. The project's research design, procedures, and data sources are reviewed in detail in appendix B; here we highlight features most relevant to *The Long Shadow's* objectives.

The Youth Panel is unusual among single-city case studies in that it is based on a probability sample. This is important because probability sampling assures internal validity (Michael and O'Muircheartaigh 2008). Schools and children were selected for participation in two stages. First, Baltimore's 123 public elementary schools were classified according to their racial-ethnic composition (segregated white, segregated black, racially integrated) and neighborhood socioeconomic status (white collar, blue collar). Twenty schools were then selected on a random basis from among the six school types defined by these two sampling frames (for example, blue-collar segregated white schools).[14] For the next step, classroom rosters were used to randomly select first-time first graders from within those schools.[15] Because of this probability sampling, the 790 beginning first graders who make up the sample are representative of conditions in Baltimore's public schools at the time.[16]

In 1980, 44 percent of Baltimore schoolchildren were in poverty-level households, fifth highest among the country's fourteen largest school districts (Abell Foundation 1989, table 4). Two-thirds of the sample were in low-income families at the project's outset, the exact percentage low-income system-wide at the time (Baltimore City Schools 1988). These low-income children are the main focus of this volume, but to understand what makes their experience distinctive requires a comparative frame of reference. For that, we also examine the upper 25 percent of the sample families. These families are decidedly better off than the larger low-income group, but *better off* is context bound. In families we characterize as disadvantaged or lower socioeconomic status (SES), the typical parent is a high school dropout; in better-off families, most parents have some college.

These family differences across social lines are large, but higher-SES families in the sample fall well short of high SES by national standards. Had the BSSYP been national in scope, it is certain that differences across family circumstances would be larger than those seen in this volume, and very likely the consequences of those difference as well. Still, comparisons along social lines in the book, though limited to the city's public school enrollment, turn out to be highly consequential for children's well-being. Owing to our robust research design, those comparisons are internally valid and can be generalized to the larger population of Baltimore school children. Although our perspective is local, there can be little doubt that *The Long Shadow's* account of the Baltimore picture understates the influence of family background in children's lives. That realization is sobering, for as we will see, differences within the sample are not just large, but profoundly so.

Data Sources

Members of the Youth Panel were six-year-old children when we first entered their lives in 1982 and young adults when we exited in 2006. Their voices are heard throughout this volume by way of wide-ranging conversations with them during the summers of 1995 and 1996, and in 2000 throughout the year, all well after high school. These sessions—162 in all—asked members of the sample to reflect on their years growing up and to look ahead to their anticipated futures. They were recorded and later transcribed. The quotes introduced in this chapter are from those interviews; background on those quoted and profiled is provided in appendix A.

These interview materials are vivid and full of insight, but the BSSYP is centrally a survey project and a rich store of survey data is on hand to help in tracking the children's development. Participants were interviewed in person up to twenty times through high school and twice after high school.[17] The latter covered experiences since high school in family life, employment, postsecondary schooling, and what we call problem behaviors—such as contact with the criminal justice system, alcohol and drug use, and smoking. None of our surveys achieved 100 percent coverage, but most years the yields were quite satisfactory, averaging 77 percent across the entire collection.[18]

The Young Adult Survey (YAS) commenced in 1998 with 82 percent of the interviews completed that year and the majority of those interviewed (55 percent) age twenty-two at the time; 38 percent were age twenty-one; the rest were twenty-three and older. For convenience, we refer to the YAS as the project's age twenty-two survey. The second after high school survey, the Mature Adult Survey (MAS), took place about eleven years after the panel's expected high school graduation in the spring of 1994. Because 70 percent of interviews were conducted in 2005 and 66 percent of those interviewed were age twenty-eight at the time (31 percent were twenty-nine), the MAS is referred to as the project's age twenty-eight survey.

Parents and teachers of the children also are represented. Parents were interviewed up to eleven times from first grade to eleventh grade and teachers interviewed up to nine times, the last in ninth grade.[19] Additionally, we use school records from Baltimore, as well as from schools outside the city to which children transferred.[20] These provide report card marks, deportment ratings, achievement test results, promotion histories, and disciplinary problems. Appendix B reviews sample attrition and retention over the project's twenty-five-year history, as well as details on the measurement of key constructs.

That the BSSYP data archive is uncommonly rich and encompassing is a decided advantage for *The Long Shadow's* agenda, which weaves together information over many years and from many sources. Our goal is to tell a complicated story with fidelity, yet keep it digestible, a challenging balance that has obliged a number of compromises (to be reviewed as they are encountered). What we have not compromised is our determination to honor the participants' experience in their key particulars.

What Comes Next

This is not the first time we have posed questions of the panel participants about their family life, their schooling, or even their transition to adulthood in relation to experiences growing up. This is a local study of national import and has supported much useful research. Its scientifically strong research design, long time frame, high sample retention over many years, and intensity of its fieldwork set it apart from other single-city case studies. Indeed, even before the age twenty-eight

Mature Adult Survey became available, the project had achieved recognition as a landmark longitudinal study of the twentieth century (Phelps, Furstenberg, and Colby 2002).[21]

Although the issues taken up in this volume are not new to us, *The Long Shadow* is altogether new and quite different from any of our previous published work. That holds for its topical breadth, the variety of data sources brought to bear in the execution of its agenda, and how those data are used. Our previous work will be brought in at times to help inform interpretations and our sense-making, but selectively and, we hope, judiciously. As well, we have tried to make this volume accessible and self-contained; no grounding in our previous studies is needed. The book presents statistical analysis, but is self-consciously nontechnical; where technical issues cannot be avoided, that material is relegated to footnotes and appendices.

Those points speak to the book's character. As regards its substance, our overriding goal is to elucidate how it is that some of the urban disadvantaged manage to get ahead in life, while others are held back by the circumstances of their early family lives. Toward that end, we use the project's rich store of survey, interview, and school record data to support close inspection of the children's unfolding lives at home and at school, beginning in first grade, continuing through the end of high school (however concluded), and then well into their third decade of life.

The majority of the sample children grew up poor or near-poor in a city that has been near the top nationally on virtually every indicator of community and family distress. Their experience of urban disadvantage is described in chapters 2 through 4. Chapter 2 reviews conditions in Baltimore City during the children's and their parents' formative years. The economic history of Baltimore over the latter half of the twentieth century spans the industrial boom of the postwar years when the parents were coming of age and the industrial bust that is backdrop to the panel participants' development. The deindustrialization, downsizing, and impoverishment of places like Baltimore is a familiar tale and its relevance for children's well-being is understood, but the earlier story of the region's industrial buildup is no less relevant because it has implications for the resources commanded by the children's parents.

The details of Baltimore's changing economy and demographics over the panel's two generations are, in ecological terms, elements of the backdrop social context that frames children's development; in the foreground are the close-up conditions children experience daily in their home lives, their neighborhoods, and their schools. These three institutional settings—home, neighborhood, and school—affect children's development all along the way, but the focus in this volume is how they are experienced in early childhood, around the time of the children's entry into "real school" as first graders. The socioeconomic standing and makeup of their birth families are reviewed in chapter 3; neighborhood and school are addressed in chapter 4. The book is a story of socioeconomic destinations constrained by socioeconomic origins; by the end of chapter 4, the origins side will be in hand.

Chapter 5 describes the children's standing with respect to several key transition to adulthood milestones over the years after high school—working full time, becoming a parent, marrying or partnering, and living apart from one's parents. It is a bridging chapter in several senses. Organizationally, it separates chapters devoted to the Youth Panel's socioeconomic origins from the chapter that describes their socioeconomic destinations. The transition to adulthood also bridges stages of the life course, from children's near complete dependence on the parental family in childhood and early adolescence to the increasing self-dependence expected of late adolescence and emergent adulthood.

The bridging imagery works well from a stratification perspective also: the transition to adulthood carries young people from an identity rooted in family socioeconomic origins to one anchored in their own socioeconomic destinations as adults. Chapter 5 reveals differences across social lines in the details of how these adult transition milestones come together in the children's lives, with distinctive patterning by race and gender and along lines of family socioeconomic background.

Consequences for their socioeconomic destinations, rooted in family, neighborhood, school, and details of their adult transition, are taken up in chapter 7, but first those destinations need to be mapped. That is done in chapter 6, which sketches the panel's socioeconomic standing at the time of the MAS (roughly age twenty-eight) in the same terms used to locate their parents in socioeconomic space: their levels of schooling, occupational status, and earnings. Because well-being in adulthood is as much a family affair as a matter of personal accomplishment, however, for members of the Youth Panel in family unions, we also examine the levels of schooling, occupational status, and earnings of their spouses and cohabiting partners.

The tendency for like to marry is well established (see, for example, Blossfeld 2009), and on that basis we expect, and do see, similar socioeconomic profiles for the partners in these relationships. However, the likelihood of marrying or partnering is quite different across social lines, and comparing two-earner families against one-earner families is certain to show the latter badly disadvantaged (Isaacs 2008) This is stratification-relevant within the sample because lower-SES white women are more likely than their African American counterparts to be in family unions as young adults. When children are in the picture, whites also are less likely to be parenting alone. The literature on intergenerational mobility does not often contrast socioeconomic standing in personal terms against that at the family level, but doing so proves to be instructive.

With a solid descriptive account of social origins and social destinations in hand, we then shift into analytic mode to examine implications of the former for the latter. At issue is the fundamental question of social stratification as a field of inquiry: who gets what and why?[22] The book identifies two mobility regimes. Chapter 7 evaluates a life-course developmental model of the sort used to study the role of schooling in status attainment. Success in school is the vehicle by which children of privileged family background maintain their privilege across generations, but also the vehicle by which some lower-SES children rise above their origins. That much is well established in the literature, but in the experience of the Youth Panel children, it is more a precious few than some: barely 5 percent of the panel's urban disadvantaged complete college, 4 percent with bachelor's degrees and fewer than 1 percent with associate's degrees.

The story of status attainment through schooling is a familiar one and *The Long Shadow* establishes how it unfolds in the urban context. A college degree is the understood way to get ahead in the modern era, but during the closing years of the twentieth century not many of Baltimore's needy children advanced on the strength of strong academic credentials. Status attainment through school instead mainly served to preserve privilege across generations: children of higher-SES families were more likely than their lower-SES counterparts to attend college, to finish college (ten times more likely), and then later to reap the labor market rewards that attach to a college degree.

For the Youth Panel children, however, college is not the only route to material well-being. Chapter 8 identifies a second mobility regime, one that privileges lower-SES whites over blacks of like background. Its benefits accrue first to white men through access to high-wage employment in the remnants of Baltimore's old industrial economy and then, derivatively, to the lower-SES white women who marry and partner with them. Working-class whites have not commanded much attention in literature on the urban poor, and because of that this second mobility regime largely has gone unremarked.[23] For status attainment through school, college completion is the major line of divide; for blue-collar attainment, it is access to well-paid, steady work.

Chapter 9, the concluding chapter, reflects on the two mobility paths taken by the Youth Panel participants on their journey from childhood to mature adulthood. Multiple assets and liabilities in childhood trigger later events and circumstances that channel higher-SES youth along one pathway and lower-SES youth along another. It is an account of cumulative disadvantage anchored in the early formative years (see, for example, Kerckhoff 1993), and offers the insight that pathways are plural. Race and gender come into play in two ways under the noncollege mobility regime: the labor market opportunities that favor white men over African American of like background and the characteristic differences by race in family life that have profound implications for women's economic well-being.

Chapter 2

The Baltimore Backdrop

U RBAN DISADVANTAGE presents itself in children's lives at every turn—at home when they awaken in the morning, outside when they head off to school, and then at destination's end when they arrive. Family, neighborhood, and school, these settings dominate children's development during their formative years and set the stage for their unfolding life scripts (Jessor 1993). But there also is a broader context to urban disadvantage, one that hovers in the background. For the children of the Beginning School Study Youth Panel (BSSYP, or Youth Panel), this backdrop is Baltimore City and its changing character over the latter half of the twentieth century.

The children were first graders in the fall of 1982, a time when wrenching changes associated with deindustrialization and shifting demographics were remaking the face of Baltimore and other old-line industrial cities. The parents, in contrast, came of age during a quite different time in the city's history. That is where we begin.

The Industrial Boom Years

The rapid industrialization that fueled America's economy during World War II and for some years after brought great prosperity to port cities along the East Coast and the industrial centers of the Midwest. Averaging twenty-four years of age in 1976 (the modal birth year), the Youth Panel parents are among the nation's many *boomers,* the familiar term used to characterize the baby boom that followed World War II. But boomer also fits well the state of the economy at the time. It too was booming, although not all of Baltimore benefited to the same extent. Mobilization for war was the initial impetus, sustained later by the rebuilding of Europe and Japan and, on the home front, a spike in demand for consumer goods once thought luxuries but mass-marketed during the good times of the 1950s and 1960s. The big-ticket items were automobiles and suburban housing, and together they transformed the urban landscape.

The sprawling Bethlehem Steel complex at Sparrows Point is the iconic image of Baltimore's industrial prowess. Employment there nearly

21

Source: Public domain, Environmental Protection Agency, photograph by Jim Pickerell 1973.

doubled during the war, peaking at thirty-five thousand and making Bethlehem Steel the world's largest steel mill at the time (see photo 2.1). Much the same was happening throughout the rest of Baltimore's industrial core. The city's workforce exploded from 150,000 manufacturing jobs in 1939 to 251,000 in 1942, with four of five jobs war-related (Durr 2003, 17). The city's population likewise swelled, from 859,000 in 1940 to 1,250,000 in late 1942, well above the totals registered during any of the decennial censuses before or since. The in-migrants were a diverse group, black and white, many from the rural South and the Appalachian belt that stretches on the diagonal from the southern tier of western New York through northern Mississippi, Alabama, and Georgia.[1]

It is hard to track Baltimore's recipient share of the Great Diaspora out of the South because national figures generally monitor flows from the South to other regions of the country. Maryland, a border state during the Civil War, is included in the South. Nevertheless, it is certain Baltimore was the destination for many. Amy Bentley (1993, 421) estimates that between 1940 and 1943, 160,000 workers moved into the city from rural Maryland, West Virginia, Virginia, North Carolina, Tennessee, and Kentucky. Many were Appalachian whites.

Jobs were the lure, and though these white migrants initially encountered considerable hostility—disparaged as hillbillies, "crackers," and "Oakies" (for example, Kolodner 1962)—being white eventually overrode their "otherness," Baltimore's southern heritage being the key:

> Although its industrial economy more closely resembled that of Philadelphia and New York, Baltimore even in the 1940s was most decidedly Southern in character. Jim Crow was alive and well; blacks and whites lived in separate and unequal worlds. (Bentley 1993, 422)

In fact, segregation in Maryland was more pronounced than in the other border states, attributed by some to racial politics focused on the state's large population of free blacks before the Civil War (Durr 2003, 9). In 1910, for example, Baltimore passed the nation's first racially restrictive residential zoning ordinance, a segregationist approach to city planning that was endorsed the following year at a citywide meeting of neighborhood improvement and protective associations (Silver 1997).

And so, we are told, "White native Baltimoreans were only temporarily ambivalent about the Southern newcomers. . . . Southerners and Appalachians lived under a distinct color line, as did Baltimore's ethnic working people. A new white working class had united with surprising ease, because in the neighborhood and on the job, everybody was white" (Durr 2003, 19). That is certainly the broad sense of it, although the white working-class alliance was not always unified (Hill 1961; Sugrue 2004) and neither were blacks altogether absent from the workplace.

These were good times for the working man: "The quarter century following World War II was a 'golden age' for most workers and their families . . . , even for men with a high school education or less. . . . Well-paying manufacturing jobs allowed many men to support a family on a single income" (Danziger and Ratner 2010, 134). This working-class success story characterized black diaspora labor as well (Gregory 2005, chapter 3; Sugrue 2004), though not in equal measure. African Americans working on the docks, in the steel mills, and on the auto-assembly shop floor were excluded from the skilled unions and relegated to the "dirtiest and least desirable jobs" (Durr 2003, 81).

Change eventually came, but it was painfully slow. In 1963, *Ebony* magazine reported that "there [was] not one Negro in building trades apprenticeship training programs in Fort Wayne Indiana, Milwaukee, Minneapolis, Baltimore, or Atlanta. Only two of 3,500 apprentices in all trades in Newark are Negro and in Chicago, where a quarter of the population is Negro, the apprentice figure is less than one percent." In similar vein, but cutting a broader swath, between 1950 and 1960 nationally the representation of African Americans in building trades apprenticeship programs rose from a mere 1.5 percent to an equally mere 2 percent (Hill 1965). African Americans who did manage to access the skilled trades typically were consigned to nonunionized construction and low-end, low-pay work (bricklaying, roofing).

The picture was much the same in Baltimore. Kenneth Durr (2003, 81) estimates that in 1960 blacks held 68 percent of all unskilled jobs and whites 92 percent of skilled jobs. Moreover, those African Americans who did manage to penetrate the skilled trades mostly were consigned to low-wage work. According to Social Security Administration data, the black graduates of Carver High's auto mechanics program from 1956 to 1969 earned barely half that of the white graduates of Mergenthaler High,[2] taking four and a half years to reach the earnings levels that Mergenthaler alums realized "after a few months" (Levenson and McDill 1966, 350).[3]

Looking back from 2014, Jim Crow segregation and racial exclusion from the skilled trades might seem ancient history, but this was Baltimore when the Youth Panel's parents were growing up, not their grandparents or great-grandparents. Interesting, you might think, but of what relevance to employment prospects today? In exactly what ways we take up later, but to anticipate just a bit: when surveyed at age twenty-eight in 2005, almost half the white men raised in families we classify as lower SES were working in the construction and manufacturing crafts (carpenter, mechanic, for example) versus 15 percent of African American men of like background.[4] Within this category of labor, white earnings averaged $43,383 and black earnings $21,569, similar to the 2:1 ratio documented by Bernard Levenson and Mary McDill for the parents' generation in the 1960s.

The *Long Shadow* of family background plays out in a host of ways. One is by facilitating college attendance, the now understood way to escape urban disadvantage—"want to move up, then stay in school" goes the message (for example, Rosenbaum 2001). The literature on family help through job contacts is less abundant and the issue is not especially prominent in the policy arena, yet job contacts are highly relevant to employment prospects. Only a handful of those with lower-SES origins make it through college (chapter 6). For the others—the vast majority—entry into the world of work will not be smoothed by a college degree. The workplace will determine how well they fare, and family help getting an economic toehold can make a huge difference. The history just reviewed suggests that white parents of modest means may be better positioned than black parents to provide such help for their children (chapter 8).

The Industrial Bust

"In 1950, Baltimore was the sixth-largest city in the country, home to 950,000 people and a thriving manufacturing and shipping industry. As the economic base of Maryland, Baltimore provided 75 percent of all jobs

Photo 2.2   Baltimore's Downtown Inner Harbor

Source: © Douglas Miller, reprinted with permission.

to workers in the region. Many were manufacturing jobs in textile and automobile production. The region's economic powerhouse was the steel industry." (Service Employees International Union 2004)

How quickly things can change. The sprawling Beth Steel complex that once housed more than thirty thousand workers by 2005 had downsized to a workforce of just 1,500 and the downward spiral continued: bankruptcy was declared in spring 2012, and in 2013 Bethlehem Steel was sold off in pieces, much of it as scrap metal. The decline and fall of this industrial powerhouse is both symbolic and practical. Most of the industry that used to provide well-paid, steady work for Baltimore's blue-collar workforce is gone. And not just manufacturing, but retail too, and just about every other sector of the city's once-vibrant postwar economy.

That is the deindustrialization script, but the region's economy has not so much stagnated as changed. Baltimore's downtown profile today is a thing of beauty. The Inner Harbor port area once dominated by decaying docks and empty warehouses now gleams with office buildings, hotels, and tourist-oriented entertainment amenities—marinas, a science center, a marvelous aquarium, shopping pavilions, an array of restaurants to satisfy every palate and budget, and all within an easy walk to the Orioles and Ravens ballparks (see photo 2.2). It is a wonderful place for a weekend visit and a great place for some to work, but this new economy is focused more on making money than on making things (Olson 1997, 392). That leaves a gaping hole in the middle, and most of the well-paid professionals laboring in those office towers head out to the suburbs at day's end. Then the second city emerges, with the low-wage night crew cleaning and security personnel standing guard.

According to Sherry Olson (1997, 396):

> Of net growth in the region, half reflects high-wage knowledge-intensive jobs, while the other half reflects low-wage jobs that pay half as much: from child care to cleaning carpets in hotel rooms, to picking up Styrofoam cups on the water-front. Nothing in-between. Nothing to replace the ninety-thousand well-paid unionized factory jobs that have disappeared.

This circumstance is hardly peculiar to Baltimore:

> The decline in manufacturing jobs has not meant fewer jobs available for less skilled workers; rather it has meant that different jobs are available. For instance, the share [nationally] of less educated men in retail trade and selected service jobs, including hotel, restaurants, and entertainment tourism grew from 24 percent to 28 percent between 1985 and 2007. For less educated women, from 36 percent to 40 percent. . . . The problem has not been job availability, but the wages these jobs pay. (Blank 2009, 16)[5]

It has become an hour-glass economy. Those with the skillset, credentials, and contacts valued in the high tech and FIRE industries—finance, insurance, and real estate—are thriving; those left behind are consigned to low-wage, low-benefit work with limited potential for advancement—bulges at the top and bottom, with little between. As yet there are no catchy descriptors for the upper and lower tiers; for this volume, the urban advantaged and the urban disadvantaged will suffice.

The Youth Panel's Baltimore

The purpose of this chapter is to sketch conditions in Baltimore as the Youth Panel made its way through the city's schools. The postwar boom's relevance is historic; the import of Baltimore's industrial bust is more immediate. The Youth Panel's Baltimore is the city as it was during the 1980s and 1990s, and as it is today. Two photographs show the Baltimore that was and is: the first, row homes in one of the city's many working-class residential enclaves during the industrial heyday, neat and tidy, with marble steps washed daily and, in close-up, the occasional painted screen; the second, what remains of too many of those communities in the modern Baltimore—blocks of boarded-up, abandoned and decaying row homes, only a handful occupied (see photos 2.3 and 2.4).

Baltimore's history over the second half of the twentieth century is captured in these two images. It is a history that parallels that of the nation's other deindustrializing cities, hemorrhaging good jobs, much of its middle-class population (whites initially, soon followed by middle-class blacks), and much of its wealth. As noted, by the mid-1980s,

Photo 2.3   Classic Baltimore Working-Class Row Homes

Photo 2.4   Distressed Row Homes

Baltimore had lost more than half its jobs in primary metals, shipbuilding and repair, transportation, and manufacturing; a decade later, the loss was 75 percent. The city's share of regional manufacturing declined from 75 percent to 30 percent between 1954 and 1997; driven by the expansion of suburban shopping malls, the city's retail sales suffered an even steeper decline, from 80 percent to 18 percent (Levine 2000, 125–26).

In 1958, for every job in the surrounding counties, there were 1.8 in the city; in 1987, only 0.47. During this time, Baltimore's share of households with earnings above the region's median declined from 46 percent to 25 percent (Lyall 1993, 35). What of those working downtown in Baltimore's new economy? The share of workers in the city's central business district living in Baltimore fell from 58 percent to 46 percent between 1969 and 1979 and included just 29 percent of those earning $50,000 and above (Levine 1987, 113).

The Changing Face of the City and Signs of Distress

Accompanying these economic changes were equally momentous demographic changes. Between 1950 and 1990, the city's population fell by more than two hundred thousand, from 949,708 to 733,014. The nation's sixth largest U.S. city was now twelfth largest, and the downward spiral continues: in 2010, Baltimore ranked twenty-first, with a population of 620,961.

The black-white balance in the city also shifted dramatically over these years—from 24 percent African American in 1950, to 46 percent in 1970, to 64 percent in 2010. In 1950, two-thirds of the region's white residents lived in Baltimore; in 1997, the figure was 13 percent. With the whites who relocated to the suburbs went much of the city's wealth: median household income citywide in 1985 was $16,700, as against $31,000 in the area's five surrounding counties (Szanton 1986, 2–3).

The consequences of this economic decline permeate city life, including conditions of family life and the resources available to children during the time the Youth Panel children were coming of age. In 1979, just before the BSSYP's launch, Baltimore's rate of child poverty stood at 33 percent, and over the next decade it hardly changed. In 1989, it was 32 percent, against a national average of 18 percent, and an average of 27 percent in the fifty large cities covered in a report by the Annie E. Casey Foundation (1997).

In 1990, 53 percent of the city's children were in single-parent families, second highest of the fifty large cities; in 1994, 14 percent of the city's births were low weight, against a statewide average of 8.4 percent and a fifty large-city average of 9.0 percent (ranking forty-seventh). During that time, the lives of many of the city's older youth took one or another unfortunate turn, often tied in with illicit drugs. Baltimore's juvenile arrest rate in 1990 was 155.5 per 10,000 over the ages of ten to seventeen. For perspective, the statewide rate in Maryland then was 57.8 and the average for the nation's fifty largest cities was 84.2. Baltimore also scored near the top in high school dropout, ranking ninth nationally, at 22.8 percent of sixteen- to nineteen-year-olds in 1990 (Mark Bomster, "City's Dropout Rate Ranked 9th-Worse in Nation in 1990," *Baltimore Sun*, September 18, 1992, pp. C1–4), four years before the Youth Panel's on-time high school graduation. Fewer than half the BSSYP graduated on time in 1994: 40 percent had already left without degrees; others were delayed owing to a history of grade retention or assignment to special education.

Neighborhood conditions followed a like path, with many plagued by the ills that often accompany high poverty. Baltimore placed fifth among the nation's hundred largest cities in the growth of severely distressed census tracts between 1970 and 1980 (Kasarda 1993, 286, 294); it ranked fourth among the nation's fifty-five largest metropolitan statistical areas in the disparity between central cities and their surrounding suburbs in unemployment, poverty, crowded housing, and other measures of hardship (Nathan and Adams 1989, 485–87). This decline is what hard census data reveal about local conditions at the time, and it mirrors broader quality of life measures, including soaring crime rates, the so-called crack invasion, increases in vacant and boarded-up housing, and escalating community concerns over vandalism, litter and the like (Taylor 2001).[6]

Baltimore's School System

Cities, as a rule, do not shrink gracefully—"undercrowding" captures the sense of it (Cohen 2001); neither do their school systems. School enrollment peaked at just under two hundred thousand in the early 1970s; by the time the Youth Panel children were entering first grade in 1982, the system was a third smaller, down to 119,789 (Casserly 1983, 10). Today only five digits are needed to tally its students: enrollment during the 2011–2012 school year was 84,212 (Maryland Department of Education 2012).

The student mix also changed. As the first major southern city to comply with the Supreme Court's landmark school desegregation decision in 1954 (Bard 1958; David 1994), Baltimore moved swiftly and boldly, but paid dearly—the push for desegregation no doubt accelerated the exodus of whites from the city's public schools. The system flipped from majority white to majority African American around 1960 (Bowler 1991, 43) and white flight continued for many years thereafter. Between 1970 and 1982 white enrollment declined by more than 60 percent (Casserly 1983, 11).[7] In 1982, enrollment system-wide was more than 75 percent African American (Maryland Department of Education 1983, 8) and heavily segregated by race. According to Douglas Massey and Nancy Denton (1993, 71), in 1980 Baltimore was the second most segregated of the twelve southern cities covered in their book *American Apartheid*. Both trends continued. In 2011–2012, African Americans accounted for 85.5 percent of Baltimore's enrollment (Maryland Department of Education 2012). In 2010–2011, practically all its black students attended majority black schools—97.1 percent (Ayscue et al. 2013, 52). A comparison with the city's immediate neighbor, Baltimore County, is instructive.

In 2010–2011, Baltimore County was Maryland's third largest school district with an enrollment of over a hundred thousand; Baltimore City then ranked fourth (Ayscue et al. 2013). Whites by then were a minority in the county schools also, making up 45.9 percent of the total, down from 78.4 percent in 1989, a demographic change largely fueled by the exodus of African Americans from Baltimore City into the county. As mentioned, virtually all of the city's African American students attended schools with a majority black enrollment. In fact, 79.3 percent attended hyper-segregated schools with a minority enrollment of 90 percent or greater and 44.3 percent attended what Jennifer Ayscue and her colleagues (2013) call apartheid schools with an African American enrollment of 99 percent to 100 percent. By way of comparison, the respective figures in Baltimore County were 48.4 percent, 20.0 percent, and 3.2 percent—two majority-minority districts with vastly different segregation profiles.[8]

Though greatly shrunken relative to its peak, in 2010–2011 Baltimore's school system still ranked fourth largest in Maryland; in the early 1980s, it was third largest. Also then and now, it exemplified the many challenges associated with big city, high-poverty schooling. Its enrollment, black and white, was majority low income.[9] As mentioned, in 1980 Baltimore's 44 percent poverty enrollment was fifth highest among the country's fourteen largest school districts (Abell Foundation 1989, table 4). Nearly 33 percent of Maryland's African American students were in Baltimore, well beyond the city's 17 percent share of the state's student enrollment. Additionally, 17 percent of city students received expensive special education services, accounting for more than 20 percent of the statewide total (Maryland Department of Education 1983, 8).

Such a high-need student profile poses obvious challenges, and against a limited resource base the challenges magnify. The city's cost per pupil (essentially expenditures) in 1981–1982 was $2,564, a bit below the state average of $2,888 but well below expenditures in Maryland's wealthiest counties: $3,371 in Montgomery County just outside Washington, D.C.; $3,234 in Baltimore County (Maryland Department of Education 1983, 16).[10]

Funding for public education is a shared responsibility of local, state, and federal government. In 1981–1982, Baltimore's wealth per pupil ranked third lowest among the state's twenty-four school districts—$54,808, against a state average of $87,821 (Maryland Department of Education 1983, 21). As a result, and despite having the highest property tax rate by far in the region (Orr, Stone, and Stumbo 2002, table 7), Baltimore's local revenues for public education K–12 increased just 30 percent between 1970 and 1982, less than half the 67 percent increase in the thirty-two large city school systems surveyed by the Council of Great City Schools and barely 25 percent of the 116 percent increase nationally during this period. Nor did other sources compensate. Baltimore's education receipts from all sources (local, state, and national) rose 51 percent between 1970 and 1982, against an average increase of 120 percent for the nation's large cities and 164 percent nationally (Casserly 1983). Shortfall of this magnitude has obvious implications for the city's ability to provide critical services.

Recap and Looking Ahead

The picture just sketched of a city in distress is backdrop to the Youth Panel's journey from childhood through adolescence and into adulthood. Conditions in the broader economy trickle down to the city's neighborhoods and schools, and, even closer in, to family. But we ought not to overstate: not all of Baltimore's children suffered such exposure. Then and now, the city includes pockets of middle-class and professional families. Most live in the city's upscale neighborhoods, and many of their children attend private schools. In 1980, 62 percent of Baltimore's white children attended public schools against 95 percent of African American children.[11]

Still, that around 40 percent of Baltimore's white children, and some of its middle-class children, attended public schools at the time is critical to *The Long Shadow*'s objectives: 25 percent of the sample families are of higher socioeconomic standing. These families were far from the area's wealthiest, but neither were they in desperate straits. Most of these parents had attended college and held middle-class or professional jobs. In contrast, most lower-SES parents, black and white, did not finish high school and when fortunate enough to be working, they held low-level jobs. Also, because neighborhoods in Baltimore are highly segregated along socioeconomic lines as well as by race, these better-off households are substantially insulated from the side of city life just profiled. The experience of their children is important as a point of contrast against which to judge what life holds for those in lower-SES families, the urban disadvantaged.

This broad sketch of Baltimore history is backdrop to the more immediate influences on life chances emanating from conditions experienced close up in families, neighborhoods, and schools. The next chapter expands on the differences in family life across social lines just alluded to; neighborhood and school are taken up in chapter 4.

$=$ Chapter 3 $=$

Family Disadvantage

T HE URBAN disadvantaged, families of low socioeconomic standing by the standards of this volume, make up half the Beginning
School Study Youth Panel (BSSYP, or Youth Panel). Most research
on the life conditions of the urban poor, including most community case
studies, looks inward, focused on poor communities of color, African
American or Latino-Hispanic. Such studies are valuable, but also limiting. Because the BSSYP is a probability sample of Baltimore's entire first
grade enrollment, it includes not just disadvantaged African American
families, but also disadvantaged white families and middle-class households. The latter were decidedly better off than the majority of the panel;
by extension, their children were better off than most who attended
Baltimore's public schools at the time. So, how disadvantaged are the
urban disadvantaged? Comparisons across the socioeconomic gradient
afford purchase on the question.

Another set of comparisons examines *variability within*, that is, differences among families ranked low by socioeconomic criteria. In urban
America, race-ethnicity (African American and white in the sample)
and gender are salient lines of divide. Here, at the outset, our focus is
race—blacks and whites of lower socioeconomic standing.[1] Poor blacks
(and Latinos) have received much attention in the literature on urban
poverty; poor whites much less so. This neglect of low-income whites
is unfortunate. As this volume shows, the experience of poor whites
affords useful perspective on the character of family disadvantage in
the urban context.

Family Conditions Early in Life

Family life during the early elementary years is our point of departure.
Lower socioeconomic status (SES) and disadvantaged minority youth
begin school already behind on all criteria commonly used to gauge
school readiness (Duncan and Magnuson 2011). With their academic
preparation weak and their deportment viewed unfavorably by teachers (see, for example, Lee and Burkam 2002), many find themselves

challenged at the outset and those challenges magnify with time: once children fall behind, it is hard for them to catch up. In our sample, 65 percent of lower-SES children repeated a grade by the end middle school whereas only 20 percent of higher-SES children did. Indeed, many were held back twice. Repeaters' and promoted children's standardized test scores differ starting in the fall of first grade, and academic deficits like these shadow children all throughout their schooling (Alexander, Entwisle, and Dauber 2003).

The impetus behind the study was to understand the importance of early schooling for children's later development. At the time this project was launched, sociologists rarely studied children below high school age and developmental psychologists and education researchers who did study younger children rarely considered the role of social context in their development. Still, the critical period when children go from home child to school child is foundational (see, for example, Entwisle and Alexander 1989), as established by our own studies (Entwisle and Alexander 1993; Entwisle, Alexander, and Olson 1997, 2010a), as well as the broader literatures on family and schooling.

James Heckman (2008, 319) favors "sensitive period" over "critical period" to avoid the connotation that deficits early in life are irreversible. Still, he concurs on the key considerations: "the ability gaps between individuals and across socioeconomic groups open up at early ages, for both cognitive and non-cognitive skills" (308). He continues that, "on average, the later remediation is given to a disadvantaged child, the less effective it is" (309).[2] Heckman's view accords with the import of relevant research. Greg Duncan and Jeanne Brooks-Gunn's review (1997, 597), for example, concludes that family and economic conditions in childhood are a stronger influence on children's school achievement than conditions during adolescence are.[3] Likewise, Aletha Huston and Alison Bentley (2010, 419), taking in more recent literature, say that "early poverty appears to be especially damaging to children's achievement trajectories and school careers." Much the same holds for school-based interventions, in that those targeted at younger children (for example, high-quality preschool programs) have larger and longer-lasting consequences than those targeted at older students (Duncan and Magnuson 2004).

Family First: The Overlapping Spheres

The Long Shadow implicates family resources and early constraints with regard to socioeconomic standing in young adulthood. The internal environment of the family is one source of influence; the larger world to which children are exposed is another. The external environments most relevant for children's development are the neighborhood and the school. In the early years, family is decisive for both: by deciding where to live, parents determine the neighborhood and school contexts to which their children are exposed.[4]

Family, neighborhood, and school jointly contribute to children's development (Jessor 1993), but given most poor children live in low-income neighborhoods and attend high-poverty schools, these linkages tend to reinforce patterns of social advantage and disadvantage. Additionally, because circumstances early in life set children on distinctive paths through school and into the labor market, for the poor this tendency toward alignment across social contexts will foster immobility rather than mobility. Poor minority children who live in high-poverty neighborhoods and attend schools that mainly enroll other needy children are trebly disadvantaged. This chapter examines family life; neighborhood and school are taken up in chapter 4.

Urban Disadvantage: Family Socioeconomics

For us, *The Long Shadow* of family disadvantage inheres in the resource limitations families suffer and the consequences that follow. The literature offers many options for measuring family socioeconomic standing but SES, conceptually, is more than level of schooling, or occupation, or family finances. Robert Bradley and Robert Corwyn (2002, 373) observe the "consensus that income, education and occupation together represent SES better than any of these alone." In other words, the family's socioeconomic profile determines its standing. Accordingly, this volume locates families along the socioeconomic gradient as a function of mother's and father's educational levels, mother's and father's occupational status levels, and family income, low or not low, based on school records. Such an approach is conceptually appropriate, but it potentially obscures important detail, and for that reason we also probe what might be hidden from view.

Two measures of the parents' socioeconomic standing are developed from these five indicators: a continuous SES interval scale for analytic use later and a categorical scale that distinguishes among lower-, middle-, and higher-SES family origins (see table 3.1).[5] Lower-SES families make up roughly half the sample, intermediate and higher-SES families about one-fourth each. Because we are interested mainly in differences across the socioeconomic extremes, table 3.1 and most of the other comparisons reported in this volume omit results for the middle category.[6] The emphasis on the word *extremes* reminds us that SES differences across family types in the sample are less pronounced than would be seen nationally or even regionally. The families we classify as lower SES are genuinely so; the higher-SES designation is more relative. These families are decidedly

Table 3.1 Family Socioeconomics and Demographics of Birth Families

	Lower SES (Lower Half of Panel)			Higher SES
	Total (N = 394)[a]	African American (N = 228)[a]	White (N = 166)[a]	Total (N = 189)[a,d]
Measures of SES				
Average mother's education level (years)	10.0	10.4	9.4	14.4
Average father's education level (years)	10.4	10.8	9.9	15.2
Percent low income (meal subsidy)	94.6	97.8	89.7	12.9
Average occupational status (SEI), mother	22.6[b]	22.5	22.7	51.2[c]
Average occupational status (SEI), father	23.4[b]	22.6	24.2	53.8[c]
Family demographics (percentages)				
Mother employed, grade 1	28.6	33.7	22.0	69.1
Father employed, grade 1	75.2	72.3	77.8	96.2
Teen mother (age nineteen and younger)	66.2	70.0	60.1	22.9
Early teen mother (ages fifteen through seventeen)	40.2	45.7	31.0	9.3
Mother never married by first grade	35.7	51.3	13.5	8.9
Mother married as of first grade	44.6	31.0	64.0	75.3
Single-parent home	24.4	29.0	18.4	12.5
Two-parent home	45.9	33.2	62.6	72.3
Mother and other adult home	25.2	32.2	16.0	12.5
Average number of children	1.8	1.7	1.8	1.1

Source: Authors' compilation.

[a]Figures are maximum sample sizes. Not all the information reported is available for everyone.

[b]Representative occupations at the midpoint of the SEI scale include cab drivers, cashiers, telephone operators, data-entry clerks, longshoremen, and brick masons; at the low end, they include garbage collectors, construction laborers, maids, cooks, and janitors.

[c]Representative occupations at the midpoint of the SEI scale include kindergarten teachers, real estate agents, and insurance brokers; at the high end, they include social workers, career counselors, electrical engineers, architects, doctors, and lawyers.

[d]The higher-SES group is 54 percent white, 46 percent African American.

better off than those of the lower and middle ranks, but by national standards probably solidly middle class, rather than higher or upper.

Beginning with the sections that follow and continuing throughout this volume, we undertake a close reading of the Youth Panel's life experiences. First grade is the point of departure, following them over a quarter century into the panel's third decade. Our focus is the Youth Panel children, but *The Long Shadow*'s goal is more ambitious. The participants are typical children of the city. Owing to our project's grounding in scientifically rigorous probability sampling, their experience affords a window on that of children like them citywide at the time, which means the picture that emerges in this volume is bigger than the BSSYP.

Family Differences Across the Socioeconomic Gradient

Although Baltimore's school system in 1982 was (and still is) overwhelmingly low-income minority, for strategic reasons we oversampled schools with large white enrollments. This is why 45 percent of the sample are white and 25 percent qualify as higher SES (see table 3.1). The typical lower-SES parent is a high school dropout and 95 percent of the children are on meal subsidy—most assuredly a disadvantaged profile. But what of the 5 percent of lower-SES children whose families are not low income according to school records? Their mothers average 8.6 years of schooling and their fathers 9.1 years (not shown in the table), well below the levels for all lower-SES families in table 3.1. This illustrates our point that socioeconomic standing inheres in a family's SES profile, not in any single criterion.

The Socioeconomic Index (SEI) metric by which jobs are ranked (Featherman and Stevens 1982) is used extensively in stratification research, but is less intuitive. It ranks occupations nationally using census data on the educational and earnings levels of incumbents, with values ranging from roughly 0 to 100. The version used to rank the parents' occupations is referenced to the 1970 census.[7] The averages of 22.6 and 23.4 for lower-SES parents correspond to lower level blue-collar and white-collar jobs, including cashiers, cabbies, telephone operators, data entry clerks (these were the days of keypunch machines), longshoremen, and brick masons. Roughly 10 percent of lower-SES parents have jobs with the lowest possible status ranks (scores of 18.5 and below). They are garbage collectors, construction laborers, maids, cooks, housekeepers, and janitors.

This lower-SES profile is stark contrast to the 25 percent classified as higher SES, whose parents average around three years of college. Half have college degrees, including some with advanced degrees (30 percent of fathers and 14 percent of mothers). In higher-SES families, SEI averages in the low 50s for both parents. They are real estate agents, managers, and insurance brokers at the midpoint; teachers K–12, social workers, electrical engineers, architects, doctors, and lawyers at the high end.

A small fraction of the higher-SES children (13 percent) were eligible for subsidized meals at school, marking their families low income despite their parents' high levels of schooling and higher-status employment. This circumstance may not be all that unusual in that most large cities are home to colleges and universities with graduate and professional schools. Most students today work part time while taking courses (for example, American Council on Education 2006) and graduate students tend to be income poor, but schooling rich. Parental schooling for these low-income but higher-SES families averages 14.2 and 13 years for mothers and fathers and their occupational status averages, at 46.9 and 49.5, as well within the higher-SES qualifying range. There is a lesson here: across a large, diverse sample, combinations of SES attributes that seem anomalous on close inspection can be perfectly reasonable.

Employment data, reported in table 3.1, add to the picture: lower-SES parents not only hold lower ranking jobs, their employment also is more erratic. We lack complete employment histories, but the gap in employment at the time of our first grade interviews in the fall of 1982, a time of nationwide recession, is vast.[8] For fathers, it is the difference between virtually total employment among the higher SES and 75 percent employment among the lower; for mothers, it is the difference between 69 percent employment among the higher and 29 percent among the lower. Most survey research affords but a moment-in-time snapshot of family conditions, but because we have tracked these families over many years we can say that these employment patterns during the first grade year are fairly characteristic of these households. In lower-SES households, the percentage of fathers employed in years 4, 6, 7, 8, 9, 10, and 11 ranges from 69 percent to 77 percent (averaging 74 percent); in higher-SES households, the range is from 94 percent to 99 percent (averaging 96 percent). The corresponding ranges over years 2, 3, and 4 are 70 percent to 80 percent for higher-SES mothers and 22 percent to 32 percent for their lower-SES counterparts.[9]

Employment uncertainty is chronic in lower-SES households and differences across social lines are huge. For most fathers no doubt the ideal is full-time, year-round work; for mothers, things are not as clear. James Coleman and Thomas Hoffer (1987) argue that maternal employment detracts from within-family social capital and so is detrimental to children's upbringing, but evidence on long-term effects is thin and conflicting (Ludwig and Mayer 2006, 184–86). Increases have been substantial in the labor force participation of women with children since

1982, and money brought into the family by a second earner, paired with increasingly favorable views of women's employment, make for a strong counterargument (for example, McLanahan 2004, 607).

Within the sample, we see both sides of the story. On the one hand, Kim, who is African American, reports that having both parents working—often two jobs—took a toll on her schoolwork, a "mistake" she vowed not to repeat with her own children (in 2000, she was a single mother with three children). On the other hand, Karen's single-parent mother worked fifty hours weekly at her own business, but Karen (who is white) had an aunt and grandmother living nearby to help look after her, an arrangement that by her account worked well. Karen was married with one child and was working part time when we last spoke with her. To work or not? Context clearly matters when it comes to implications for children's development, but context often is lacking in research on the topic, which might help explain why the question remains unresolved.

Bear in mind that higher SES in the sample does not mean wealthy, so we cannot know whether maternal employment is discretionary, obligated by family finances, or some combination of the two. In today's economy, two earners often are needed to achieve a family wage (the amount needed to support a family comfortably) and going it alone can mean financial hardship. That being the case, it is striking that levels of maternal employment in higher-SES households rival those of paternal employment in lower-SES households. Because approximately 25 percent of lower-SES mothers parent alone, including almost 30 percent of African American mothers (see table 3.1), the stresses on them must be enormous.

This pattern matches national trends, in that highly educated women are the ones most prone to work outside the home.[10] Among married mothers ages twenty-five and older with young children and a bachelor's or an advanced degree, labor force participation nationally has not dipped below 60 percent since at least 1994. Over this same span of years, employment figures for high school dropout mothers ranged between 35 percent (in 1997) and 27 percent (in 2000); for mothers with a high school degree, employment hovered around 50 percent (Cohany and Sok 2007). The picture in table 3.1 is much the same.

For lower-SES women, work is a necessity, not discretionary, but deindustrialization and suburbanization have left many central cities bereft of accessible jobs (Wilson 1997). The remaining good jobs are mostly white collar and so out of reach of the urban disadvantaged owing to a skills mismatch (Kasarda 1990; Blank 2009). The issue for Wilson is male joblessness, but given the many inner-city women also shouldering weighty parenting responsibilities, the same forces that leave inner-city men without attractive job opportunities may be even more limiting for women.

Variation Within: Race Differences at the Low End

The urban disadvantaged are not all disadvantaged to the same extent and there are reasons to think the conditions of life experienced by disadvantaged racial and ethnic minorities will be harsher than those typical of lower-income whites. Nationally, black poverty is both deeper and longer lasting than white poverty is (Magnuson and Votruba-Drzal 2009; Timberlake 2007). In 2011, for example, 12.8 percent of blacks but just 4.4 percent of whites had incomes below 50 percent of the poverty threshold; by the more relaxed standard of low income (meaning income under two times the poverty threshold), the respective figures are 51.3 percent and 25.7 percent (Kneebone, Nadeau, and Berube 2011, 17).

Also, a higher percentage of poor blacks than whites live in areas of concentrated poverty—nationally in 2000, 18.6 percent versus 5.9 percent (Jargowsky 2003). Blacks also make up a much larger fraction of the concentrated poverty population—in 2009, 44.5 percent African American versus 16.5 percent white (Kneebone, Nadeau, and Berube 2011, 16).[11]

Notwithstanding these national trends, the socioeconomic profiles of lower-SES blacks and whites in table 3.1 are virtually interchangeable. This might seem counterintuitive, but we believe it is absolutely the case, and not just in our sample. The explanation is somewhat involved, but worth pursuing because it sheds light on submerged racial dynamics with respect to big city schooling.

The White Presence in Baltimore's Schools

The Youth Panel sampled first graders attending Baltimore City public schools. Because many white families in the city send their children to private schools, the white subsample likely is more disadvantaged than Baltimore's overall white population is.[12] Still, the city system enrollment does include some better-off white families, and they too are represented in the panel.

The typical lower-SES parent, white or black, is a high school dropout. In fact, overall more white parents than black failed to finish high school; for mothers, 44 percent versus 33 percent; for fathers, 33 percent versus 30 percent. At the same time, more white parents also completed college: for mothers, 14 percent versus 9 percent; for fathers, 20 percent versus 8 percent. Whites thus are overrepresented at both ends of the education distribution.

At the high end are parents of some means. They have options, but elect to stay in the city, at least through the elementary grades. No doubt for some it is a principled commitment, but one made easier by the existence of upper-income white residential enclaves and, at least in the early grades, of neighborhood schools with a comfortable white presence. During the 1990–1991 school year, thirteen of Baltimore's 122 public elementary schools had white enrollments of 90 percent or greater, eighteen had white enrollments of 75 percent or greater, and twenty-six had enrollments at least half white. These twenty-six elementary schools accounted for 73 percent of the city's white elementary students; the thirteen hypersegregated schools alone enrolled 43 percent.[13]

The middle grades (twenty-seven schools) draw from wider catchments areas. Not a single school had a white enrollment of 90 percent or greater, one school had an enrollment over 75 percent white, and just four were majority white. These four schools together accounted for 43 percent of the total white middle school enrollment, but between elementary school and middle school, the percentage white system-wide dropped from 18.8 percent to 13.2 percent.

At the high school level, with still wider attendance zones, just two of twenty schools—both citywide academic magnet schools—had majority white student bodies. These schools accounted for 27.8 percent of the city's remaining white pupils and just 4.1 percent of its black pupils.[14] Between elementary and middle school, many whites left the system (see also Alexander, Entwisle, and Dauber 1996), and those who stayed tended to stay put: 76 percent of Youth Panel whites but just 57 percent of blacks resided in the same census tract in the first and fifth grades.

Upper-income whites in high-poverty cities tend to reside in comfortable, middle-class neighborhoods and three of the Youth Panel's elementary schools fit this description. But Baltimore also includes stable lower-SES white neighborhoods, many of long standing. Sherry Olson (1976, 5), for example, describes the area around the B&O railroad yards in West Baltimore as "hidden valleys of white poverty persisting from one generation to the next." These neighborhoods were first established in the 1840s and 1850s and today retain much the same character: a railroad museum now occupies the site of the switching yard, but not much else has changed and the area's low-income white residential enclaves remain substantially intact.

Long-time locals think of Baltimore as an overgrown small town—a mosaic of "urban islands," in Christopher Silver's phrase (1997). During the 1970s, the city sponsored a popular annual fair. Neighborhoods were its centerpiece, and a host of community association booths displayed their community's virtues. Community identities were strong then and widely understood, and the situation is much the same today. Many of these neighborhoods are set off geographically by natural barriers (the Jones Falls, parks and ravines, the Chesapeake Bay inlet) and man-made barriers (highways, rail lines, industrial complexes) that help preserve their distinctiveness and, as regards race, their exclusiveness. Several such neighborhoods—black and white—were included in the original sampling. Box 3.1 gives a sense of their geography.

Box 3.1   Neighborhoods Apart: Natural and Man-Made Boundaries

The fabric of the city's life is a patchwork of clearly recognizable neighborhoods, each possessing a shared ethnic, cultural, and class identity as well as a colorful history. Baltimore's neighborhood pattern had its roots in the physical landscape—the network of streams, valleys, and harbor inlets forced strong natural boundaries. On this natural foundation, cultural and social patterns further differentiate the city into distinct neighborhoods, many with their own miniature "downtown" shopping areas, powerful community associations, building and loan societies, and political clubs. In addition to natural boundaries, some neighborhoods are bounded by parks, highways, and industrial zones, creating further barriers to pedestrian traffic and enhancing their isolation. These physical barriers produce and reinforce patterns of class and racial segregation.

Hampden originated as a company town created by cotton mill owners in the nineteenth century. Its location along streams of the Jones Falls Valley created a physical barrier separating Hampden from the surrounding community. The mills are long gone, but Hampden survives as a white segregated enclave (in 1980, it was more than 99 percent white), bounded by the Jones Falls Valley on the west and south and Wyman Park on the east. Its physical separation has helped perpetuate its cultural and ethnic distinctiveness and insulated it from demographic changes that overwhelmed the city (even in 2000, its population was 94 percent white).

By the mid-twentieth century, Baltimore had become a highly industrialized manufacturing and shipping center. World War II brought thousands of new workers and transformed the city into a major industrial city, but Baltimore still retained its southern cultural heritage and its residential patterns reflected this Jim Crow influence. The residences of the white working class that provided the manpower for this industrial base were conveniently located near the industrial zones in which residents worked. The southern tip of the city contains three neighborhoods within our sample that illustrate this pattern.

Curtis Bay and Brooklyn are white working-class neighborhoods located adjacent to the Curtis Bay Industrial zone, isolated along the inner harbor inlet of the city. In 1980, African American residents made up less than 1 percent of Curtis Bay and 2 percent of Brooklyn. In fact, most blacks who lived in the area did so in the racially integrated Brooklyn Homes public housing project located in an isolated corner between the Brooklyn and Curtis Bay neighborhoods. Children from Brooklyn Homes attended a separate elementary school (Bay Brook), rather than Brooklyn's main elementary school, Maree Faring, which remained 96 percent white.

Morrell Park, located in the southwestern part of the city not far from Cherry Hill, is another white working-class neighborhood whose racial segregation is maintained by natural and man-made boundaries. It is bounded by the Gwynns Falls, Carroll Park, a major highway, several

(*Box continues on p. 42.*)

Box 3.1   *Continued*

---

major roads, and two sets of railroad tracks. Aided by these physical boundaries, today it is still more than 90 percent white.

Armisted Gardens, a white working-class fenced enclave, was originally built during World War II as public housing for workers in defense plants. Located in east Baltimore along an extension of Herring Run Park and adjacent to a major industrial zone (Pulaski Industrial Area), even today it remains a physically isolated neighborhood. A major electric transmission line extends across the northern edge of the community, and a set of major roads and highways run along the borders of the neighborhood. The continued racial segregation of Armisted Gardens is striking: by 2000, its African American population was still less than 2 percent.

African American neighborhoods are not so dramatically bounded, and tend to fill in areas not taken by whites. Cherry Hill, a highly segregated neighborhood near Brooklyn, is an isolated black enclave bounded by the harbor inlet, a park, and a residential dead zone of empty space. The neighborhood is further circumscribed by major roads, highways, and railroad tracks, with few roads into or out of the community. In 2000, Cherry Hill's population remained 96 percent African American.

These lower-SES urban enclaves are just as distinct as those inhabited by the city's well-to-do whites, with one critical difference: those who call them home are some of Baltimore's neediest, white and black. And as regards school, they have few options. They cannot afford private school tuition or housing in the suburbs, and often family ties to place are strong. These low-income residential enclaves are key to the continued presence of working-class whites in Baltimore's public schools, and to the blue-collar attainment regime that privileges them over blacks of like socioeconomic background.

Family Makeup and History

The large changes in family life that played out nationally over the latter half of the twentieth century include increases in single parenting, in the number of never-married mothers, and in the prevalence of female-headed households (McLanahan and Perchesik 2008; Ellwood and Jencks 2004), all consequential for children's well-being. David Eggebeen and Daniel Lichter (1991), for example, estimate that the child poverty rate in 1988 would have been about 33 percent lower had the percentage of single-parent households then been the same as in 1960.

These changes in family life are most pronounced among African Americans, but hardly exclusive to them.[15] In 1993, Charles Murray directed attention to some disquieting statistics: 22 percent of white babies in 1991 were born to single women, 82 percent of them high school dropouts.[16] Murray used these figures to sound an alarm, and he has returned to this theme in his recent book *Coming Apart: The State of White America, 1960–2010* (2012). In his 1993 *Wall Street Journal* article, he argued that low-income whites were following the path forged by black Americans decades earlier, one leading to a horrid future: "illegitimacy is the single most important social problem of our time—more important than crime, drugs, poverty, illiteracy, welfare or homelessness because it drives everything else" ("The Coming White Underclass," October 29, p. A14).[17]

Murray is correct that unwed parenting is associated with social problems like welfare dependency and persistent poverty, but which lead and which follow is not easily determined. Economic privation no doubt accounts for some portion of children's adverse outcomes in solo-parent households, most often female-headed. These households are disproportionately low income, and children's health, schooling, and overall well-being are compromised by low income (Duncan and Brooks-Gunn 1997; Magnuson and Votruba-Drzal 2009). But it is not just a matter of low income, as the achievement gap separating children in single-parent families from those in two-parent families is greater than can be accounted for by economics alone (McLanahan and Sandefur 1994).

These are politically charged issues, even without race in the mix. Race, however, is very much in the mix, especially in explaining persistent poverty. Overall, many more poor whites than poor blacks are in single-parent families and many more whites than blacks are in poverty, but rates—the proportion subject to poverty—tell a different story: rates of single parenting are much higher among blacks than among whites, and so the impact of single parenting is felt disproportionately by black children.

But is single parenting the real issue? Andrew Cherlin (2009) argues that family instability is key, not the configuration of caregivers, because a stable single-parent household probably is better for children than a revolving door of short-term relationships. Given that more than half of unmarried biological parents are expected to have a child with a different partner (Smeeding, Garfinkel, and Mincy 2011), Maceo's unsettled family life is illustrative. Maceo never knew his biological father and moved between households often when growing up. His three siblings have three different biological fathers, and of his youngest sister's father he says, "That was just somebody she [their mother] was messin' with. They weren't even livin' together."

Box 3.2   White Working-Class Family Support

While in elementary school, Karen lived in an ethnically diverse Baltimore City neighborhood of mostly low-income and lower-middle-class residents. She was an only child and her parents divorced when she was three. Karen's grandmother and an aunt immediately stepped in to help with day care. When Karen started school, it was to their home that she went at the end of the school day and where she spent her days in the summer. Evening meals often included her mother, grandmother, and aunt. Karen happily relates how she and her mother (despite working up to fifty hours a week) would sit down together to work on homework. When Karen was twelve, her mom remarried and the newly formed family moved outside the city to one of the surrounding counties. Karen says that it was great to leave the city and the violence she encountered in middle school, but that "it was hard to leave her grandmother, aunt, and cousin who had lived just around the corner."

Writ large, it is much the same nationally:

> U.S. children born into low-education and minority households spend a substantial and rising share of their childhoods in single-parent, divorced and remarried households; they are exposed to a disproportionate number of adult partner relationships through cohabitation and remarriage among their primary caregivers; and they experience a comparatively smaller number of years in which a stable father is present in the household. (Autor and Wasserman 2013, 37–38)

However, in societies with a strong social safety net—for example, universal health-care and child-care subsidies (Pong, Dronkers, and Hampden-Thompson 2003; Hampden-Thompson and Pong 2005; Rainwater and Smeeding 2004)—adverse child outcomes associated with single parenting are mitigated, suggesting single parenting per se is not the issue.

A strong family support system—often grandmothers in African American extended families (see, for example, Entwisle and Alexander 2000; McLoyd et al. 2000)—also can mitigate problems associated with single parenting. The likelihood of extended family living arrangements is greater among African American than whites,[18] but kin ties are important in lower-SES white families too. Consider Karen, profiled in box 3.2. In elementary school she lived close to her grandmother and usually went there after school instead of returning to an empty house.

Table 3.1 provides an overview of family makeup in the study, contrasting lower-SES families with higher-SES families, and, among those of lower SES, blacks with whites. Paralleling national trends, differences in family life across socioeconomic levels are large, and racial differences within them are sizeable. Two-thirds of the panel's lower-SES mothers were teenagers at the birth of their first child, roughly three times the level in higher-SES families. Among the lower SES specifically, teen parenthood was more common among blacks than among whites: 70 percent of black first births were to teenage mothers, almost 10 percent higher than the white percentage.

The teen years cover a broad range, however, and the consequences of having a baby at age nineteen may be less severe depending on the circumstances (for example, finished school and married). What, however, of becoming a mother at age fifteen, sixteen, or seventeen, when teens are unambiguously of high school age and we would prefer they be focused on their studies?[19] These kinds of off-time events or accelerated role transitions signify "precocious development" (see Pallas 1993; Wickrama and Baltimore 2010), which can be a good thing, but not when it entails taking on the adult responsibility of parenting without the resources, financial and otherwise, to do the job properly. In this light, it is troubling that teen births at age seventeen and below account for 46 percent of African American mothers' first births and 31 percent of white mothers'.

Almost 70 percent of lower-SES black mothers were not married when their child was in first grade; more than half had never married.[20] Both levels are well above those registered by higher-SES mothers, as might be expected, but also above those of lower-SES whites, 36 percent of whom were unmarried when their child finished first grade and 14 percent of whom never married.[21] Single parenting often pairs with low levels of schooling, which is why the three tips Isabel Sawhill and Ron Haskins give for avoiding poverty include marrying before having children ("Five Myths About Our Land of Opportunity," *Washington Post*, November 1, 2009). The other two are finishing high school and working full time. For those who heed this counsel, the poverty rate nationally is 2 percent, about as low as poverty rates go.

Against that standard, this lower-SES African American family profile does not augur well for the future, but is hardly peculiar to family life in Baltimore. Taking stock of the literature from around this time, William Julius Wilson and Robert Aponte (1985, 241) tell us that:

> female-headed families are heavily represented in the poverty population, are highly urbanized, and are disproportionately black; . . . black female heads are much less likely to marry if single or to remarry if divorced or

widowed . . . female-headed families among whites tend to be of relatively short duration, whereas among blacks they tend to be prolonged; . . . black children are increasingly growing up in families without fathers.

Wilson and Aponte go on to implicate joblessness among black men as a root cause, and that problem too has grown more severe, a "crisis ignored" according to Andrew Sum and his colleagues (2004).

Data on family size in table 3.1—number of children (a tally of siblings) and number of parents and other adults in the household—add onto this picture. Lower-SES families have more children (almost one more, on average, than higher-SES families) and fewer parents to care for them (just 46 percent of lower-SES children are in two-parent households in first grade versus 72 percent of higher-SES children).

Managing a large family is challenging, and single parenting magnifies the challenge. Among lower-SES families, black mothers began parenting earlier and were much more likely to be parenting without the benefit of a father coresident. Just 33 percent of lower-SES black households included two parents, versus 63 percent of lower-SES white households.

Having many children dilutes the parental resources available to any one of them, and children in large families generally have poorer schooling outcomes (see, for example, Blake 1989). To see whether these family circumstances persist, we examined family makeup in 1984 and 1985 and the same patterns hold. The two-parent household percentages for lower-SES African Americans are well below the lower-SES white figures each occasion: 29 percent to 36 percent versus 54 percent to 63 percent. Among higher-SES families, the percentages are higher still, and more stable: 72 percent to 75 percent across occasions. These patterns pertain to the parents; later we will see whether they are repeated in the Youth Panel's experience of family life as young adults.

Extended Family, Within the Household and Beyond

Another consideration is extended family living arrangements or, if not coresident family then family nearby. Table 3.1 reports the percentage of solo mother households with another adult present. In 1982, almost a third of lower-SES black mothers (32 percent) were living with another adult, a much higher percentage than in higher-SES households (13 percent) or in lower-SES white households (16 percent). A like pattern, not displayed, persisted in second grade and fourth grade, so African American children in the study, at least in the early years, had greater access than white children to extended family within the household. In the study (for example, Entwisle and Alexander 2000) as generally (Furstenberg 1976; Furstenberg, Brooks-Gunn, and Morgan 1987; Kellam et al. 1975), that often is a grandparent. But nearby kin outside the household are important also. Consider Geraldine's and Gail's experiences.

Geraldine, an African American, went to live with her grandmother in tenth grade, following a brother who had made the move some years earlier. Life at home, she told us, was too unstable:

> Well, it was like, at home I didn't have any structure, and I just ran, I was buck-wild when I was a teenager. . . . I was hooking school, I wasn't going to school. I think like my tenth grade year, that was like my worst year of school. I went to school like maybe out of a hundred and eighty days, I think I went to school ninety days, out of a hundred eighty. And like I failed, like, there was social studies and math, I failed all three quarters, and then the fourth quarter I passed, and they passed me to the eleventh grade, so that's why, I knew that I needed to be with my grandmother because I had to go to school, I had to make up my bed, I had to do this, I had to do that, . . . and that was the structure that I needed. So I really, really needed that structure.

It may well be that the structure Geraldine sought saved her—hers is the story of a young survivor who went on to complete a master's degree and was working toward her doctorate when we talked with her in 2005.

Gail, a white high school dropout, spoke of her experience shuttling between her parents' home and her grandparents' when things were too unsettled with her parents: her parents fought often, her mother used drugs, she had brothers in jail, and a sister had turned to prostitution:

> I mean, sometimes . . . uh . . . I guess I . . . um . . . well, sometimes my mom and dad would fight sometimes. . . . And I didn't like to be around that so, you know . . . I mean, I liked bein' at my grandmother's cause, you know, I guess they showed more attention to me or somethin' like that . . . bein' around for me, you know, they get my clothes for me or, you know, or just stuff like that. Make me dinner and so . . . I mean, my mom did it but she wasn't really there, you know.

Continuing, Gail went on to speak of her special relationship with her grandfather:

> Well . . . um . . . he would do just about everything for me. . . . he took care of me, you know. I mean, he more or less showed me what was right from wrong and so forth. We were just really close and we still are close.

Although expressed differently, Gail's account too is about the need for structure paired with caring, qualities Gail's parents apparently weren't able to provide but her grandparents could. In these stories, extended family support is a safe refuge from family dysfunction. Karen's situation is rather different in that those extra hands added onto a sturdy foundation. Still, helping hands can fall short, as in Bess's experience.

Bess, who grew up in what she described as chaotic family environment, had her first baby at age fourteen in the summer of eighth grade, then a second in tenth grade. She tried to finish high school, indeed worked hard at it, but was unable to trust her mother to watch her first baby and eventually gave up. Bess would call home from school, she told us, and her mother would not be there; she would come home to find her baby soiled and unfed. "If I had somebody to watch who I knew, you know, was a good person to watch and I knew she was gonna' be all right, then, you know I woulda' stayed [in school]." Bess was surrounded by an abundance of family—a cousin who supported a drug habit by prostituting herself and her mother, who, according to Bess, was drunk "morning to night." Bess is one of the Youth Panel's many permanent dropouts, a victim, she says, of a neglectful mother and extended family dysfunction.

These sharply contrasting accounts of family support for Geraldine, Karen, Gail, and Bess blur together in typical survey data (including ours), as the surrounding context is hard to capture in the clipped survey format. In addition, household rosters of coresident family will miss help from kin living nearby. Bruce's white working-class extended family, for example, owned three adjacent houses on a block of row houses on Baltimore's West Side, effectively a family enclave. Although nearby kin can provide help with child care and be a safe refuge from dysfunctional family dynamics, a large networked family is no guarantee of either. With extended kin often come obligations and a tight-knit but troubled family, as in Bess's situation, is more likely to drag down than to lift up.

Urban Disadvantage at the Interior of Family Life

The socioeconomic profiles reviewed in this chapter make concrete our sense of urban disadvantage. This disadvantage inheres first in a short-fall of material resources, but extends beyond the purely economic (see, for example, Mayer 1997, 2010). Dollars are important, but so too are the other pillars that contribute to a family's socioeconomic standing. Parents with little formal education and an erratic history of employment in low-level work are not well positioned to model the kinds of behaviors and encourage the kinds of values that will help their children to succeed at school, and the stresses that often accompany urban disadvantage add to their challenges (to be taken up in chapter 7). That is not to say lower-SES parents cannot parent well or establish a sturdy foundation for success at school, but for them to do so is vastly more difficult. The higher-SES to lower-SES comparisons presented in this chapter identify huge differences in family resources across social lines even within a high-poverty urban school system, where family privilege at the upper end falls far short of what would be seen against, say, the suburban advantaged.

The demographics of family life also matter. Though not strictly socioeconomic, solo parenting and precocious parenting add to the burdens associated with low levels of schooling, low-status work, and low income. Our profiles reveal expected differences along the socioeconomic gradient, but also variability within when comparing black and white families of lower socioeconomic standing. These instances of intersectionality (see, for example, Browne and Misra 2003) align with national data on family life and so in that sense also are expected. Still, to see them juxtaposed against the nearly interchangeable white and black lower-SES profiles points up facets of *The Long Shadow* that are likely to weigh more on African American children's development than on white children's. The urban disadvantaged thus are not all similarly disadvantaged. That is true at the interior of family life; it also characterizes children's first grade neighborhoods and schools, to which we now turn.

= Chapter 4 =

Neighborhood and School

O UR COVERAGE of urban disadvantage to this point has centered
on the interior of family life, but the family also is gateway to
the world beyond, first through its choice of neighborhood and
then by determining the school its children attend. Neighborhood and
school, when added to family, round out the overlapping spheres of
influence that children experience firsthand, day in and day out.

Neighborhood and Family Disadvantage

The urban disadvantaged live in the poorest parts of the city. The
worst of these neighborhoods are distressed in many ways associated with urban decay—crime, drugs, boarded-up houses, and empty
businesses—and family life in them can be ugly.

Peter describes the high-poverty African American neighborhood of
his upbringing:

> Well some of the families that used to live around here, they was like,
> like junkies and stuff like that, and half of them didn't even respect their,
> their mother and father. . . . Like this one guy, him and his father started
> fighting because the son was fixing a pack of Oodles Noodles, but his
> father wanted to eat it . . . and they was fighting over a pack of Oodles and
> Noodles in the street . . . [And the Mom], she was after getting drunk, so
> she didn't really care who, who had the Oodles Noodles.

Ken, who is white but, like Peter, also of lower-SES background,
describes his:

> You know, I'd get home, I'd get home like three-thirty, four o'clock in
> the afternoon, depending on what time we got out [from school]. And
> people'd be standing on the corners. That's when the prostitutes were
> running in and out of the neighborhood, and I couldn't even walk my
> grandfather's dog without getting harassed, you know.

William Julius Wilson (1978) attributes these kinds of conditions in
low-income neighborhoods to the exodus of jobs, the middle class, and

50

stabilizing institutions. Robert Sampson (2000) adds that weak cohesion at the community level opens the door for crime and other forms of predatory behavior, and residential segregation adds a racial layer to urban disadvantage (Massey and Denton 1993). Compared with whites of similar income, blacks tend to live in lower-quality neighborhoods where their children attend lower-quality schools (for example, Pattillo 2005). These patterns are one way disadvantaged family life casts its long shadow. We begin with neighborhood.

Neighborhood Profiles Versus Neighborhood Effects

Whether neighborhoods are consequential for children's development as distinct from family conditions is not easily established. Adverse family and community conditions often co-occur, so how can we say which has primacy? And within neighborhoods, it is much the same: for example, in 1980 census data for Baltimore, the correlation between neighborhood median family income and the percentage African American residents is 0.60, large enough to cloud clear-cut interpretation. When adverse outcomes are observed, as in high rates of dropout or incarceration, this conflation makes it hard to know which feature of neighborhood is responsible—concentrated poverty, racial segregation, or something else?

The available research elevates neighborhood socioeconomic disadvantage over other contenders because low income and joblessness define what makes a disadvantaged neighborhood disadvantaged (Leventhal and Brooks-Gunn 1998). But neighborhood quality is not simply a matter of employment or poverty levels, and poor does not necessarily mean distressed. A community's commitment to civility and upkeep can stem the "broken windows" dynamic of community decay (Taylor 2001) and help tamp down crime (Sampson 2000). As Katherine Newman and Rebekah Massengill (2006, 432) put it, "Collective efficacy [at the community level] is not just merely a function of 'percent poor' because even when controlling for poverty rates, we see differential rates of community cohesion, trust, and willingness to intervene in the face of threatening disorder."

Research now has moved beyond the surface capture of neighborhood conditions that can be culled from census data. The best of these studies bring to bear rich observational and ethnographic data to get closer to what life is like close in, on the ground (for example, Sampson 2012; Sampson and Raudenbusch 1999).

A second strand of this new generation of neighborhood research turns to experimental interventions to gauge how neighborhood affects children. Typically these involve housing voucher programs that allow some low-income residents of racially segregated or high-poverty communities to relocate to communities where poverty rates are lower or where the residential mix more diverse (for example, Ludwig et al. 2012). The question is whether movers and their children fare better in their new neighborhoods than would be expected had they remained in their former neighborhoods. "Would be expected" asks about something that did not happen, but the question can be informed by the experience of those left behind who were eligible for vouchers but not randomly selected to receive them. With random assignment, the personal and family circumstances of movers and stayers should be comparable. If that is the case and their neighborhoods differ in ways intended by the voucher plan, then differences in children's developmental outcomes, including the quality of their school performance, likely trace to those differences in neighborhood conditions.

The Beginning School Survey Youth Panel (BSSYP, or Youth Panel) entails no such interventions, nor is it a neighborhood study per se. We cannot evaluate the panel's experience by way of rich ethnographic observation or experimentation. Still, we have in hand an uncommonly rich store of information about where the Youth Panel were living around the time they began first grade and, unlike studies that identify neighborhood crudely by way of zip codes or census tracts, our data map onto authentic neighborhood boundaries.

Our data sources include census data for a fairly standard portrait of neighborhood conditions, but also official crime statistics and residents' perceptions of neighborhood quality. When juxtaposed, these reveal critical distinctions missed in depictions of neighborhood from census sources alone. And though we cannot assess consequences for children's development with the kind of authority conferred by experimentation, there is reason to suppose that neighborhood levels of criminal victimization and social cohesion count for a great deal. For example, a recent attempt to reconcile findings from nonexperimental and experimental neighborhood studies concludes that children's schooling is most affected by violence in the community, with Baltimore and Chicago highlighted as cities burdened by especially dangerous neighborhoods (Burdick-Will et al. 2011, 256). Consistent with this, Patrick Sharkey (2010), examining homicides within a week of testing, finds that exposure to neighborhood violence depresses children's vocabulary and reading scores. His results hold for African American children in Chicago, the only group with exposure to neighborhood homicides sufficient to test the proposition—a dubious distinction indeed.

Neighborhood Conditions via Census Data

Table 4.1 profiles the Youth Panel's first grade neighborhoods by way of census data, but configured as locally meaningful communities using the Baltimore Neighborhood Statistical Areas developed by the City Housing Authority. Neighborhoods have distinctive identities in Baltimore and the table rendering is faithful to them. Here is how Alice, a white woman from Baltimore's low-income West Side, replied when asked at age twenty-eight to think back to whether neighborhood kids hung together at school:

> You know . . . I was in the middle because where we live at, on this side of Fulton Avenue . . . called Lumberyard, and then on this side of Monroe Street is Doghouse, and in the middle, they just call it the Corner. So I, I mean, I lived at West Side, you know, I know a lot of people at West Side, I know people in Doghouse, I know people, you know, Pigtown, you know, I just, I know people all around. But the majority of them would stay in their groups.

To a local, the areas she ticks off—Lumberyard, Doghouse, The Corner, Pigtown, and West Side—make perfect sense.

First grade school addresses are used to attach neighborhood attributes to families.[1] This is serviceable for nineteen of the original twenty schools, which are neighborhood schools in the traditional sense.[2] The twentieth school was located at the boundary of black and white low-income neighborhoods to promote racial integration, and with a 63 percent white enrollment, it was successful. This school's uncommonly broad catchment area obliged us to use household addresses to attach neighborhoods to families.

Also reported in table 4.1 are figures for all of Baltimore (bottom row) and for all twenty neighborhoods averaged. The Youth Panel was designed to afford a window on conditions citywide. How well the two profiles align is one standard of its success, and it is reassuring that they are practically interchangeable.

So what do the neighborhoods experienced by the urban disadvantaged look like and how do they compare with higher-SES children's neighborhoods? The conditions depicted in table 4.1 reflect what children encounter travelling to and from school, as well as what they see when out and about where they live. Neighborhood racial makeup is one clear difference: just 13.6 percent of the residents in lower-SES white neighborhoods are African American against 75.6 percent in lower-SES black neighborhoods. In higher-SES neighborhoods, the corresponding figures are 11 percent and 41 percent, which average to the 25.1 percent figure reported in table 4.1 for all higher-SES neighborhoods.

Table 4.1   Neighborhood Conditions, Circa 1980

	Black in Neighborhood	Below 75% Poverty Level	Poverty Level	Below 200% Poverty Level	Women Head Household with Child in Poverty
Lower SES (N = 394)	49.5	20.4	28.1	55.0	50.0
White (N = 166)	13.6	17.4	23.8	48.4	50.7
Black (N = 228)	75.6	22.5	31.3	59.7	49.5
Higher SES (N = 189)	25.1	7.3	11.4	28.6	29.3
Overall (N = 787)	42.3	15.3	21.5	45.4	41.4
Baltimore City	54.8	17.0	22.9	45.9	49.7

Source: Authors' compilation based on data from the 1980 Census (U.S. Bureau of the Census 1983).
Note: All numbers except income are percentages.

Residential patterns in Baltimore are highly segregated by race so these differences in racial makeup hardly surprise. More surprising is that, notwithstanding their physical separation, the lower-SES black and white neighborhoods included in the study display strikingly similar socioeconomic profiles. We saw this in chapter 1 for the West Side neighborhoods bordering The Corner; we now see that it is much the same citywide.

In the lower-SES African American communities, the poverty rate averages 31.3 percent and 59.7 percent of residents have incomes less than twice the poverty line, qualifying them as low income. It is well known that cities like Baltimore harbor large swaths of concentrated black poverty, but what of white poverty? Conditions in the lower-SES white neighborhoods are not quite as extreme, but neither are they all that different: nearly 50 percent of their residents are low income by the standard just given and 23.8 percent are at or below the poverty level. For perspective, 28.6 percent of those in higher-SES communities are low income and their poverty rate averages 11.4 percent.

In addition to these poverty figures, lower-SES neighborhoods, African American and white, show high levels of male unemployment and their median family incomes lag well behind the citywide average. Lower-SES white neighborhoods again are not quite as disadvantaged,

Women Head Household with Child	High School Graduate Age Twenty-Five Plus	Male Unemployment	Professional and Manager	Laborer and Service	Median Family Income
43.2	36.8	26.9	11.9	32.1	$13,042
32.9	33.6	24.1	10.0	26.3	$14,084
50.7	39.2	28.9	13.4	36.3	$12,284
24.5	64.9	16.8	34.5	16.3	$24,758
36.2	46.0	23.3	18.4	26.9	$16,747
40.5	48.4	23.2	19.5	25.6	$15,721

but they are close, which runs counter to popular perception of urban disadvantage as peculiar to people of color.

This kind of equivalence mirrors that seen for lower-SES parents in chapter 3. Unexpected perhaps, but as argued there, it may be fairly characteristic of whites and blacks whose children attend public schools in places like Baltimore. Black-white comparisons across the entire city would look rather different, as they combine better-off white children who attend private schools with those less well off, for whom private school is not an option.

This comparability does not extend to neighborhood demographics however, also paralleling the pattern seen for family demographics in chapter 3: in lower-SES African American communities half of all households with dependent children are headed by women (50.7 percent), many more than the 32.9 percent in lower-SES white neighborhoods and the 24.5 percent in higher-SES neighborhoods. There is one commonality though: in lower-SES communities, the poverty levels of black (49.5 percent) and white (50.7 percent) households with children headed by women are almost identical. This is the feminization of poverty alluded to in chapter 1. It starts with single parenting and trickles down to children regardless of race. Nevertheless, and despite this parity, African American children are at substantially greater risk of poverty because

African American mothers are much more likely than white mothers, including those of comparable SES, to be parenting alone.

Neighborhood profiles like these establish that the disadvantage the Youth Panel children experience growing up is not just within the family: many poor children also grow up in poor neighborhoods.[3] Poor neighborhoods, yes, but are they also distressed neighborhoods? A sense of that is afforded by their crime levels and what residents of these communities have to say about neighborhood conditions, features of neighborhood life taken up in the next sections.

Neighborhoods and Criminality

In many parts of any big city, crime and the fear of it top the list of neighborhood concerns. Table 4.2 reports detailed crime rates for the twenty original neighborhoods, organized to allow comparisons across family socioeconomic levels. These are official crime statistics, averaged across 1980, 1981, and 1982 for stability.[4]

The crime rates in table 4.2 represent the number of incidents per hundred thousand residents. Summary indices also are reported for two crime composites: violent crimes, which include assault, homicide, rape, and robbery; and property crimes, which include burglary, larceny, auto theft, and robbery.[5] The summary measures are standard or Z scores. Neighborhood crime rates by type were first standardized and then averaged together.[6] Across the entire sample, the mean value of the two summary scales is zero by construction (hence the zero entries in the Overall columns). This fulcrum is used for interpreting the group-specific values reported in table 4.2, which present deviations from the overall average and so gauge relative standing: positive values indicate a higher-than-average rate of crime exposure within the sample and negative values a lower-than-average rate.

That the disparity in table 4.2 across lower-SES and higher-SES neighborhoods for property crimes is so small—0.04 standard deviations (SD) versus −0.04 SD—might seem odd, but these are crimes of opportunity: robbers go where the goods are. Even so, distinguishing lower-SES African American neighborhoods from lower-SES white neighborhoods reveals a striking disparity: the average is −0.43 SD for whites, almost half a standard deviation below the average, and 0.38 SD for blacks. In fact, rates for property crimes of every type are highest by considerable margins in lower-SES black communities—for burglary, as an example, 2,670.8 per hundred thousand in lower-SES African American communities versus 1,973.7 in lower-SES white communities. Averaging the black and white figures yields the lower-SES composite value of 0.04 SD, but this is highly misleading: the neighborhood crime victimiza-

Table 4.2   Crime Exposure, Neighborhood Rates/100,000, 1980–1982 Averaged

	Assault	Homicide	Rape	Violent Crimes (Z score)	Robbery	Property Crimes (Z score)	Burglary	Larceny	Auto Theft
Lower SES (N = 394)	1,014.1	28.3	75.4	.31	1,347.3	.04	2,377.1	4,170.6	634.6
White (N = 166)	732.0	15.8	45.9	-.32	655.4	-.43	1,973.7	3,704.5	582.1
Black (N = 228)	1,219.5	37.4	96.9	.77	1,851.0	.38	2,670.8	4,509.9	672.8
Higher SES (N = 189)	426.7	11.2	33.2	-.54	787.8	-.04	2,899.1	4,309.4	555.5
Overall (N = 787)	794.6	21.5	60.3	0.0	1,166.9	0.0	2,481.6	4,156.1	622.9
Baltimore City	783.5	28.2	70.8		1,266.4		2,221.9	4,704.0	649.7

Source: Authors' compilation based on Taylor 1999; Governor's Office of Crime Control and Prevention 2013.

tion lower-SES African Americans encounter is far above that lower-SES whites do.

The pattern for violent crime is much the same, with the exception that violent crime is more concentrated altogether in lower-SES communities: at a standard deviation of −0.54, the higher-SES summary value is more than a half standard deviation below the panel average. In large cities no one is altogether immune from the threat of violent crime, but the threat is much greater in some places than others—indeed, for the Youth Panel, three times greater across the extremes. The homicide rate is 11.2 per hundred thousand in higher-SES communities against 15.8 in lower-SES white communities and 37.4 in lower-SES African American communities. For rape, the corresponding figures are 33.2, 45.9, and 96.9 SD. With the exception of robbery, violent crime rates in higher-SES neighborhoods are about half the corresponding lower-SES white rates, which are half or less the lower-SES black rates, a striking and disquieting orderliness.

Census data on poverty, income, occupation, and the like leave the impression that the neighborhood disadvantage that lower-SES blacks and whites in Baltimore experience is much the same. By conventional socioeconomic criteria, that appears to be the case, but crime exposure is vastly greater in poor black neighborhoods than in poor white ones. Implications of this for quality of life seem obvious, but that is from our perspective as outsiders. Would the residents of these communities agree? That they indeed do is seen in the next section.

Neighborhood Quality Through Residents' Perceptions

In 1981, the year before the study launch, the *Crime Changes* project (Taylor 1999), the source of the neighborhood crime data just reviewed, also fielded resident surveys in sixty-six neighborhoods throughout the city, using random block sampling to achieve representativeness. The surveys averaged twenty-four residents per neighborhood. Ten of the original twenty neighborhoods were among the sixty-six; eight others bordered one of the sampled neighborhoods and were of similar sociodemographic makeup. Including the close matches, table 4.3 covers eighteen neighborhoods and 90 percent of the panel (713 of 790).

These are not the perceptions of the parents or of the students themselves (as are most quotes throughout this book). Rather, they are contextual, in the same sense as the census data reported in table 4.1, and the sense of context they convey is perfectly aligned with the patterning of criminality just reviewed.

These surveys asked about crime, civility, sociability, sense of community, and neighborhood upkeep, as well as the respondents' feelings about life there. We selected thirty items for consideration that seemed most relevant, later setting aside three that did not align well with the others. The remaining twenty-seven are reported in table 4.3 grouped into four clusters:

attachment to community,[7]

perception of crime,[8]

quality of life,[9] and

social cohesion.[10]

High values indicate positive sentiment. After conversion to Z or standard scores to adjust for differences across items in the number of response options provided, the clustered items were averaged and the averages assigned to members of the Youth Panel based on their neighborhood of residence. Also reported are values for a summary scale (*Overall Quality*), calculated across all twenty-seven items. As with the crime scales just reviewed, the Overall entries in table 4.3 are zero by construction and the other entries are interpretable relative to that average—positive values indicate an above average, more favorable view of community and negative values a below average, less favorable view (in standard deviation units).[11]

In every instance, perceptions of community are much more favorable in higher-SES neighborhoods than in lower-SES ones, with the differences large, ranging from a half to a full standard deviation. Here again, though, the lower-SES figures are misleading in that they average together the quite negative perceptions of neighborhood characteristic of lower-SES African Americans with the much more favorable views held by lower-SES whites. It is the difference between –0.55 SD and –0.195 SD in expressions of attachment to community (the smallest disparity comparing across the five) or between –0.54 SD and 0.37 SD for social cohesion (the largest).

The *Overall Quality* contrasts seem a fair summary: the lower-SES average value is –0.26 SD, well below the higher-SES average of 0.49 SD (a difference of 0.75 SD), but lower-SES African Americans hold a much less favorable view of their communities than lower-SES whites do: –0.53 SD versus 0.13 SD. These calculations are relative, not absolute, but they accord with neighborhood crime statistics: both identify lower-SES African Americans as subject to much harsher neighborhood conditions than similarly lower-SES whites, despite similar neighborhood

Table 4.3   Neighborhood Quality Through Resident Surveys, 1980

	Attachment	Quality of Life	Perception of Crime	Social Cohesion	Overall Quality
Lower SES	−.21	−.40	−.22	−.16	−.26
(N = 342)					
White	.10	−.19	.24	.37	.13
(N = 143)					
Black	−.44	−.55	−.56	−.54	−.53
(N = 199)					
Higher SES	.56	.71	.33	.36	.49
(N = 182)					
Overall	.00[a]	.00	.00	.00	.00
(N = 713)					

Source: Authors' compilation based on Taylor (1999).
Note: Entries are Z score averages across items from the neighborhood survey project fielded in sixty-six Baltimore neighborhoods in 1982. Eighteen of the original twenty neighborhoods were matched to the sample sixty-six neighborhoods, nine being exact matches (the remaining nine were nearby neighborhoods of similar sociodemographic makeup). Item averages aggregated to the neighborhood level were assigned based on first grade neighborhood of residence. These averages were then normalized based on their distributions. Table entries are in the Z score metric. The overall entries are zero by construction, the Z score distribution having a mean of 0 and standard deviation of 1.

socioeconomic profiles. We review some possibilities for the why of such strikingly different neighborhood conditions in the next section.

Fractured Communities, Weakened Social Cohesion, and Urban Disadvantage

Census data on poverty, income, occupation, and the like give the impression that lower-SES black and white neighborhood disadvantage in Baltimore is much the same, but neighborhood crime exposure and residents' sentiments tell a different story: in every comparison, African American quality of life lags behind—indeed, far behind. All of Baltimore, white and black, has suffered from disinvestment and deindustrialization (chapter 2), but additional hardships weigh especially on the African American community. These include segregated residential enclaves that trace back to World War II and before, the politics of urban renewal, and the still simmering aftermath of the urban unrest of the 1960s.

A neighborhood that looks bleak and threatening to outsiders can feel very different to those who call it home. Alice, introduced earlier, tells how her relatives living up the street in her low-income West Side neighborhood reacted when she suffered a seizure at their home:

> Yeah, my uncle called nine-one-one, and I laugh about this, because my cousin tells me about it all the time. My brothers had run down, because

the family lived on the same block, and he had run down to my uncle's house, and my cousin run outside in his underwears to come up to see what was going on. And I just laugh about that to this day, so. And then my uncle had to, when the paramedics and all got there, he was like, hey, you know you're in your underwears? You know, and he was like, well, I didn't think about it at that time.

These are happy memories about a neighborhood most outsiders avoid in daylight, let alone after dark. Having family nearby is as characteristic of African Americans in these communities as it is of whites, but other conditions of community life make it harder for blacks to maintain strong, cohesive neighborhoods. Dilapidated housing, evictions, family emergencies, and the desire to escape a threatening environment contribute to high rates of residential mobility in many low-income communities (DeLuca, Rosenblatt, and Wood 2012). Additionally, single-parent households, which are more prevalent among African Americans, in the Youth Panel and nationally, move more often than two-parent households do (McLanahan and Sandefur 1994). Those conditions, and the instability they prompt, mitigate against forming strong bonds to place. Added on is criminality, and the fear of it, which encourages families to withdraw into the safe or safer confines of the home (DeLuca, Rosenblatt, and Wood 2012; Furstenberg et al. 1999; Jarrett 1997).

Consider how Aubrey's parents—whites living in a low-income white neighborhood—tried to insulate him from conditions outside:

We had a big old back yard that we played in. That's basically what we did, to keep us out of trouble, because our parents were very much concerned about us in that neighborhood, so they didn't let us just run wild on the streets. They kept a good watch on us and kept us in line.

Mae's parents, continuing her account from chapter 1, imposed a curfew to keep her out of harm's way:

right in my street where I lived at, I seen somebody die there. . . . That's how it was for me, you know. It didn't bother me, because actually, I had a curfew, I had to be in the house before it got dark outside. And I know they only did that for my own safety. . . . So I mean, I would come home from school . . . and I would go in the house, and I could—I had other things to occupy my mind. I watched a lot of TV, you know. . . . I really wasn't out there. I didn't involve myself, actually, I couldn't involve myself, cause like I said, I had a curfew. By the time I got home, did my chores, homework, what's the use in going outside? You know, it's almost dark.

Joe grew up in a tough southwest Baltimore neighborhood. His mother would not let him play in the local playgrounds for fear of him seeing "drugs being sold, people getting beat up, somebody getting shot."

Two forces are at play in this account of urban disadvantage. The first, residential instability, is centripetal; it scatters families. The second, the retreat from public space into the protective cocoon of family life, is centrifugal; it isolates families from one another. Both forces weaken community cohesion: "as . . . families withdraw from local neighboring relations, the prospect for revitalizing inner-city neighborhoods is . . . discouraged" (Jarrett 1999, 48).

Lower-SES whites, we have seen, have a higher percentage of two-parent households, live in less crime-ridden neighborhoods, and tend to remain in their racially isolated community enclaves, all of which can strengthen community cohesion.[12]

Additional destabilizing forces originate beyond the community. One is urban renewal, famously equated to "black removal" by James Baldwin (1963). That characterization seems altogether apt for Baltimore in the era at issue: between 1951 and 1971, 80 percent—90 percent of the twenty-five thousand families and seventy-five thousand persons displaced by highway construction, school construction, and public housing projects and the like were African American (Olson 1976, 54).

The West Side neighborhood of Harlem Park is an example. Early in the twentieth century, Harlem Park was a center of black residential life in Baltimore, a lovely community with a strong sense of identity. Its downward slide did not begin in the 1970s, but problems magnified when a highway project from that era split the neighborhood down the middle, literally and figuratively. This six-lane East-West Expressway project met fierce resistance from more powerful community groups on the east side and eventually was cancelled,[13] but not before a 1.4 mile stretch of construction had demolished twenty blocks of Harlem Park: "Entire neighborhoods were wiped out and nearly 3000 people displaced" (Shen 2010).[14]

Former residents recount fond memories of outdoor life in Harlem Park before the demolition, hanging out and playing in the neighborhood's twenty-nine "pocket parks," all swept away by the highway construction (Giguere 2009, 260). One resident recalls that:

> for the young adults growing up in the area . . . Harlem Park was a close-knit, caring community in which residents looked out for one another, respected one another and emphasized education and values. . . . there was crime, and drugs but . . . some of the older guys, well [they would drink, but] they wouldn't sit out publically and drink. They respected somebody's kids, or nephews, or little brother to that degree. (261)

That was then; Harlem Park today is one of Baltimore's many distressed African American neighborhoods.

These neighborhoods also bore the brunt of the rioting triggered by Martin Luther King's assassination. The turmoil resulted in six fatalities, seven hundred injured, and more than a thousand businesses looted or destroyed (Zumbrum 1968). And what of today?

As Andrew Giguere (2009, 243) reports,

> Large sections of Edmondson Avenue through Harlem Park westward to Edmondson Village were devastated by looting and fires. Many of these areas have not yet recovered. According to the *Baltimore Sun*, homes and businesses have long been replaced by "abandoned houses with collapsed roofs, vacant lots overrun with trash and weeds, and residents desperate for something better" (Kiehl 2008, B1+).[15]

This fracturing of community under the pressure of assaults from within and without is the opening for predatory crime, which tears at the heart of Baltimore's low-income African American neighborhoods. Baltimore's poor whites have not been immune from this perfect storm but the African American community has suffered disproportionately from these:

> crippling trends and tragic events—the dramatic loss of manufacturing jobs and tax base, the ruinous riots of 1967 and 1968; the exodus of first white then African American middle-class families; the sequential epidemics of heroin, crack cocaine and HIV; the intensified crime and gang activity that fed and feasted off the drug trade; and the activities of slumlords, property flippers and predatory lenders. The end result has been an ever-deepening cycle of disinvestment and decline. (Annie E. Casey Foundation 2010, 2)

All these events are reflected as well in the Youth Panel's remembrances in box 4.1.

Wilson (1987) argues that neighborhood distress is driven by society-wide forces and knows no color. No doubt he is right, but if a meaningful distinction can be made between the disadvantaged, as used here, and the truly disadvantaged, as in his account, these neighborhood profiles and their historic backdrop elevate black urban disadvantage over white. In light of them, the weakened community cohesion that is so striking in survey data from the 1980s hardly surprises.

Of what relevance is this history to this volume's agenda? That Baltimore's lower-SES white communities have been spared the worst of the ravages that plagued their African American counterparts is, we think, one key to *The Long Shadow's* account of white working-class privilege in the socioeconomic destinations of the Youth Panel children grown up (developed in chapter 8). Neighborhood, however, is not the

---

Box 4.1   Loss of Community: Social Capital in Baltimore's
Poor Black Communities

"Where I lived, it was more or less like, I guess you'd say family ori-
ented. Because everybody knew everybody. . . . When you hear everybody talking about how someone could spank you whether they were
family or not. Well, that's what it was like on the block . . . and maybe
one or two parents was watching us and stuff. . . . Then after a while the
neighborhood started going down. . . . Basically the kids were getting
badder and badder and . . . the people you thought was really nice was
changing, you know what I mean?" [Sona]

"The neighborhood [when I was young] was kind of close-knit . . .
and the people that grew up with me were like family. Then I moved
from there to West Baltimore . . . and the neighborhood we had moved
to was a rough neighborhood. . . . It was a lot of drugs, drug activity, a lot
of, you know, shooting and homicide, stuff like that going on." [Floyd]

"I saw on TV was what I had, so that's my idea of family life. It's as
though it's everybody all together, all loving, . . . that was how it was, it
was family. And then . . . the area becoming drug-infested, is what really
deteriorated my family. . . . It was the drug game itself that made my life
what it was. . . . I was ripped from my family. . . . So the pain, . . . it was
just a homesick pain. It was, I was missing my family." [Terry]

---

only setting beyond the family that bears on the Youth Panel's development and life chances; another, the school, is taken up next.

Schools and Family Disadvantage

Chapter 2 recounted some of the history of Baltimore's public schools
over the latter half of the twentieth century—shrinking enrollments,
changing demographics, and resource shortfall. Now we shift from the
general to the specific, profiling the elementary schools. We begin there
because the Youth Panel is anchored in first grade; however, exposure
to schools and school-like settings of different quality begins earlier.
Disadvantaged children less often go to center-based child care and
organized preschools, and the ones they do attend are lower quality: the
wealthiest 20 percent of families spend almost five times more for preschool than the poorest 20 percent (Huston and Bentley 2010, 416, 426).

Archival material about the Baltimore City public school system
from the early 1980s, when the Youth Panel children were in elementary school, is thin. Recordkeeping then was neither centralized nor

computerized, but we have two useful documents from that time: "School Profiles: School Year 1987–1988," published by the school system, and *Take This School and Love It: A Reference Manual on the Baltimore City Elementary Schools,* compiled in 1990 by the Citizens Planning and Housing Association. "School Profiles," which covers all but one of the elementary schools then extant (the missing school is one of the original twenty), contains school-level achievement test results and enrollment demographics, starting with the 1986–1987 school year and extending back to 1982–1983, the Youth Panel's inaugural year. *Take This School* covers elementary school resources and staffing, but mostly for the 1989–1990 school year. The timing is not ideal, because the Youth Panel children would have advanced to middle school two years earlier, but the gap in time is small and wholesale changes over that interval seem unlikely.[16]

School Racial and Socioeconomic Composition

We start with the distribution of schools by income level and racial composition, the two criteria used to sample schools for the study. The oversampling of schools with large white enrollments is apparent in table 4.4. The first panel covers the entire city system; the second panel the twenty selected schools. Schools are classified by income and racial makeup. The income cutoffs used are as follows:

high income, between zero and 29 percent receiving free or reduced price meals (the sample range is 11 percent to 17 percent);

middle income, between 30 percent and 67 percent receiving free or reduced price meals, the latter being just under the citywide average at the time (the range is 30 percent to 53 percent); and

low income, between 68 percent and 100 percent (the range is 68 percent to 90 percent).

For racial context, we distinguish among:

hypersegregated white schools, with 10 percent or less African American enrollment (the range is 1 percent to 10 percent);

hypersegregated African American schools, with 90 percent or more African American enrollments (enrollment is 99 percent or 100 percent African American in just under half the city's elementary schools, also the range for schools in this category); and

racially integrated schools, with the percentage African American 11 percent to 89 percent (the range is 17 percent to 87 percent).

Table 4.4 Racial and Income Composition of Baltimore Elementary Schools, 1982

| | City[a] | | Sample | | BSSYP Distribution Across Sample School Types | | | | | | |
| | | | | | Lower-SES | | Middle-SES | | Higher-SES | | Overall |
	#	%	#	%	Blacks	Whites	Blacks	Whites	Blacks	Whites	
High-income schools[b]	**12**	**9.8**	**4**	**20.0**	**1.8**	**7.2**	**5.2**	**31.8**	**32.5**	**68.6**	**18.7**
Segregated white[c]	3	2.4	1	5.0	0.0	4.2	0.0	12.5	0.0	14.7	4.2
Segregated black	1	0.8	0	—	0.0	0.0	0.0	0.0	0.0	0.0	0.0
Integrated	8	6.5	3	15.0	1.8	3.0	5.2	19.3	32.5	53.9	14.5
Mid-range income schools	**37**	**30.1**	**8**	**40.0**	**15.8**	**58.4**	**40.5**	**52.3**	**48.2**	**22.5**	**37.2**
Segregated white	10	8.1	5	25.0	—	57.2	0.0	48.9	0.0	18.6	20.4
Segregated black	15	12.2	1	5.0	5.7	0.6	13.8	0.0	14.5	0.0	5.3
Integrated	12	8.1	2	10.0	10.1	0.6	26.7	3.4	33.7	3.9	11.5
Low-income schools	**74**	**60.2**	**8**	**40.0**	**82.5**	**34.3**	**54.3**	**15.9**	**19.3**	**8.8**	**44.1**
Segregated white	0	—	0	—	—	—	0.0	0.0	0.0	0.0	0.0
Segregated black	56	45.5	4	20.0	57.0	—	45.7	0.0	18.1	0.0	25.2
Integrated	18	14.6	4	20.0	25.4	34.3	8.6	15.9	1.2	8.8	19.0
Totals	**123**		**20**		**228**	**166**	**116**	**88**	**83**	**102**	**783**

Source: Authors' compilation.

[a]Baltimore City Public Schools 1988.

[b]The income categories are high, between zero and 29 percent free or reduced price meals; midrange, between 30 percent and 67 percent; low, between 68 percent and 100 percent.

[c]The racial composition categories are segregated white, 10 percent or less black enrollment; segregated black, 90 percent or greater black enrollment; integrated, between 11 percent and 89 percent black enrollment.

How race and income intersect as dimensions of diversity citywide is revealing. Sixty percent of city elementary schools are low income. Most of these are segregated black and none is segregated white. At the high end of the income distribution are twelve schools; most are integrated (eight of the twelve), but three are segregated white, and just one is seg- regated black, a rare school type indeed. The study includes four high- income schools—a third of the system total; none is segregated black.

We said earlier that the existence of white residential enclaves helps account for the continuing presence of whites in Baltimore's public schools. That certainly seems apt in table 4.4 for higher-SES whites who are substantially segregated from blacks, but what of lower-SES whites, a third of whom (34.3 percent) attend low-income integrated schools? Our standard for integration identifies settings where meaningful cross-racial contact is at least possible, a broad range. The highest percentage African American enrollment in these low-income integrated schools, 37 percent, is the West Side school located at the boundary of low-income black and white neighborhoods to promote school desegregation. Its enrollment is 63 percent white, well integrated by Baltimore standards. However, we saw in chapter 1 that the school's feeder neighborhoods are segregated black and segregated white. The three other low-SES integrated schools have mostly white enrollments, at 75 percent and above.

School Types

The right panel of table 4.4 shows the distribution of children, classified by race and SES level, across school contexts. These are the schools the Youth Panel children actually attended, or did not.

Consider first those they did not attend: no whites of any income level attend low-income black segregated schools and no black student attends the lone high-income white segregated school. Hypersegregation means just that, and it is striking when made visible this way. Additionally, null cells at the school level preclude attendance by anyone. White segre- gated low-income schools and black segregated high-income schools are not represented in the study, and from the left-side panels of table 4.4 we see that hardly any schools of these two types exist system-wide. Baltimore's public schools at the time were constructed around rigid racial separation overlaid on income, privileging whites at the high end and disadvantaging African Americans at the low end.

That said, these schools were not altogether homogeneous. SES diversity within race-typed schools is considerable: most lower-SES blacks (57.0 percent), a near majority of mid-SES blacks (45.7 per- cent), and almost 20 percent of higher-SES blacks attend low-income segregated black schools with no white classmates; correspondingly, most lower-SES whites (57.2 percent), a near majority of mid-SES whites (48.9 percent), and 20 percent of higher-SES whites attend white segregated middle-income schools with no black classmates. The distributions are parallel, but offset by one income level: many blacks, regardless of family circumstance, attend low-income schools and many whites, regardless of family circumstance, attend middle-income schools.

This pattern of downward socioeconomic integration is reminiscent of Douglas Massey and Nancy Denton's (1993) observation that residential barriers relegate black families of means to less desirable neighborhoods and schools, making it harder for middle-class black parents to support their children's academic development.[17] From their research in Philadelphia circa 1980, they conclude that:

> Blacks . . . face strong barriers to residential mobility. As a result, high status blacks must live in neighborhoods with fewer amenities than whites of similar background. . . . They live in poorer, more dilapidated areas characterized by higher rates of poverty, dependency, crime, and mortality, and they must send their children to public schools populated by low-income students who score badly on standardized tests. (Massey, Condran, and Denton 1987, 29)

Their last point is of most immediate relevance. Baltimore's black pupils attend schools with a much higher low-income enrollment than whites do—42.4 percent, on average, in 1999–2000 versus 19.6 percent (Logan 2002). This asymmetry matters because a school's percentage low-income enrollment predicts reading gains over the elementary school years (Huston and Bentley 2010, 427) and, too, a socioeconomically integrated school environment is demonstrably advantageous for lower-SES children's learning (Kahlenberg 2001, 2012). Other things equal, the distribution across school types seen in table 4.4 will tend to enhance the learning of lower-SES white children, many of whom attend schools with children of higher SES than their own, but not the learning of downwardly integrated higher-SES African American children.

High-poverty schools often are struggling schools; high-poverty minority schools, like many in Baltimore, especially so (Orfield and Lee 2005). Such schools can be strong academically (Carter 2000; Quane and Wilson 2011), but they are the exception. More often, their test scores are low and their academic press weak. The next section takes up these and other educationally important resources, asking whether they too are stratified along lines of race and family SES.

Stratified School Resources: Academic Context

Many disadvantaged children fall behind academically; indeed many start school already behind (Lee and Burkam 2002). But school context can make a difference, and our nation's public schools on the whole help lift these children (Alexander 1997; Entwisle, Alexander, and Olson 1997; Heyns 1978; Downey, von Hippel, and Broh 2004). Disadvantaged youth, in the language of the Coleman et al. (1966), are "differentially sensitive" to school influence, a conclusion sustained many times since, most notably in the Tennessee class size reduction experiment (Krueger and Whitmore 2002). These children benefit from the high standards and good role models found in high performing schools (Kahlenberg 2001), whereas failing schools lack the resources to support their learning.

Baltimore's school demographics are far from encouraging, but perhaps tangible resources in support of children's learning are more equitably distributed. We begin with academic context or climate as reflected in a school's achievement profile, promotion rate, and attendance. A successful school has children coming to school regularly, scoring at or above prescribed grade level on achievement tests, and moving up to the next grade at year's end. None of these characteristics can be taken for granted in high-poverty school systems: 17 percent of the Youth Panel repeated first grade, including almost 25 percent of lower-SES children; by the end of eighth grade (the last year of middle school), half the children had been held back at least once (Alexander, Entwisle, and Dauber 2003).

The low-income schools attended by lower-SES blacks have the highest concentrations of both African American (83 percent) and low-income (74 percent) enrollments (column 2 of table 4.5). Lower-SES whites, in contrast, attend schools with an average African American enrollment of 17.2 percent and a low-income enrollment of 54 percent. Do schools with such different sociodemographic profiles also present different academic profiles?[18] Table 4.5 confirms that they do.

Promotion and attendance data are referenced to the 1988–1999 school year, two years after most of the Youth Panel children had moved to middle school (sixth grade); the achievement data, though, are time-appropriate. They are second grade spring averages on the math and reading sections of the California Achievement Test battery, averaged for stability over the 1983–1984, 1984–1985, and 1985–1986 school years. Children promoted from first grade to second on the first try would have been in second grade in 1983–1984. Scores are reported as grade-equivalent (GE) and benchmarks are determined by national norms.[19]

Across the entire panel, the standard deviations for the test score averages reported in table 4.5 are 0.29 GE units in reading and 0.49 in math; for the lower SES specifically, they are 0.26 and 0.34 GE units, so an average difference across groups in any one year as small as 0.25 to 0.30 GE would be large enough to be considered educationally meaningful. Many of the differences in table 4.5 exceed that level, with those across the socioeconomic extremes largest: 0.3 GE in math and 0.6 GE in reading.

Table 4.5   Academic Profile for the Schools[a]

	% Low Income	% Black Enrollment	Math[b] Average	Reading[b] Average	%[c] Promoted	%[c] Attendance
Lower SES (N)	65.1 (371)	53.6 (371)	3.0 (371)	2.7 (371)	91.9 (343)	89.2 (343)
White (N)	54.0 (166)	17.2 (166)	3.2 (166)	2.7 (166)	89.8 (127)	89.2 (127)
Black (N)	74.0 (205)	83.1 (205)	2.9 (205)	2.6 (205)	93.2 (216)	89.2 (216)
Higher SES (N)	30.6 (189)	49.7 (189)	3.3 (189)	3.3 (189)	93.0 (139)	91.6 (139)
BSSYP Overall (N)	52.3 (745)	52.1 (745)	3.1 (745)	2.9 (745)	92.1 (652)	90.0 (652)

Source: Authors' compilation.

[a]Baltimore City Public Schools 1988.

[b]Averages are school-wide second grade spring averages on the California Achievement Test averaged across the 1983–1984, 1984–1985, and 1985–1986 school years, reported as grade equivalents.

[c]Entries pertain to the 1988–1989 school years.

A higher-SES–lower-SES difference of this magnitude in reading at the end of second grade is ominous, and that most poor children spend all of their elementary years in such settings even more so. The tendency is for poor children to fall further and further behind academically over time. Certainly that is the case within the sample: the gap between lower- and higher-SES reading comprehension scores explodes from 0.5 GE in the fall of first grade to 3.0 GE by the end of fifth grade. That school context differences overlap these achievement disparities is hardly a good sign, as Baltimore's children are not realizing the academic benefits that flow from attending socioeconomically integrated schools (for example, Kahlenberg 2001, 2012).[20]

The promotion and attendance figures in table 4.5 are time-offset in that they pertain to 1988–1989, which would be the second year of middle school. Still, the comparisons are similar to those for achievement scores, and here too, seemingly small differences can be of large import. Commenting on Chicago's school reform in the 1990s, for example, Anthony Bryk and his colleagues (2010, 30) note that "a good elementary school might report an average daily attendance in the 95- to 96-percent range. . . . [while] in contrast, an elementary school that reports attendance around 90 percent or lower would likely be a troubled place." The differences in table 4.5 show lower-SES children attending schools with somewhat lower promotion and attendance rates than their higher-SES counterparts. Note, though, that in lower-SES schools, nonpromotion is more common in the schools attended by whites.

Stratified School Resources: Staffing and Infrastructure

Do school resources follow the same lines as academic achievement? The resources displayed in table 4.6, which again pertain to the 1988–1989 school year, seem self-evidently relevant: per pupil expenditures, student-teacher class ratio (akin to class size), principal and staff turnover, enrollment level relative to the school's approved capacity (percent utilization), and the number of separately funded special programs at a school. Special programs range from one to thirteen across schools and run the gamut. They include Chapter 1 and Head Start programs targeted to needy children, academic interventions (Writing to Read and Writing to Learn), parent involvement and volunteer programs (Coordination for Parent and Community Citizens in Volunteerism in City Schools Program), and programs to insulate children from drugs (Drug Free Schools), abuse (Child Abuse and Neglect), and dropout (School Dropout Demonstration Assistance Program).

Table 4.6   School Resources: Staffing and Infrastructure for the Schools[a]

	Expenditures per Pupil ($1,000s)[b]	# of Special Programs	# of Principals (last 5 years)	Principal Tenure (years)	Student/ Teacher Ratio	% Staff Continuity (across years)	School Utilization (% of capacity)
Lower SES (N)	2.3 (343)	6.6 (343)	1.9 (343)	2.8 (343)	32.1 (343)	87.1 (343)	72.7 (343)
White (N)	2.4 (127)	5.7 (127)	1.7 (127)	3.3 (127)	35.2 (127)	86.9 (127)	71.9 (127)
Black (N)	2.2 (216)	7.1 (216)	1.9 (216)	2.5 (216)	30.3 (216)	87.2 (216)	73.1 (216)
Higher SES (N)	2.1 (139)	4.8 (139)	2.0 (139)	3.4 (139)	30.9 (139)	87.6 (139)	76.1 (139)
BSSYP Overall (N)	2.2 (652)	5.8 (652)	1.9 (652)	3.0 (652)	31.9 (652)	87.4 (652)	73.5 (652)

Source: Authors' compilation.
[a]Citizens Planning & Housing Association 1990.
[b]All entries are referenced to the 1988–1989 school year.

A 2001 survey of high schools across Maryland (Kerr 2002) found that schools serving high-needs students were most prone to adopt so-called best practice reforms like interdisciplinary teaming, ninth grade transition programs, and school-within-school restructuring. Why should this be? Kerr surmised these schools desperately want to help their students succeed but do not know how, so they eagerly embrace possible solutions. This reasoning seems plausible, and likely holds at the elementary level also.

Nationally, funding levels in high-poverty school systems lag far behind those in wealthier communities (Baker, Sciarra, and Farrie 2010; Arroyo 2008), but the resource disparities in table 4.6 are of a different character.[21] At the district level (Baltimore City), funding streams—such as federal Title 1 or Chapter 1 monies—often favor the neediest schools. Accordingly, in table 4.6 per pupil expenditures in the schools attended by lower-SES children average a bit above expenditures in the schools attended by higher-SES children ($2,300 versus $2,100). Likewise, special programs are more numerous in lower-SES schools, averaging 6.6 versus 4.8, and are most numerous (7.1) in lower-SES African American schools. Against a standard deviation of 2.2, these are large differences. That these extra resources and programs are need driven and do not in themselves indicate fundamental school quality differences seems obvious; to know whether they also are solutions requires a different kind of assessment.

Staffing patterns, the other major element of table 4.6, also yield a clear picture, but, again, not as might have been supposed. Differences across school types are exceptional in that they are small and go against the grain of the across-the-board advantages that otherwise accrue to higher-SES youth over those disadvantaged. As well, among lower-SES children, in most instances the white profile seems the more favorable, but not in all instances—for example, principalships are somewhat more stable in the schools attended by lower-SES whites (averaging 3.3 years versus 2.5), but their student-teacher ratios are higher (35.2 versus 30.3).

On the whole, the distribution of human and infrastructure resources across Baltimore's schools appears reasonably equitable. Apart from monies targeted specifically to high-need schools, table 4.6 identifies no glaring biases. This is not to say that the city school system harbors no pockets of privilege. To the contrary, privilege is fully evident in school academic and sociodemographic profiles that faithfully follow lines of advantage and disadvantage. Residential patterns, not school policy, drive these differences, however, whereas the allocation of resources managed by the school system seems reasonably balanced.[22]

Family, Neighborhood, and School: Recapitulation and Next Steps

This chapter completes our survey of conditions the Youth Panel children experienced in their home lives (see chapter 2), neighborhoods, and first grade schools in the early 1980s in Baltimore. The overlapping spheres of influence imagery implies that family socioeconomic level, neighborhood, and school are vehicles, at least potentially, for the transmission of social advantage and disadvantage across generations. The urban disadvantage portrayed in these chapters is multifaceted, quite real, and, as we will see, consequential in the lives of the children who experience it.

Patterning was evident too in how race intersects socioeconomic disadvantage in Baltimore. Lower-SES whites in the study are authentically lower SES, but owing to resources linked to family, neighborhood, and school, they are less disadvantaged than lower-SES blacks. Fewer of them grew up in single-parent families, levels of criminality where they lived were lower and the sense of community stronger, they experienced less concentrated poverty in their schools, patterns of segregation afforded them a semblance of racial isolation, and their schools' academic press was somewhat more favorable. These contrasts also favored children of higher-SES background over lower.

The picture to this point implicates the socioeconomic gradient—higher versus lower—as governing access to resources in childhood that promise to resonate over time. Toward the lower end of the SES distribution, the advantages mainly fall to whites. Such conditions at the launch of children's formal schooling—their social origins—would seem to foreshadow very different later life trajectories—or social destinations. Having now achieved solid grounding in the former, it is time to transition to the latter.

Chapter 5

Transitioning to Adulthood

W E BEGIN life wholly dependent on our birth families; as adults, we are expected to be substantially self-sufficient. The transition to adulthood involves several role transitions that we use as touchstones to monitor progress: take a full-time job, marry, live apart from one's parents, and then, the final step, become a parent.

We are beyond the once-held notion that everyone ought to traverse the life course following the same predetermined sequence (Rindfuss, Swicegood, and Rosenfeld 1987). Indeed, so much has changed that the order in which these roles are assumed and their timing largely have become matters of individual taste. Consider that since the early 1990s, women's average age of first birth has been below their average age of marriage, and the difference is increasing.[1] Although the norms governing such matters have relaxed, exactly how these milestones are managed still matters. For example, the earnings of college-educated women who delay marriage until their mid-thirties exceed by almost $20,000 those of their counterparts who marry in their twenties, and an earnings premium for delayed marriage also is evident among women with lower levels of completed schooling (Hymowitz et al. 2013, 18).

At the other extreme are the adverse consequences that accompany early parenting outside of marriage. A teen pregnancy, for example, can compromise a woman's life prospects by making it difficult for her to stay in school and later may limit her employment opportunities (Swartz 2009, 205).[2] *Accelerated role transitions*—taking on adult-like responsibilities before being socioemotionally or financially ready— often characterize youth who are less mature than they are pseudo-mature. Often they suffer role strain (Pallas 1993), and adverse consequences are likely.

Consider Bedelia's premature parenting: "I came home from school, then I went to work, then I picked them up from school, then I came home, I got them doin' their homework, I fed them, I gave them their baths and I put them to bed And I had no life."

This situation is precisely what makes having babies young and without a partner so difficult, but Bedelia's case includes a heart-wrenching twist. Her account continues:

> He [her father] . . . was making me raise his kids so he can have a life. . . . from the age of thirteen to sixteen I was a mommy, you know, to their kids. . . . I was depressed, I tried to commit suicide because nobody would listen to me when I said, "Look, I want to have a life."

Many of the urban disadvantaged are obliged to grow up quickly. For Bedelia, a white lower-SES woman who never finished high school, the price paid was dear indeed. As an adult, she turned to drugs and found herself in an abusive relationship with a boyfriend.

How young people go about establishing independence from their birth families intersects with other threads of their life development, including the transition into work and out of school. That makes it relevant to *The Long Shadow's* agenda: the transition to adulthood carries young people from their socioeconomic origins (chapters 2 through 4) to their socioeconomic destinations as young adults (the focus of chapter 6), with these consequential role transitions the bridge (for example, Settersten and Ray 2010).

Markers of the Transition to Adulthood

The two after high school surveys at ages twenty-two and twenty-eight asked members of the Beginning School Study Youth Panel (BSSYP, or Youth Panel) at what age they expected to complete five milestone events: finish full-time school, marry, become a parent, live in a house or apartment apart from parents, and work full time. The response option "have already done that" monitors transition milestones.

This chapter centers on a set of Done (coded 1) and Not Done (coded 0) life events to identify milestones completed, with the exception of school. A completed education often signifies a move to adult self-sufficiency, but schooling differs from these other milestones in that it is effectively open ended. The idea that lifelong learning is requisite in today's world to keep pace with workplace changes has wide currency, even among the urban disadvantaged: at age twenty-eight, an extraordinary 80 percent said they intend to acquire additional schooling, including 85 percent of high school dropouts. Once a parent, always a parent, once married, never again never married, but with schooling there is no limit. Instead of treating education as a milestone event, we defer consideration of it until chapter 6, where attained level of schooling at age twenty-eight is examined as a facet of socioeconomic destinations.

Family life transitions raise another question: is a cohabiting relationship a milestone event? By age twenty-eight, 40 percent of the panel had

married, but the figure almost doubles to 78 percent counting cohabitations of at least three months' duration, so deciding how to treat cohabitation is of some consequence.[3]

Marriage and cohabitation obviously differ in many ways, not the least
of which being the legal obligations that attach to marriage. But they also
are similar in ways germane: both entail strong emotional bonds and,
given that 40 percent of nonmarital births are now to cohabiting partners,
cohabitation often is the foundation for parenting (Cherlin 2005, 36). Also,
both arrangements represent a large step for claiming adult standing.

In the Youth Panel, as nationally, African Americans are much less
likely to marry than are whites: among women, 29 percent versus 59 percent ever married through age twenty-eight. In recognition of these
realities, and the increasing acceptance of cohabitation, we treat partnerships of at least three months' duration as functionally comparable to
marriage. There also is a practical consideration: the size of the sample
makes it is impractical to keep marriage and cohabitation distinct, so we
combine them under the rubric *unions*.[4]

Pathways to Adulthood

The twenties is a decade of momentous change for young people. Ronald
Rindfuss (1991) refers to these years as "demographically dense," as the
checklist of completed milestones in table 5.1 shows. For our sample,
age twenty-eight Done levels are higher across the board than those at
age twenty-two. However, full-time work, here defined as a job held at
least three months, spikes early, at 86.5 percent by age twenty-two, and
by age twenty-eight is close to universal at 97.1 percent. Completion
rates for other milestones also are high at age twenty-eight, ranging
from 67 percent to almost 80 percent. Marriage, as noted, is an exception: barely 40 percent of the panel has married by age twenty-eight.

Between ages twenty-two and twenty-eight, the average number of
milestones completed increases from 2.2 to 3.2 (table 5.1, last row). But
though most of the panel can check off most of the milestones as their
third decade draws to a close, beneath this overall picture is a multiplicity of distinct pathways into adulthood. The most common of those are
reviewed in the next section.

Across Milestones: Transition
Patterns and Profiles

If checking off all four milestones is requisite for achieving adulthood,
then many in the panel have a distance yet to travel: on average, the
Youth Panel at age twenty-eight is almost one milestone short. And the
road traveled is not the same for everyone. Of the sixteen possible distinct
combinations of these four transition markers, fifteen are represented in
the Youth Panel's collective experience. The six most frequent (table 5.2)

Table 5.1   Transitioning to Adulthood, Milestones Passed

	Percent Already Done	Age Twenty-Two	Age Twenty-Eight
✓	First full-time job	86.5%	97.1%
✓	Marry-cohabit [marry]	42.8% [13.2%]	78.2% [39.5%]
✓	Live without parents	46.8%	75.8%
✓	Become parent	41.9%	67.4%
	Transitions completed	2.2	3.2
	(N)	(630)	(625)

Source: Authors' compilation.

Table 5.2   Milestones to Adulthood: High-Prevalence Configurations

						Lower-SES Family Background			
	Work	Union	Live without Parents	Parent	% of BSSYP	White Men	Black Men	White Women	Black Women
1	✓	✓	✓	✓	47.2ᵃ	50.8	51.2	65.6	50.5
2	✓	✓	✓	X	16.7	11.9	—ᵇ	14.1	7.5
3	✓	✓	X	✓	9.1	15.3	16.7	—	9.3
4	✓	X	X	X	6.9	—	6.0	—	5.6
5	✓	X	✓	X	5.5	—	—	—	—
6	✓	X	✓	✓	5.1	—	—	—	14.0

Source: Authors' compilation.
Note: All numbers are percentages. High prevalence are patterns that account for at least 5 percent of the sample.
ᵃLow-prevalence patterns are not reported, which is why percentages do not sum to 100 in columns.
ᵇPercentages involving five or fewer observations are not reported.

account for at least 5 percent of the panel each and 90 percent together, but a wide gap separates the first from the rest.

At 47.2 percent, Done All is by far the most common pattern (table 5.2). Under our coding, this group has completed the entire journey, though that depends on exactly how the journey is construed. Restricting adult unions to marriages, the completion total plummets to 14 percent (not shown in tables). This is a huge difference, but it cannot be said one is correct and the other wrong. The lesson, rather, is that how one thinks of family counts for a great deal.

Table 5.2 displays the sociodemographic composition of the six most common transition patterns defined around the four milestones. To illustrate, nearly half the panel has completed all four transition benchmarks (column 6). That degree of commonality is impressive, but variability is impressive too: among lower-SES white women, the figure is 65.6 percent (the highest); among higher-SES white men, it is 22.5 percent (the lowest).

Mid-Level Family Background				Higher-SES Family Background				
White Men	Black Men	White Women	Black Women	White Men	Black Men	White Women	Black Women	(N)
39.4	37.2	57.1	51.2	22.5	32.4	30.4	57.1	(294)
30.3	—	22.9	20.9	47.5	17.6	41.3	—	(104)
—	16.3	—	—	—	—	—	—	(57)
—	—	—	—	—	—	13.0	—	(43)
—	—	—	—	12.5	14.7	—	—	(34)
—	—	—	14.0	—	—	—	—	(32)
								(564)

This difference exposes a gulf across social lines in precisely how the transition to adulthood is negotiated, one overlaid on race, gender, and SES background. It is instructive to consider exactly who follows each of these patterns, because their sociodemographic profiles are quite distinct.

Pattern 1 (47.2 percent): Work-Union-Home-Parent

Pattern 1, Done All, is the fast track into adulthood and youth of modest family origins are the ones most prone to take it: all four lower-SES figures exceed 50 percent, white women highest by a considerable margin.

Women also tend to predominate among the Done Alls of mid- and higher-SES background, but higher-SES white women are an exception. Just 30.4 percent fit into this pattern, well below the 47.2 percent share overall. In the next chapter, we will learn that these higher-SES women have the highest level of completed schooling, and in table 5.2 they are overrepresented in pattern 2 at more than 41.3 percent (against 16.7 percent across the entire sample). Those in pattern 2 have lived apart from their parents and have had partners and jobs, but not children. For the highly educated women among them, it seems the traditional gendered division of labor holds little appeal, at least not at this point in their lives and not to the extent as women of modest socioeconomic origins.

This Done All pattern once was, and for many still is, the ideal (see Karen's account in box 5.1). But as the participants' lives have unfolded,

---

Box 5.1   Transitioning to Adulthood the Old-Fashioned Way

In 1998, Karen married and left the diverse Baltimore City working-class neighborhood of her upbringing for a home in the suburbs. Their first child arrived two and a half years later.

Karen credits her family life to the way she was raised:

> We waited to get married. We both lived at home so we could save our money towards a house. . . . You know, do everything the right way that you're supposed to do it, you know. You're supposed to not live together and then get married, and then have a kid and all that, so, you know, that's what we tried to do, so.

Karen was still living in the suburbs when we last spoke with her in 2004. She hoped some day to finish her community college degree, which she interrupted with forty-two credits owing to her pregnancy, but not until her daughter was older. Karen was almost twenty-nine at the time, well beyond the traditional college-going age.

it has been honored more by some than by others. Its prevalence is both gendered (within social class levels, women have the largest proportionate representation) and conditioned by social class (all four lower-SES figures exceed 50 percent). However, higher-SES white women appear to be caught in something of a tug of war between the two, and their SES origins seemingly win out.

This all seem clear from table 5.2, but a word of caution is in order. A checklist approach to characterizing attained adulthood gives the impression that a large number of the sample have arrived at more or less the same place in the same way—they all have families, have had jobs, and have lived independently of their parents. That description is true, but also not quite true: among lower-SES whites in this pattern, most unions are marriages (80 percent for men and 76 percent for women); among African Americans, most unions are partnerships (67 percent for both men and women).

Another not quite true item involves absentee fathers: though the Done Alls are parents, they are not all parenting in the same way: the figures for men coresident with their children are 83 percent among whites, 44 percent among African Americans. An overlay of family SES reveals additional differences. Mothers of all SES levels live with their children, but not so fathers. From higher-SES origins to middle to lower, the percentage of African American men coresident with their children all of the time drops from 64 percent to 50 percent to 36 percent. White males, too, evidence a gradient, though their lowest level of full-time coresidence (77 percent, for lower-SES men) exceeds the highest level for African American men (64 percent). None of this is unexpected given that nationally the number of young men living with a related child has declined precipitously in recent years, from 75 percent of white men with a high school education or less in 1970 to 40 percent in 2010. For African American men, the drop-off has been even sharper: with a high school degree, from 65 percent to 25 percent; without a degree, from 65 percent to 20 percent (Autor and Wasserman 2013, 34–35).

A checklist accounting of adult standing thus exaggerates the appearance of uniformity, as the surrounding context clearly matters. The figures just reported probe the point by way of survey data; Phil's account in box 5.2 illustrates what can be gleaned from a more richly textured account of life circumstances.

Pattern 2 (16.7 percent): Work-Union-Home

The second most popular pattern applies to fewer than 20 percent of the sample. It has three of the four milestones completed, the omission

---

Box 5.2   Done All, the Back Story

Phil, a white male of working-class background, graduated high school with a clear "next step" plan. Unfortunately, a congenital hearing problem kept him from entering the police academy, then the fire department, then the marines. Thwarted, he instead undertook a three-year union apprenticeship for operating engineers at a local community college. That opened the door to well-paid, steady work in construction, but a history of substance use haunted him—alcohol at eleven, marijuana at seventeen, and crack cocaine at twenty-one. Firings followed, he had brushes with the law, and he and his pregnant girlfriend lost their apartment. They, with their baby, eventually moved in with Phil's parents, a move he credits with saving him, literally. Speaking of drugs, he recounts,

> I don't even remember how it started. I just know that it got bad. My face was shrunk; I just looked terrible. . . . It had to change. . . . I had a good job. I was making more money than I had ever seen, and that's what it was all getting spent on. If it weren't for my stepdad and Mom, I'd probably be dead now on the street somewhere you know.

When we last spoke with Phil in 2005, he had gone through a detox program, was back working in construction, had purchased a home, and, having left his girlfriend, had sole custody of their child—all milestones checked. However, he also was drinking heavily, enough to qualify as a binge drinker, and had an arrest record for domestic disputes and intent to purchase drugs, though he had no convictions. Of parenthood, Phil recalls, "I always wanted to wait until I was settled like my brother did, to have a house, have everything set, and then have your family, you know." Continuing, he offers a word of advice to others: "Don't have a family, then work into everything else, that's the way I see it."

---

being children. Those following this path have held full-time jobs, lived apart from their parents, and married or partnered, but are not parents. Delayed childbearing thus distinguishes pattern 2 from the Done Alls and they are further distinguished by their sociodemographic makeup.

Where youth of modest social origins dominate the Done Alls, deferred parenthood is more characteristic of the more privileged segment of the panel, who, we suppose, favor other priorities. School and career are likely candidates (Hymowitz et al. 2013; Settersten and Ray 2010), along with a better understanding of family planning and possibly cultural tastes regarding the centrality of parenthood and children.

This second pattern also is quite striking in how race and social class intersect. More than 40 percent of higher-SES whites, men and women, fall into this pattern, against a panel-wide average just under 17 percent. Higher-SES African Americans, on the other hand, are underrepresented and their parenting behavior holds the key. In the study, more African Americans than whites are parents—76 percent versus 57 percent—and the largest disparity is among those of higher-SES background, with 61 percent of African Americans parents, but just a third of whites.

The next two transition configurations are discussed together because neither includes leaving the family nest. They appear to be different in other respects—in terms of family formation, for example—but in fact they are more similar than they appear. We mention differences first.

Pattern 3 (9.1 percent): Work-Union-Parent

Pattern 4 (6.9 percent): Work

The pattern 3 checks off both family milestones—they have been in unions and are parents; pattern 4 entails neither. These family differences make them seem worlds apart, but when probed the distinctiveness blurs. Sixty-three percent of the pattern 3 group have lower-SES origins, and African American men are 42 percent of the total. Their family life consists mainly of partnerships (71 percent) and their parenting is mostly absentee (43 percent are never coresident with their children; another 7 percent respond "some of the time," meaning less than half the time). By contrast, of lower-SES African American women in this pattern, all but one live with their children all of the time (the other "most of the time"). Also, roughly 40 percent of pattern 3 African American men and women were no longer in unions at age twenty-eight.

So, parents often are absentee and unions can be unstable. The ever-never distinction is meaningful, but the lines are not as cleanly drawn as might be supposed. Another commonality, the one that prompts us to discuss them together, is that these members of the panel had yet to live apart from their parents.

It is not unusual for young people who have "launched" to return to their parents' home in a tight economy. In popular imagery, they are boomerang kids (Parker 2012). A twenty-something survey of college seniors in May 2010 found that 85 percent anticipated moving in with their parents after graduation, an increase from 67 percent in 2006 (Dickler 2010; for a life-course perspective on this phenomenon, see Goldscheider and Goldscheider 2000). The standard here is rather different though: never having lived on one's own. This pattern long has been a staple of family life in other cultures (Newman 2012), but it is rather new to the United States. More properly, it has only recently begun to attract attention.

For the Youth Panel, unsurprisingly, the challenge of getting a toe-hold in an unwelcoming economy seems to play a role. Having worked full time indeed is a defining feature of both patterns 3 and 4, but when contacted at age twenty-eight, more than 40 percent were without jobs, well above the 24 percent unemployment overall, and men more so than women: 48 percent of white men and 44 percent of African American.

However, difficulty in the licit workforce likely is not the sole expla-nation. Steven Levitt and Stephen Dubner (2005) suggest another in their book *Freakonomics*, which applies the logic of cost-benefit analy-sis to situations typically outside the purview of academic economics, including, of relevance here, inner-city drug-dealing. Drawing on eth-nographic research conducted in Chicago (see, for example, Levitt and Venkatesh 2000), they note that many at the lowest rung of the drug trade live at home. Why? It turns out these men, young and black in the Chicago study, simply cannot afford a place of their own: despite the imagined riches that draw them into the world of drug dealing, their earnings on an hourly basis average below minimum wage.

Circumstantial evidence in the Baltimore sample suggests much the same. For example, the lower-SES men in these two patterns (thirty-two of the hundred) are much more likely than other lower-SES men to have used drugs (mostly marijuana). They also are much more likely to have run afoul of the criminal justice system. Among those arrested, a drug offense is much more often implicated. For patterns 3 and 4, the figures are 81 percent drug use and 81 percent arrested versus, in other patterns, 69 percent lower-SES male drug use and 62 percent arrested.[5] Differentials involving convictions (62 percent versus 41 percent) and incarceration (52 percent versus 28 percent) are even greater, and more of the pattern 3 and 4 arrests are for drug-related offenses: 65 percent versus 59 percent.

Twenty-eight-year-old lower-SES African American men still living at home thus rank high in problem behaviors, and drugs are prominent. What might surprise is that this problem behavior profile holds as well for lower-SES white men living at home. Indeed, in some respects, their profile is even more troublesome—for any drug use, 85 percent versus 79 percent for their African American counterparts; for drug use other than marijuana, 54 percent versus 11 percent; for arrests, 100 percent versus 68 percent; and for time behind bars, 55 percent versus 50 per-cent. In the media and much popular thought, the nexus of drugs and criminality exemplifies the scary face of urban disadvantage: predatory young black men. These figures challenge that narrative, in that the "face" is not exclusively one of color.

Patterns 3 and 4 also include a significant minority of women who have yet to live apart from their birth families. At 17 percent of the total, lower-SES African American women are the second largest demographic in pattern 3, but unlike their male counterparts, most live with their children all of the time (the one who does not is coresident "most of the time"). For these women, living at home affords extended family support for their parenting and probably financial assistance. The men in this situation no doubt get help too, but likely less so in their role as parents.

Pattern 5 (5.5 percent): Work-Home

In pattern 5, family formation is deferred—no children yet and no marriage or partnership.[6] It is, rather, defined by two elements: these youth have worked full time and lived apart from their parents. It is a path most often followed by men of higher-SES background, white and black—they are the only groups with representation above 10 percent against 5.5 percent overall. As we will see in chapter 6, these men also are high achievers in their SES destinations. It seems reasonable to suppose that status aspirations play a role—focused on school and career, it is easy to see how family might be put off; and too, as young men of means, a single lifestyle no doubt holds appeal.

Pattern 6 (5.1 percent): Work-Home-Parent

Pattern 6 includes parents who have lived independently and worked full time, but have yet to marry or partner. It makes up just 5.1 percent of the Youth Panel overall, but 14 percent of lower-SES and mid-level African American women. Although a low frequency pattern, its sociodemographic profile is troubling—at 46.7 percent of the total, lower-SES origins African American women dominate this pattern, the most pronounced distributional skew across all six patterns.

If the live-at-home men of patterns 3 and 4 embody the male face of urban disadvantage, these women are the female counterpart: black single mothers on their own. They absolutely qualify as disadvantaged, whether in terms of their family background or, as we will see, of SES destinations characterized by economic hardship and low levels of schooling.

However, though their family life to this point has been different from that of the lower-SES white women in pattern 1, all but two of these women expect some day to marry. From their perspective, the difference is a matter of timing, not of kind, but even if they are correct that it is only a matter of time until they marry, timing can count for a great deal in women's life-course development. In 2004, at age twenty-five, 78 percent of high school dropouts and 64 percent of women who went no further than high school were mothers; of college graduates, just 20 percent. By age forty, the gaps were much narrower—86 percent and 83 percent versus 74 percent (Smeeding, Garfinkel, and Mincy 2011, 9)—but those who deferred parenting in favor of school and career will be better off financially than their contemporaries who were parents at a young age, and especially than the young mothers among them parenting without partners (Hymowitz et al. 2013; Settersten and Ray 2010; Rector 2010).

The role of family and children in women's lives is key to understanding these pathway differences across social lines. For lower-SES women of both races, the likelihood is high of becoming a parent at an early age, but white parenting is more often within unions and black parenting more often alone. This difference puts lower-SES white and black women on opposite sides of the economic hardship associated with single parenting: in 2008, single parents were six times more likely to be poor than married couples with children were (Rector 2010).

Whether the dollar costs associated with single parenting are outweighed by compensating advantages is quite another matter. If family comes first for these women, their financial sacrifices could be calculated and acceptable. Much hinges on the presumption that career-family priorities differ across social and possibly racial lines.

Kathryn Edin and Maria Kefalas (2005, 170) report, based on 162 interviews with black and white mothers from the Philadelphia area, that lower-income unmarried mothers view parenting not as a hardship, but, rather, as "the best of what life offers." Parenthood, they say, validates their lives and gives them a sense of purpose. Indeed, these women "credit virtually every bit of good in their lives to the fact that they have children—they believe motherhood has 'saved' them" (11). Andrew Cherlin and his colleagues (2008) add that today a birth outside of marriage carries little stigma among low-income women.

The centrality of children in disadvantaged women's lives appears to hold in the BSSYP also (table 5.3). When asked at age twenty-eight about the best thing that has happened to them since high school, 58 percent of lower-SES white women mention the birth of a child or their relationship with a child but only 29 percent of higher SES white women do. Among African Americans, however, the SES gradient is muted: 52 percent and 60 percent of lower-SES and higher-SES background women, respectively, mention children.[7] A like question asked at age twenty-two (but with predefined response options) shows much the same.

And what of the salience of priorities outside family? Choices of career as "best" weren't especially prominent in replies at either age, but

Table 5.3   **Women's Priorities Across Social Lines**

	Age Twenty-Eight	Age Twenty-Two			
	Children Most Positive[a]	Most Important Thing[b]		Last Twelve Months[c]	
		Education	Children	Education	Children
Higher SES					
White	29%	37%	14%	41%	0.0%
(N)	(35)	(49)	(49)	(32)	(32)
Black	60%	31%	37%	30%	26%
(N)	(35)	(35)	(35)	(23)	(23)
Lower SES					
White	58%	8%	55%	7%	29%
(N)	(64)	(53)	(53)	(28)	(28)
Black	52%	15%	44%	8%	41%
(N)	(106)	(114)	(114)	(63)	(63)

Source: Authors' compilation.
[a]Item wording: Over the years since high school, what is the most positive thing that has happened to you? Response code for open-ended replies: birth of or relationship with child or children.
[b]Item wording: Think about your life since high school. What would you say is the most important thing that has happened in your life? Responses (of ten provided): education, child.
[c]Item wording: During the last twelve months, did something happen to you that was really good or particularly important? Responses (of ten provided): education, child.

school received frequent comment at age twenty-two, with large differences across social lines: higher-SES origins women, African American (31 percent) and white (37 percent), were much more likely to mention school as the arena of greatest satisfaction since high school than lower-SES women were (8 percent of whites, 15 percent of blacks). A like pattern holds when asked about events during the previous year specifically: school was mentioned by 41 percent of higher-SES white women, but just 7 percent of lower-SES white women, and not a single higher-SES white woman mentioned children, whereas 29 percent of their lower-SES counterparts did. Higher-SES African American women also referenced schooling more often than their lower-SES counterparts did, 30 percent versus 8 percent.

These sharply contrasting perspectives on sources of satisfaction in young adulthood give context to the transition patterns in table 5.2. Differences in family life align with preferences: for higher-SES women, school, and by implication career, loom large; for their lower-SES counterparts, family is more salient. One might well ask why lower-SES African American women do not simply hold off parenting until they marry or, in today's world, partner, but that question asks a great deal of women who lack attractive partnering prospects, are desperate for meaning in their lives, and foresee roadblocks to advancement through school (see Edin and Reed 2005). Wanting to feel good about oneself is fundamental to human nature. Given that other avenues are cut off, it hardly surprises that some women turn to family, but at what cost? Recall Bess from chapter 3, who had to leave high school to care for her babies because she dared not entrust them to her mother. Here is what she told us in 2000 when asked to look ahead ten or fifteen years:

> I can promise you that I would have been working in one place for a while, and happy there, hopefully have my own home; would have bought a home by then, maybe two, and just being happy. Just putting my kids through school, being able to do for them in the way that I, the way that I want to. And just be a good mommy, I want to take care of my kids. That's all I really want to do. I don't ask for too much out of life, I just, right now, I just want to get a home for my kids, and get me a car, and just work and pay my bills, that's it. And be able to provide for them and teach them how to provide for theirself, you know, that's it. That's all I want. And that's not hard, and, it'll work. I'll do it.

We hope Bess achieves her goals, but in 2005 there was still no car and no house, she was making $7.00 an hour stocking shelves in a convenience store, and living in an apartment with the father of her two youngest children, a musician who also did "street promotions" for a marketing company. And how does Bess view her life? Her children, she says, are the high point, adding that life has gotten much better since high school. Who is to say otherwise?

Looking Ahead: the Transition to Adulthood and Socioeconomic Attainment

These pathways into adulthood combine milestones in different ways that lead to large differences across social lines. The transition to adulthood being the bridge between socioeconomic origins and destinations, the characteristic patterning of these pathways along social lines exposes plural bridges, ones that could well lead to different stratified destinations at journey's end. If that proves to be the case, they also stand as potential carriers of the long shadow's reach.

Patterns 1 (the Done Alls) and 6 (those parenting without partners) illustrate that possibility. Both signify a strong lower-SES familial orientation, but they are distinctively race-typed and one suspects they will have rather different implications for lower-SES women's mobility and economic well-being. Additionally, the deferred childbearing that is more characteristic of women of higher-SES background can smooth the path into and through college, illustrating the life-course principle that strands of development intersect across domains. At issue here are the developmental paths of family and schooling, an intersection likely to contribute to the preservation of advantaged origins.

Diversity Versus Disorder in Life-Course Development

The modern era presents many possibilities for moving into adulthood. Against milestones reached, the children of the study are well along their journey, but is that a reasonable way to gauge adulthood? Achieved adulthood may be more a state of mind than a matter of having done this or that (see, for example, Arnett 2004), and no doubt many of the Youth Panel would subscribe to that position. The imagery that adulthood vests in checking off some definable endpoints could well be misplaced, but in this chapter that approach has proven useful as an organizing frame.

We are reminded of Ronald Rindfuss's (1991) distinction between diversity and disorder. Diversity is simply difference; it is neither good nor bad. Disorder, on the other hand, involves transition sequences that violate social expectations. The collective experience among the sample reveals a multiplicity of transition patterns, but in an era of changing norms, how can we say whether any qualify as disorderly? To help clarify, Rindfuss adds a second stipulation—for him, adverse consequences make disorder interesting (see Rindfuss 503 and note 7).

Becoming a parent before marrying or ever marrying can be problematic or not, depending on a host of considerations. On the surface, the situation of the jobless teen mother who drops out to care for her asthmatic daughter with no support from the baby's father and no parents or extended kin to help looks the same as the situation of the thirty-year-old never-married mother with a close-knit family and on leave from a good job. By the standard of yesterday's expectations, the family transitions of both would be considered disorderly, but the conditions of their parenting in fact are radically different. To see that difference requires a broader view that encompasses strands of development in other domains, and one suspects the road ahead will be bumpier for the younger unmarried mother.

A focus on anticipated consequences thus sets some parameters. The transition sequences and supplementary materials reviewed in this chapter trace the paths followed by the Youth Panel children to age twenty-eight, but to what end points have those paths led? Our interest in this volume is the panel's socioeconomic destinations, for which there is no set end point. Still, taking stock as the panel nears the end of its third decade will afford a fairly good gauge of adult prospects. The next chapter profiles the socioeconomic standing of study participants at age twenty-eight in the same terms used for their parents in chapter 3: progress through school as of that point, the rewards realized through work (earnings), and the status of their jobs. These three criteria of socioeconomic attainment are markers too, not of adulthood, but as rough barometers of quality of life in material terms.

= Chapter 6 =

Socioeconomic Destinations

T HE MILESTONES along the path to adulthood taken up in the previous chapter differ from progress along the socioeconomic status (SES) gradient in obvious ways, but as well in a way that might not be so obvious. Marrying and becoming a parent are discrete events. The birthdates of children, anniversaries, and even leaving the parental home can be marked on a calendar, whereas progress through school and experience in the workplace are infinitely changeable. When some college students take twenty or more years to finish their degrees (Attewell and Lavin 2007) and dropouts sit for the general educational development (GED) certificate well into their thirties (American Council on Education 2011), who can say when done really is done? When asked at age twenty-eight, 80 percent of the Beginning School Survey Youth Panel (BSSYP, or Youth Panel) participants said they intended to further their educations.

So both the transition to adulthood and socioeconomic accomplishment unfold over time. That back story is where we begin with this chapter's agenda, which is to sketch the panel's socioeconomic attainments a decade after high school along the same lines as done for their parents in chapter 3 and at about the same age.[1] This will set the stage in chapter 7 for an uncommon like-for-like comparison of parents' and their children's socioeconomic standing as young adults. The Mature Adult Survey (MAS) interview at age twenty-eight is the reference point for destinations: levels of education, occupational status, and earnings.

Building Human Capital
Through School and Work

The modern economy offers two well-understood paths for getting ahead in life. One is school, the other the workplace. Both entail investments in human capital. Schooling enhances skills and technical knowledge and confers credentials, and the workplace provides experience and often specialized training. Continuing the analogy, investments are expected to yield returns: employers who value these productivity-enhancing commitments of time reward workers through higher wages, promotions, and more generous benefits. Despite many exceptions (for example, not all jobs offer the same opportunities for advancement, years of hard work can yield little in return, and the *working poor* would seem an oxymoron were it not for their large numbers), that account still holds in the main: bypassing school and an erratic work history make it hard to advance in the modern era.[2]

Table 6.1 offers a first look at the sample's history of investment in its human capital; later in the chapter we review the associated returns. Two time horizons are used: the two years before the MAS (left panel) and from the end of high school (right panel).[3] Investments are calculated as the percentage of months enrolled in school and the percentage of months employed. Time out of the workforce and not in school are tallied as periods of idleness. The everyday meaning of *idleness* connotes just hanging around, but there are many ways to occupy one's time when not in school or employed, parenting being the most obvious. Still, regardless of the reason, foregoing school and spells out of the workforce promise to compromise later employment prospects. As used in the economics literature (for example, Edelman, Holzer, and Offner 2006) and here, the word *idleness* is intended to convey that idea.

From table 6.1, we see that employment, mostly full-time, dominates throughout the BSSYP, ranging upward from almost 60 percent to 80 percent of lapsed months across both intervals. Work is steadier during the recent period as school enrollments recede, but even over the longer span since high school (including the most recent twenty-four months), the Youth Panel was employed, on average, 70 percent of the months (61 percent full time).

School enrollment comes in a distant second over both periods. Differences across social lines are not large but are gendered: women were enrolled for a higher percentage of months than men (since leaving high school, 21 percent versus 16 percent for both races). These investments would be expected to pay dividends, but though "college for all" may be the currently popular exhortation, "work for all" is closer to the urban disadvantaged's reality.

In fact, "for all" is not quite right, and table 6.1 shows large disparities across social lines in work histories. White men's experience stands out especially. They register the lowest levels of school participation and the highest levels of workforce participation. In fact, not a single white man was enrolled in school full time when interviewed at age twenty-eight (not presented). Employment profiles otherwise are similar, women and African American men working full-time about 58 percent of the months since high school and 68 percent of the months over the previous two years.

Table 6.1 Percent Months Employed and Percent Months in School

	Past Twenty-Four Months					Since High School, Including Past Twenty-Four Months				
	Full Time	Part Time	Full Time or Part Time	In School	Idle	Full Time	Part Time	Full Time or Part Time	In School	Idle[a]
Overall	70	12	77	11	20	61	14	70	19	24
White men	80	11	87	8	13	72	12	79	16	17
Black men	68	7	71	9	25	58	10	65	16	29
White women	67	15	76	10	22	58	16	70	21	23
Black women	69	16	76	15	20	57	16	68	21	26
Lower SES	63	11	69	10	28	57	9	63	10	34
White men	77	5	79	2	20	70	6	73	6	26
Black men	56	7	59	10	36	52	8	58	10	39
White women	58	16	69	8	28	57	10	63	11	33
Black women	63	13	72	14	25	55	11	63	13	34

Source: Authors' compilation.
Note: All numbers in percentages; from retrospective histories at age twenty-eight.
[a]Idle is defined as not working and not in school

These calculations make it seem that African American men approximate women's employment pattern, but the underlying dynamics are different. That is easier to see in the idleness tallies, which monitor time out from both school and work.

On average, the panel was idle about 24 percent of the months after high school and 20 percent of those during the previous two years, but showed large differences across groups. Lower-SES African American men were idle more than 35 percent of the time over both intervals; white men, mainly owing to their superior employment histories, were least often idle.[4] For those who forgo college, a sustained history of employment over the years after high school is the way to advance in the workplace. In the sample, working-class white men are best positioned to realize those benefits.

It also is important to note the heterogeneity subsumed under idleness. Most idle women (forty-two of the fifty-two) were involved with parenting—nearly 90 percent with children, 75 percent with children under age six.[5] Many idle men were parents also, but one suspects their parenting did not command as much of their time as for the idle mothers: most lower-SES men did not live with their children and more than 10 percent of African American men were incarcerated at the time of the MAS, nearly double the percentage of white men (11.7 percent versus 6.1 percent).

For young African American men in this age range, additional considerations come into play, overcoming negative stereotypes in finding employment is one (Kirschenman and Neckerman 1991; Pager and Karafin 2009; Moss and Tilly 2001). The urban disadvantaged are not constitutionally averse to low-level work (Newman 2000; Edin and Lein 1997; Dohan 2003). In fact, black men spend significantly more time than do white men looking for work (Tomaskovic-Devey, Thomas, and Johnson 2005) and are more likely to experience involuntary unemployment (Wilson, Tienda, and Wu 1995).

Another consideration is the stain of a criminal record (Holzer 2009; Western 2006). Incarceration rates nationally increased nearly fivefold between 1973 and 2003, drug offenses leading the way (Pager 2007). In a none-too-flattering instance of American exceptionalism, incarceration levels in the United States exceed the combined total of thirty-five European counties. The U.S. incarceration rate is an outlier also: 753 per hundred thousand in 2010, far ahead of Russia, a distant second at 609 (Pew Charitable Trusts 2010, 7).

Marijuana use and distribution accounted for more than 50 percent of all drug arrests in 2010 (88 percent for possession), with a disturbing disproportionality by race. Although marijuana use is similar among blacks and white, the consequences are decidedly skewed, as the arrest rate for blacks is almost four times the white rate. In Baltimore, 91.7 percent of those arrested for marijuana possession in 2010 were African American, the largest racial disparity in the country (ACLU 2013).

Nationally in 2008, 11.4 percent of African American men ages twenty to thirty-four were incarcerated; for those without a high school diploma or GED, the figure skyrockets to 37.1 percent—more than one in three.[6] According to the Pew Charitable Trusts (2010, 8), "as adults in their twenties and early thirties, when they should be launching careers, black men without a high school diploma are more likely to be found in a cell than in the workplace."

These national figures give perspective to the experience of the Youth Panel: at age twenty-eight, 34 percent of black men had a criminal conviction and 54 percent an arrest; for those of lower-SES background, the figures are 49 percent and 68 percent. Unlike the national figures just cited, however, lower-SES whites in the Youth Panel also run afoul of the law in large numbers: 41 percent with convictions and 63 percent with arrests. In fact, white men, higher SES and lower, report more drug use than African American men of the same class background, and whites are much more likely than are blacks to experiment with hard drugs (taken up in the next chapter).

Such high levels of arrest and conviction among lower-SES whites may surprise, but research hardly ever centers on the white urban disadvantaged who are comparable to African Americans in terms of family and neighborhood SES.[7] So far as we can tell the picture just sketched is altogether accurate, but what of consequences? Nationally, a criminal record weighs more heavily on African Americans than on whites (Holzer, Raphael, and Stoll 2004; Pager 2007; Western 2006) and table 6.1 hints at that: despite similar arrest and incarceration histories, lower-SES white men enjoy a 20 percentage point labor force participation advantage over African American men during the years immediately preceding the MAS and a 15 percent advantage over the longer interval back to high school. Among high school dropouts, the difference is larger still: at age twenty-two, 89 percent of white dropouts were working against 40 percent of black dropouts.

These comparisons leave many questions unanswered: there is no screen on the nature of the offense, the number of repeat offenses, or how much time was spent behind bars. Still, to see such near parity in involvement with the criminal justice system, even in broad stroke terms, makes it clear that problem behaviors among the urban disadvantaged are far from exclusive to African Americans.

These schooling, employment, and idleness histories identify differences by race and SES that would be expected to affect socioeconomic prospects as the Youth Panel near age thirty, although how much and

in what ways remains to be seen. Will white men profit from their superior accumulated work experience and women from their greater attachment to school? What of African American men, whose shortfall in both
domains is cause for concern? Will lower-SES men, white and black, who
get caught up in the criminal justice system be held back by their mis-
steps? The perspective afforded by table 6.1 helps identify the issues, but
is too broad brush for answers. Those are deferred until chapters 7 and 8.

Socioeconomic Attainments as Young Adults

We next take up the end states to which these investments in human
capital have led, turning first to schooling.

Schooling Undertaken and Completed

Low-income students often attend college part time and intermittently,
such that more calendar months of enrollment will not necessarily yield
more degrees. Our tallies from the previous section are not sensitive
to this. Nor do they reflect that these investments of time are directed
toward different forms of postsecondary certification. Study participants
were working toward vocational certificates, two-year community college degrees, and baccalaureate degrees, which typically yield very different labor market returns (for example, Danziger 2004).

Schooling may not have been the Youth Panel's principal pursuit over
the years after high school, but it is one that is almost certain to pay off.
However, for the urban disadvantaged, college enrollment and completion are not to be taken for granted. Compared with their better-off
counterparts, low-income youth more often delay their transition from
high school to college, attend part time, or stop out. Against the straight-
through, full-time fast track, a slow, meandering route does not auger
well (for an overview, see Goldrick-Rab and Roksa 2008). At present
roughly 40 percent of college students attend part time and 75 percent
are commuters, many juggling school with family and work. Part-time
students who are successful typically take twice as long to finish a
degree or certificate as those who attend full time, yet even then, far
fewer complete their programs (Complete College America 2011).

Much stratification research focuses on inequalities at the highest
level of schooling attained, jumping straight to the final resolution. This
skips over the paths traveled, hiding the unsuccessful attempts. Almost
65 percent of lower-SES youth in the study who try for a four-year
degree fall short, a glimpse of how educational stratification works "on
the ground" (see table 6.2).

Table 6.2   Highest Levels of Educational Enrollment and Completion at Age Twenty-Eight

	Permanent Dropout		GED		High School Diploma		Certificate-License[a]			Associate's[a]			Bachelor's[b]		
	Enroll	Earned	Enroll	Earned	Enroll	Earned	Enroll	Yield[d]	Earned	Enroll	Yield[c,d]	Earned	Enroll	Yield[d]	Earned
Overall	14.0	14.8	9.1	14.2	12.1	33.9	19.3	66.9	12.9	17.5	7.3	1.3	28.0	57.4	16.1
White men	18.9	19.7	11.4	12.9	18.9	36.4	12.9	70.6	9.1	15.2	—	—	22.7	73.3	16.7
White women	11.5	11.5	8.1	14.2	12.8	36.5	18.2	55.6	10.1	18.2	—	—	31.1	78.3	24.3
Black men	15.4	15.4	12.3	19.1	11.7	32.1	21.0	76.5	16.0	14.8	—	—	24.7	42.5	10.5
Black women	11.3	13.4	5.4	10.8	7.0	31.7	23.1	65.1	15.1	21.0	—	—	32.3	43.3	14.0
Lower SES	23.2	24.5	13.1	18.5	13.4	29.6	22.9	76.4	17.5	15.3	—	—	12.1	34.2	4.1
Medium SES	8.4	9.0	4.5	10.3	16.1	44.5	23.2	52.8	12.3	20.6	—	—	27.1	40.5	11.0
Higher SES	1.3	1.3	5.7	9.6	5.1	31.2	7.6	58.3	4.5	19.1	—	—	61.1	74.0	45.2
(N)		(88)		(57)		(76)	(121)		(81)	(110)		(8)	(176)		(101)

Source: Authors' compilation.

Note: All numbers are percentage distributions.

[a] Tallies for certificate-license and associate degrees earned do not include those who earned a credential but then enrolled in a higher-level program. For example, certificate-license was the highest credential earned for 18.0 percent of the panel and associate's was the highest credential for 3.0 percent, both higher than the table entries of 12.9 percent and 1.3 percent.

[b] Figures for the bachelor's degree include those who have earned a bachelor's and later enrolled in graduate degree programs.

[c] Given the total of just eight highest earned associate's degrees, the percentage distributions are not reported.

[d] Yield is the completion rate for enrollments undertaken.

High School and Less   Given more than 63 percent of the panel is at high school or less at age twenty-eight, schooling is concentrated toward the low end: 33.9 percent are terminal high school graduates, 14.2 percent completed high school with the GED, and 14.8 percent are permanent dropouts, meaning without high school certification of any kind at the time of the MAS. White men (19.7 percent) and those of lower-SES (24.5 percent) are most numerous among the permanent dropouts, and the socioeconomic gradient is steep: just 9 percent of those of middle SES and 1.3 percent of higher SES failed to complete high school.

The permanent distinction is important, as most dropouts eventually complete high school, either by reenrolling or alternative certification, most often the GED. These recovered dropouts make up about 60 percent of the total, about the same percentage as nationally (Barton 2005, 39; Berktold, Geis, and Kaufman 1998). Most—90 percent—complete high school by completing the GED.[8] The other 10 percent graduated with a regular diploma after returning to high school.[9]

When we last spoke with them as they were approaching age thirty, 85 percent of permanent dropouts said they expect to get more education.[10] The spark, we see, does not extinguish easily, and just about every dropout with whom we spoke expressed regret over the decision. As would be expected, limited job and earnings prospects top the list, but other voices also are heard—wanting to be a better role model for their children, feeling remorse at disappointing their parents, and, not infrequently, believing that college might have helped keep them out of trouble with the law: "maybe if I had finished school, I would not be in prison," said one (Ricardo, white); "Wouldn't be locked up. Would have had structure in my life instead of negative things," said another (Brendon, African American).

Baltimore's deindustrialization was well under way in the early 1980s, but even then men without a college degree, or even a high school diploma, could find well-paid work in Baltimore's shipyards, steel mills, and construction sites. Those opportunities now are less abundant, locally and nationally: a high school degree "is hardly enough to ensure reasonable prospects. Like it or not, at least some form of postsecondary education is increasingly necessary" (Berlin, Furstenberg, and Waters 2010, 4).

Unfortunately, college has proven an elusive goal for the urban disadvantaged. For them, high school is the modal level of completed schooling, yet just 13.4 percent stopped at high school as their highest enrollment (table 6.2). The discrepancy between schooling undertaken and schooling completed is especially large for African American women: 76 percent pursued some form of postsecondary education (bachelor's being the most popular at 32.3 percent), but only just over 30 percent finished a program.[11] The disparity is large also for those of lower-SES family background—50 percent pursued higher education, but as of age twenty-eight, only a little over 20 percent had attained a certificate or degree. That so many of the urban disadvantaged try to lift themselves up through schooling only to fall short is disheartening: across the entire panel, unsuccessful attempts at a postsecondary degree or certificate exceed successes, 217 versus 190.

Higher Education   Nonetheless, the panel's schooling spans the full spectrum of possibilities. Sixteen percent have bachelor's degrees and some graduate degrees, but these overall figures mask large differences across social lines.[12] Completion rates for those who undertake a four-year degree are one issue. At the low end are African Americans (a little over 40 percent for both men and women) and lower-SES youth (just over 34 percent), who lag far behind whites and higher-SES youth (in the vicinity of 75 percent). This shortfall is one concern; access is another, and higher-SES youth are doubly advantaged. Not only do more of them finish what they begin, more of them also begin: 61 percent undertake a four-year degree, more than double those in the middle-SES range (27 percent) and five times those in the lower (12 percent).

Bachelor's degree completion falls short of 100 percent for two reasons: no longer being enrolled, being a postsecondary dropout, or being enrolled and still working on the degree.[13] At age twenty-eight, those still enrolled would be considered nontraditional or overage students, but "swirling" in and out of college or between colleges nowadays is common (Goldrick-Rab 2006), so today's enrollee could easily be tomorrow's dropout, and vice versa.[14]

Perhaps the bachelor's degree sets too high a standard for the urban disadvantaged. Certificate programs and community colleges are more accessible by design, which is why so many disadvantaged minority and low-income students rely on them as the postsecondary point of entry.[15] The time commitment of these programs is shorter, typically they are more affordable than four-year degree programs, cater to commuter students, and are less selective in their admissions. For those reasons, we might expect to see high levels of program completion, but do not, either in the study or nationally.

Almost equal numbers undertake certificate programs (19.3 percent) and associate's degrees (17.5 percent), with uneven success.[16] In table 6.2, the associate's degree completion rate is shockingly low, at 7.3 percent. When applied to the 17.5 percent for whom community college was the highest level of enrollment, the yield is just 8 degrees, too few to sustain a more detailed breakdown across social lines. However, some associate's degree successes are hidden from view in table 6.2. Associate's degree holders who undertook a four-year program

(N = 37) are not displayed because their highest attempted degree is the bachelor's. Crediting them raises the associate's degree success rate to 31 percent (45 of 147), of line with associate's degree programs nationally (Adelman 2004).

The experience of those who undertook certificate or licensure programs is more favorable, with a completion rate of 67 percent. Cosmetology and medical assistant are the two most popular certificate programs. Both make sense. "Doing hair" is a popular route to entrepreneurship in the African American community and Baltimore's thriving health-care industry provides good employment opportunities for medical assistants. As a practical matter, the certificate-license path is the only postsecondary sector open to high school dropouts (16 percent of permanent dropouts pursue certificate programs and 75 percent finish them), but whether these programs improve their graduates' labor market prospects is unclear (see Cellini 2008). Harry Holzer (2010) concludes that sub-baccalaureate vocational training has proven effective only for specific categories of middle-skills occupations, such as LPNs, technicians, therapists in health care, and the construction crafts.

It is unfortunate that the verdict is not more clear on the value of these certificates and licensure programs because they occupy a distinctive niche in the postsecondary landscape. Nationally in 2009, some 305,000 students, just over 15 percent of all for-profit postsecondary enrollments, were at less than two-year certificate and licensure programs (Knapp, Kelly-Reid, and Ginder 2011).[17] The more popular programs include real estate, travel and tourism, personal service (such as barbering, hair styling, cosmetology), nursing assistance, auto mechanics, data processing, welding, and commercial truck driving. Typically of short duration (Apling 1993), these programs cater to low-income nontraditional students (U.S. Government Accountability Office 2009, 7–8; Phipps, Harrison, and Merisotis 1999, 7–9).

The community college system has received more attention from the perspective of educational stratification than have certificate programs, in part because of the possibility of transfer to a four-year program.[18] Successful transfer is uncommon, though, and community colleges characteristically suffer high levels of noncompletion: across the nation, the completion rate for full-time students pursuing an associate's degree is just 18.8 percent after four years; for part-time students, it is a dismal 7.8 percent (Complete College America 2011).

Clifford Adelman (2004) contends that such shocking statistics are misleading because many who attend community colleges are not serious or viable students. Screening on credit hour accumulation, he finds graduation rates are much higher among two-year matriculants who accumulate at least ten credit hours. James Rosenbaum (2001) and several of his colleagues (for example, Deil-Amen 2006) agree, attributing high levels of attrition to weak preparation and poor counseling, in high school and at college. Entering with weak skills, many of these students are shunted into noncredit remedial courses (Attewell et al. 2006) and quickly come up against academic standards they cannot satisfy.

Academic preparation no doubt is the downfall of many community college students, but the daunting practical obstacles they face apart from academics, including transportation, inflexible work schedules, finances, family obligations, job pressures, and, yes, run-ins with the law, receive little comment in critiques of the community college student profile. We cannot screen on credit hours accumulated, but those who completed associate's degree programs averaged 19.8 quarters of enrollment, so what are nominally two-year degrees often stretch to five calendar years or more.[19] These students cycle in and out, picking up credits as they can, and many ultimately fall short, like Tami (see box 6.1). Her story encapsulates the life-course principle that multiple strands of development intersect, in her case family and school, with consequences that cross domain boundaries.

Multiply Tami's experience many times over to understand why those still taking courses toward the associate's degree averaged 12.9 calendar quarters of enrollment at age twenty-eight, and those no longer enrolled were not far behind, at 9.6 calendar quarters. Three-fourths of those who began an associate's degree program withdrew and were degreeless when we last spoke with them. To invest two-plus years in pursuit of a two-year degree successfully is one thing—perhaps it will pay off (Marcotte et al. 2005; Furchtgott-Roth, Jacobson, and Mokher 2009)—but to make that investment with nothing to show for it is quite another.

Community colleges provide an affordable, accessible higher education option for students who otherwise might not be able to attend college, but with such unconscionably low rates of completion, the needed reforms go well beyond improved academic support. The larger, and arguably more formidable, challenge is to accommodate to the complicated lives of college students who do not fit the middle-class profile (Brock 2010; Goldrick-Rab and Roksa 2008).

Such reforms will not be easy because they come up against daunting resource constraints. Anthony Carnevale and Jeff Strohl (2010) argue that as a nation we have underinvested, and badly so, in precisely those schools that service our neediest students: community colleges and minimally selective colleges and universities. In 2006, the average institutional subsidy beyond net tuition was $18,542 at private research universities, $7,574 at public research universities, and $6,622 at public colleges offering the associate's degree (Wellman 2008, figure 2).

Box 6.1   Three Community College Enrollment Spells Without a Degree

All her life through high school, Tami lived in the same blue-collar Baltimore neighborhood. A student at one of the rougher city high schools, she had a baby during her junior year, but was able to graduate on time and in the top 10 percent of her class by taking turns attending with the baby's father. After high school, Tami completed two semesters toward an associate's degree at a local community college by taking advantage of on-campus day care, but stopped, a combination of financial pressures and wanting to wait until her daughter was in school full time. Employee benefits as a receptionist at a law firm later allowed her to complete a semester of law classes at a different community college. Now interested in law, she took classes in legal research and advanced law, thinking to apply her accumulating credits toward a four-year jurisprudence program, but upon marrying and relocating, she withdrew from school in 2004, a decade after high school, with thirty-five earned credits. Still without an associate's degree at twenty-eight, her goal is a doctoral degree but she expects to make it only as far as the bachelor's. Referring to her responsibilities as a parent, she says, "Just sometimes I get frustrated. Because I like, when I want something, I want it now. You know. I want—and there's a lot of things that stand in my way. Like, I mean, I don't mean to say she stands in my way, but she has to come first, you know. I'm sure if I didn't have her, I probably would be in law school right now."

These and other like considerations prompt Carnevale and Strohl (2010, 120) to conclude that "Much of the decline in college graduation rates [from 50 percent to 45 percent since the 1980s] can be accounted for by community colleges, and the overwhelming cause is the difference in resources available by level of selectivity." The authors also note that "it seems clear that no more than a third of declining completions are due to student preparedness" (74). So while Rosenbaum implicates academic deficiencies, Adelman depth of commitment, and we life's practical challenges beyond the academy, Carnevale and Strohl remind us to look also to structural differences across postsecondary sectors when pondering the why of uneven success.

Turning now to baccalaureate programs, the bachelor's degree completion rate (57 percent in table 6.2) falls between that of certificate-licensure and associate's degree programs, and at age twenty-eight 25 percent of those who had started a program but not yet finished were still enrolled. The bachelor's degree requires a substantially greater time commitment than sub-baccalaureate programs do and enrollment often extends beyond the traditional college-going age. However, given that almost 60 percent are already graduated, the experience of our study participants through age twenty-eight compares favorably with completion rates nationally (Wirt et al. 2004): for example, 60.1 percent within eight years for those attending full time, 24.3 percent for those attending part time (Complete College America 2011, 10).[20]

The typical terminal bachelor's degree recipient in the study averaged 18.2 quarters of enrollment. Had they attended full time, straight through, and were our data actually aligned with academic quarters, sixteen to twenty quarters would be expected. Our calculations are but a rough approximation, but it is interesting that those who also earned the master's degree averaged 16.5 quarters to complete the bachelor's degree, and the handful with doctoral degrees did so in 15.9 quarters.

Fast-track students finish quickly and get on with their lives, which for some means yet more school. Others not on the fast track meander, cycling in and out of school, often inconclusively. Across all three school types, successful bachelor's degree earners averaged 20.5 quarters of enrollment, a small increase over the bachelor's-only tally (18.2), whereas those still enrolled averaged 21.5 quarters, and those withdrawn 14.5 quarters.

That there are successes should not be ignored, but too many invest considerable time in school after high school with little to show for it. Their higher education path is roundabout and uncertain, and prospects for success often depend on the long shadow of family background: nationally, 60 percent of bachelor's candidates whose parents have college degrees finish in the expected four years versus just 10 percent of those whose parents do not (Settersten and Ray 2010).[21]

The Youth Panel record of four-year degree completion is much the same. To see almost 30 percent of the entire sample, including 44 percent of those with a high school diploma, attending four-year programs is welcome. Not so welcome are the pronounced disparities across social lines (see table 6.2). Women, especially white women, have a noticeable advantage in earning a bachelor's degree: at 24.3 percent, they have the highest percentage of any race-gender group, and by a comfortable margin. African American men lag furthest back: just 10.5 percent hold bachelor's degrees, for a high-low difference by race and gender of 13.8 percent (24.3 percent to 10.5 percent).

Disparities of that magnitude in levels of bachelor's degree attainment across lines of race and gender are certain to have consequences later, but they pale against a 41 percent difference across the SES extremes: 45.2 percent of those of higher-SES background complete bachelor's programs against just 4.1 percent of lower-SES youth, and this with the socioeconomic distribution of the sample truncated at the high end. Nationally it is much the same, with a 40 percent difference in bachelor's completion across the bottom and top quartiles of family income (Goldrick-Rab and Roksa 2008).

The Urban Disadvantaged and Higher Education   Given that fewer than 5 percent of the Youth Panel's urban disadvantaged earn a bachelor's degree, and even fewer an associate's, the strong relationship between socioeconomic origins and educational destinations presented in table 6.2 accords with the status-preserving side of status attainment: despite aspiring to more, precious few children of lower-SES origins achieve upward mobility through higher education. Many start down the college path, but few make it all the way, which has predictable implications for the two other pillars of socioeconomic standing: occupational status and earnings, which are taken up next.

Employment and Its Rewards

Occupational status is one tangible reward of work. Physicians are more highly educated and remunerated than are janitors, and so have higher status as a class. Symbolic or honorific rewards tend to follow a like gradient—for example, physicians also are more highly regarded by virtue of the work they do.[22]

The panel's most recent full-time jobs over the two years preceding the MAS are displayed in table 6.3 using the Census Bureau classification that ranges from executives and managers to laborers. Here we contrast the experience of the urban disadvantaged (half the sample, reported in the right panel) and those of higher-SES family background (a fourth of the panel, reported in the left panel). With eleven occupational categories distinguished and comparisons broken out by race and gender as well as by family background, this display stretches the sample to the limit—subsample sizes, especially for the higher-SES segment of the panel, are quite small. Nevertheless, the differences are striking, likely broadly generalizable, and suggest fundamentally different labor market processes at play. These do not involve only the obvious higher-SES and lower-SES divide, but also segmentation by gender and race.

For those of higher-SES background, employment is concentrated in the two highest occupational types: executive and managerial combined, and professional. These account for 38.2 percent of the higher-SES total, but just 5.1 percent of those of lower-SES origins. The SES difference is almost as large as that seen in the previous section for college completion, which no doubt plays into the disparities evident here.

Differences by gender are also significant. Higher-SES men are more numerous in executive and managerial positions: among whites,

Table 6.3 Most Recent Full-Time Job

Occupational Type	Higher SES					Lower SES				
	Overall	White Men	Black Men	White Women	Black Women	Overall	White Men	Black Men	White Women	Black Women
Executive-manager	14.7	17.1	29.0	5.1	9.7	2.1	0.0	0.0	8.5	1.2
Professional	23.5	20.0	6.5	38.5	25.8	3.0	4.3	0.0	4.3	3.7
Technical	5.9	2.9	6.5	5.1	9.7	3.0	2.1	1.6	2.1	4.9
Sales	8.1	17.1	9.7	5.1	0.0	9.3	4.3	8.2	12.8	11.1
Clerical	16.9	11.4	6.5	25.6	22.6	21.2	6.4	8.2	23.4	38.3
Protective	2.9	2.9	9.7	0.0	0.0	4.2	0.0	8.2	2.1	4.9
Service	19.1	11.4	16.1	17.9	32.3	22.5	2.1	14.8	34.0	33.3
Craft[a]	4.4	11.4	6.5	0.0	0.0	13.1	44.7	14.8	2.1	0.0
Operator	0.7	2.9	0.0	0.0	0.0	4.7	10.6	4.9	4.3	1.2
Transport	2.2	2.9	6.5	0.0	0.0	6.8	10.6	14.8	2.1	1.2
Laborer	1.5	0.0	3.2	2.6	0.0	10.2	14.9	24.6	4.3	0.0
(N)	(136)	(35)	(31)	(39)	(31)	(236)	(47)	(61)	(47)	(81)

Source: Authors' compilation.
Note: All numbers in percentages; in twenty-four months before Mature Adult Survey.
[a]Examples from within the sample include carpenter, mechanic, installer, electrical apprentice, plumber, painter, and refrigeration technician.

17.1 percent men versus 5.1 percent for women; among blacks, 29.0 percent versus 9.7 percent. Higher-SES women are more numerous in the professions: among whites, 38.5 percent versus 20.0 percent for men; among African Americans, 25.8 percent versus 6.5 percent. The only other sectors of employment with any significant higher-SES presence are the service sector and, for women exclusively, the clerical sector.

Access to these high-level positions reflects a gendered advantage in which not only educational credentials come into play, but also valued social contacts (Granovetter 1995; Nelson Schwartz, "In Hiring, a Friend in Need Is a Prospect, Indeed," *New York Times*, January 28, 2013, p. A1). For accessing professional employment, it is advantageous that white women register the highest level of bachelor's degree completion (seen earlier, 24.3 percent) and more often continue in school beyond the bachelor's (12.5 percent attained an advanced degree, followed by white men at 7.4 percent),[23] but those credentials apparently do not afford the same access to executive and managerial positions, which remain dominated by men. Also, the percentage of higher-SES women in the clerical sector is striking.

A gendered division of labor also characterizes the lower-SES end of the occupational divide. Their work is more highly concentrated at the low end (just 8.1 percent total in the executive-managerial, professional, and technical categories) and overlap across genders in employment patterns is minimal. To illustrate the kind of distinctions at issue, table 6.4 presents specific job titles within the sample that fall under these broad groupings.

More than half of lower-SES white women (57.4 percent) and almost three-quarters of lower-SES African American women (71.6 percent) work in the traditional pink-collar service and clerical sectors. Hardly any are employed as laborers, in construction or in transportation. In contrast, lower-SES white men are concentrated heavily in the industrial and construction crafts (44.7 percent of their total), whereas African Americans are distributed across several sectors of blue-collar employment—25 percent as laborers and another 14.8 percent each in transportation, the skilled crafts, and the service sector. The preponderance of lower-SES white men working in the crafts is noteworthy for two reasons: it is unexpected under the deindustrialization script and in the next section we will see that it affords them a substantial earnings advantage over others.

Occupations and Their Benefits: Earnings and Status   What we do to earn a living is a personal insignia of our standing in the wider world. It is integral to how we think of ourselves and to how others relate to us. The stranger will not know whether the woman clinician sipping wine is good at her work or has several malpractice suits pending; neither will he know, or much care, whether the trash hauler is reliable, honest,

Table 6.4   Representative Occupations at Age Twenty-Eight

Executive-manager	General manager, marketing specialist, senior accountant, financial analyst, mortgage broker, VP event planning, purchasing manager
Professional	Attorney, engineer, computer analyst, public defender, registered nurse, social worker, teacher, architect, clinical dietician, photographer
Technical	EMT, programmer, veterinary technician, web producer, paralegal, medical lab technician, medical assistant, orthopedic technician
Clerical	Billing specialist, bookkeeper, customer service representative, secretary, medical office coordinator, retail inventory, administrative assistant, warehouse clerk, data entry, front desk clerk
Protective	Security guard, police officer, house arrest officer, prisoner supervisor, range instructor
Sales	Sales clerk, salesman, insurance agent
Service	Barber, chef, cleaner, hostess, janitor, usher, bar maid, bartender, cook, cosmetologist, manicurist
Craft	Carpenter, mechanic, installer, plumber, painter, refrigeration technician, forklift operator, crane operator, welder
Operator	Exhaust cleaner, shot blaster, Corian fabricator, mill operator, bindery worker
Transport	Towing, truck driver, cab driver, bus driver
Laborer	Utility person, packer, laborer, demolition, warehouse, truck loader, carpenter helper

Source: Authors' compilation.
Note: U.S. Census categories; examples listed are the most recent jobs held as of the Mature Adult Survey.

and hard working. The job title seems to "say it all," but what exactly is the it? A stratification perspective emphasizes: a job's associated level of education; its material benefits; and the prestige or status level it confers. Table 6.5 uses these distinctions to describe the sample's most recent full-time jobs over the twenty-four months preceding the MAS.[24]

Overall, the sample's median earnings are $30,000. To know whether this figure fairly reflects young adults in the Baltimore area, we report two sources from roughly the same period. According to the 2000 Census, the median personal income for twenty-eight- and twenty-nine-year-olds in Baltimore in 1999 was $23,000 (N = 661, excluding those with no income). Adjusted for inflation, that becomes $26,962 in 2005 dollars, the reference year for most of the earnings reported in table 6.5 (Ruggles et al. 2008). That is fairly close to the study figure, but what we really would prefer is earnings in 2005, which is not the same as an inflation-adjusted estimate from 1999.

Table 6.5 Schooling, Earnings, and Occupational Status

Occupational Category[a]	Self			Spouse-Partner		
	Years of Schooling	Median Earnings ($1,000s)	Occupational Status (SEI)	Years of Schooling	Median Earnings ($1,000s)	Occupational Status (SEI)
Executive-manager	14.6	49.0	48.3	14.7	43.5	43.5
Professional	16.5	42.0	58.8	15.8	42.0	47.9
Technical	13.9	32.8	43.0	14.4	45.0	40.9
Sales	12.7	30.0	35.8	13.3	30.0	35.5
Clerical	13.0	26.0	31.3	13.1	39.0	35.8
Protective	13.2	36.0	37.6	12.9	27.0	34.7
Service	12.4	21.6	23.3	12.4	25.0	29.8
Craft	11.8	35.0	31.0	12.1	28.0	31.3
Operator	11.9	28.0	23.8	12.0	25.0	26.6
Transport	12.7	30.6	26.6	12.7	31.5	34.7
Laborer	11.8	25.0	23.7	12.0	18.0	26.1
Overall	13.1	30.0	33.3	13.1	31.0	35.3
(N)	(507)	(503)	(507)	(298)	(244)	(235)

Source: Authors' compilation.

Note: At age twenty-eight, for self and spouse or partner.

[a]The MAS occupational category is the panel member's most recent full-time employment as far back as last twenty-four months. Spouse and partner averages are grouped through their ties to one of the sample.

The 2005 American Community Survey (U.S. Census Bureau 2005) is a more time-appropriate source, although with a smaller sample size (N = 272). According to it, the median earnings that year for twenty-seven- to thirty-year-old Baltimoreans "with some earnings" was $29,250. The comparability of these census sources with the sample is only approximate (for example, many of those living and working in the city in 2005 did not grow up in the city); still, it is reassuring that earnings levels seem reasonable for young adult workers in Baltimore around the time of the MAS.[25]

As expected, the panel's socioeconomic attainments are highly variable across occupational types. With the standard deviation for years of schooling across the entire sample at 2.02, a difference in education level across occupational categories as small as a single year (roughly half a standard deviation) would be considered large. Laborers, those in the crafts, and machine operatives average just below twelve years of schooling (equivalent in our coding to a high school degree or GED), the lowest education averages of the eleven categories. At 16.5 years, professionals have the highest average, followed by managers (14.6 years) and higher level technical workers (13.9 years).

Earnings differences across occupational categories likewise are large, but do not mirror exactly the pattern for level of schooling. Professionals, for example, suffer an earnings deficit of roughly $7,000 against executives and managers.[26] One implication is that, compared with men, women's high level of professional employment seen in table 6.3 is not matched by commensurately high levels of earnings.

The construction trades also run counter to the schooling gradient—they have one of the lowest education averages, but pay much better than service and clerical jobs do. By this standard, the skilled crafts are the elite stratum of blue-collar work, and much of it is situated in what remains of the Baltimore's old industrial economy. That lower-SES white men have a near monopoly on this sector of employment accounts for their edge in earnings.

Considering all that has been written about deindustrialization's impact on the economy of places like Baltimore, this concentration of high-paying work in the skilled trades might seem anomalous, but the deindustrialization script plays out at the level of the macro-economy. On the ground, "decimated" is not quite right. As reviewed in chapter 2, Baltimore has without question suffered enormously as a result of deindustrialization, but not too long ago the arrival of the largest cargo ship in the ninety-year history of its Domino Sugar refinery was front-page news in the *Baltimore Sun* (Lorraine Mirabella, "95.5 Million Pounds of Raw Sugar," April 10, 2012, p. 1) and the state's 2012 exports hit an all-time high ("Maryland Exports Reach Record $11.8 Billion, Up 9%," February 27, 2013, p. 14). Elsewhere in the city, ships are in dry dock for refurbishing, commuters grumble over traffic congestion caused by road resurfacing and repairs to the infrastructure beneath, and the city's skyline is dotted with construction cranes for new building projects. These are the large employers and large projects; additionally, a small army of independent contractors and small jobbers stand ready to help—need a room addition, or electrical service upgraded, or a hot water tank replaced, Baltimore's Yellow Pages include hundreds of listings.

This sector of labor may not be as abundant or as lucrative as during the boom times of the 1950s and 1960s, but it is striking nonetheless to find nearly half of the sample's lower-SES white men working in the industrial and construction crafts. Equally striking is the racial disparity: the crafts employ just 15 percent of lower-SES African American men. Also, within that sector of employment is yet a second imbalance: whites earn roughly double that of African Americans, a long-standing disparity in Maryland (see Levenson and McDill 1966).

Occupational status rounds out coverage of socioeconomic standing. Averaging within the eleven occupational categories in table 6.5 shades extreme differences, but differences across occupational types are large nonetheless.[27] Across the sample, the standard deviation for the SEI scale is 12.4 points. Professionals average just below 60 points, and laborers, service workers, and machine operatives average around 24—a huge spread. Occupational status, it will be recalled, derives from census data on the earnings and educational levels of occupational incumbents nationally. Table 6.5 reveals that the broad distinctions among occupational types used to classify work approximate a status hierarchy, with professional employment at the top and lower level blue-collar work at the bottom.

Status Attainment as a Family Affair   We now have a sense of the status-conferring attributes that follow from the Youth Panel's schooling and employment at age twenty-eight, but status is not just a matter of individual accomplishment at school and in the workplace, it resides in the family also. To begin our exploration of that side of status attainment, we return to table 6.5, which also describes the status attributes of spouses and partners, as reported in the MAS. The Overall row averages across all partners. Spouses and partners have exactly the same average years of schooling as the sample, their average occupational status is within 2 SEI points, and their earnings are close, averaging just $1,000 higher.

Owing to a strong and increasing tendency for like to marry like (*assortative mating* is the technical term), spouses tend to be similar in many ways—for example, by ethnic background, religious affiliation, hobbies, and, our present focus, socioeconomic levels (Blossfeld 2009; Kalmijn 1998).[28] People often meet their life partners at school—high school sweethearts or biology lab partners from college—and with level of schooling the basis of the match, other similarities follow, for example, bachelor's degrees and above usually have higher-paying, higher-status jobs.

In the aggregate, the Youth Panel have gravitated to partners very much like themselves. This is reflected also in the interior elements of table 6.5. An important detail makes the alignment evident in these figures even more impressive, however: members of the panel are classified according to their most recent full-time occupation, whereas their partners fall into one or another of the eleven categories by virtue of ties to a member of the Youth Panel. That is to say, the data in table 6.5 signify personal accomplishment through jobs; and spouses and partners could be in different occupational categories.

The tendency for like to marry (or partner) like overrides such differences. The occupational status rankings of the sample and their partners' mostly move in parallel, and the exceptions are minor: professionals, managers, and higher-level technical workers tend, on average, to marry down; laborers and service workers tend to marry up.[29] In the middle range of occupational types, sample-partner status pairings are a few SEI points apart in both directions—the differences are trivial.

Alignment for earnings is an exception though, because it is much looser. For example, earnings differences across higher-status occupations are large among the sample but quite close among their partners. Across managers, professionals, and high-level technical occupations, the sample's median earnings range between $49,000 and $33,000, a difference of $16,000. The range for their partners is just $3,000. More generally, partners' median earnings range widely around the sample values, higher in the case of clerks, lower for laborers.

A hidden gender component is also at work here: among men, the median managerial earnings is $54,000, but their (women) partners' median is $35,000. Among women, the median managerial salary is $36,000 and the figure for their partners is $61,000. Men earn more than women in both instances, and though this is the most extreme disparity, it is not the only one. Among service workers, for example, the earnings differentials by gender and their partners are $11,800 and $5,900, respectively, both favoring men.

Partnering, Parenting, and Women's Economic Well-Being

The comparisons just reviewed suggest that personal and family socioeconomic well-being could differ, and that proves to be the case. We illustrate the point here through inspection of lower and higher-SES women's earnings, treating women without partners as families of one, in which case personal and family earnings are the same.[30] Most partner households include two earners, and differences in family formation across social lines have predictable implications for family earnings, and through earnings, for socioeconomic status level. A second consideration is whether the partners' earnings are high or low: partner up, and financial standing improves; partner down, and financial standing degrades.

The feminization of poverty directs attention to low-income women's financial struggles, but the feminization of poverty and the risk of childhood poverty go hand in hand: when these women experience hardship, so do their children. Table 6.6 compares the finances of lower-SES-origin women, African American and white, as a function of their partnering and parenthood statuses. With no partners, the children-no children entries are close and both low. Nearly 60 percent of lower-SES African Americans find themselves in this situation, and nearly 75 percent shoulder additional burdens associated with parenting alone. Lower-SES white women without partners are a bit better off financially, but the more consequential distinctions involve family life: just 19 percent of lower-SES whites are without partners and only 50 percent are parents.

A second earner in the household improves economic conditions markedly, though the white family premium is the larger: an increase of 125 percent over personal earnings versus 88 percent among African Americans. This is because African American spouses and partners earn less, on average. Still, these women, 45 percent of the African American total, are vastly better off financially than those without spouses or partners.

The experience of higher-SES women provides a revealing contrast. Those in unions and without children enjoy the highest standard of living, white family earnings averaging $94,000 and African American $70,000.[31] We said at the start of this book that comparisons across social lines can afford useful perspective on conditions of life among the urban disadvantaged, and the path these higher-SES women have followed does just that: having forgone parenthood to this point in their lives in favor of college and career, they have achieved an impressive standard of living.[32] This is the case nationally as well (see, for example, Hymowitz et al. 2013).

The feminine stereotype of urban poverty is epitomized by black single mothers. They indeed are represented in the Youth Panel, but make up less than 25 percent of the lower-SES African American total. The stereotype thus is exaggerated, as stereotypes are wont to be. Nevertheless, single parenting is prevalent among African Americans and these families face severe financial challenge, a circumstance hardly peculiar to the sample. In 2005 nationally, the median family income in black and white mother-only households was $22,004 and $28,543, respectively; in married couple households, $57,498 and $70,948 (Lindsey 2009). African Americans lag behind in both instances, signifying racial disadvantage,

Table 6.6   Women's Personal and Family Earnings

	Lower-SES White		Lower-SES Black		Higher-SES White		Higher-SES Black	
	Personal	Family	Personal	Family	Personal	Family	Personal	Family
No children, no partner (N)	26.0 (5)	26.0 (5)	30.0 (13)	30.0 (13)	40.0 (13)	40.0 (13)	28.5 (8)	28.5 (8)
Children, no partner (N)	30.0 (5)	30.0 (5)	20.0 (41)	20.0 (41)	20.5 (2)	20.5 (2)	25.5 (6)	25.5 (6)
No children, with partner (N)	25.0 (9)	48.0 (9)	24.0 (5)	54.0 (5)	37.5 (16)	94.0 (16)	40.0 (2)	70.0 (2)
Children, with partner (N)	21.0 (34)	52.0 (41)	24.5 (36)	41.5 (39)	25.0 (11)	62.0 (14)	33.5 (17)	63.0 (18)

Source: Authors' compilation.
Note: All earnings are medians in thousands of dollars, at age twenty-eight, for lower- and higher-SES women.

but they additionally suffer an enormous single-parent earnings short-fall. It is much the same in the sample, and though this holds across SES levels, the impact is hardly the same: 41.8 percent of lower-SES African American women (forty-one of ninety-five (or 41 of 95) were parenting without a partner versus just 8.3 percent of lower-SES white women (5 of 63); among their higher-SES counterparts, the respective figures are 13.6 percent and 4.4 percent (just two of forty-five).

Lawrence Bobo, James Kluegel, and Ryan Smith (1997, 23) observe that a "kernel of truth [is] needed to regularly breathe life into old stereotypes about putative black proclivities toward involvement in crime, violence, and welfare dependence." Their observation applies to these women also: the differences in family life that burden many African American women are quite real, and often they parallel those seen for their mothers in chapter 3.[33] Generational consistency typifies the experience of lower-SES white women too, but with vastly different implications: most of them also are parents, but mainly parents with partners.

Socioeconomic Standing in Adulthood: The Youth Panel Comes of Age

Workplace successes, along with levels of attained schooling, define socioeconomic destinations, but what if one or two of what we are calling the three pillars is missing? Our goal is to gauge socioeconomic standing in mature adulthood (age twenty-eight), and success in the world of work is integral to that. More than one in ten of the sample, however, had no full-time employment of at least three months' duration during the two years preceding the MAS. That gap means there is no qualifying occupational status or earnings from work. For them, we rely on schooling alone to determine socioeconomic standing.[34] The same considerations apply to socioeconomic standing at the family level, which requires information on the spouses and partners.

A spouse or partner in the picture raises another issue: does socioeconomic standing reside in the person or in the family? It seems odd, but one rarely sees the question taken up in mobility research. For the parents, SES is measured at the family level, combining mothers' and fathers' levels of schooling and job status with meal subsidy school record data to identify low-income families. The sample, though, is a panel of individuals, not families. Moreover, at age twenty-eight, more than 40 percent—including more than 50 percent of African Americans—were neither married nor cohabitating (see table 6.7). In socioeconomic space, they are "families of one" and implications for their material well-being are predictable. As Julia Isaacs (2008, 3) notes, "having two earners is critical to the economic success of many of today's families."

Table 6.7 Employment History and Marital-Partnership Status

Work History	Employment History Most Recent in Last Two Years						Marital-Partnership Status Age Twenty-Eight					
	Overall	White Men	Black Men	White Women	Black Women	Family Status	Overall	White Men	Black Men	White Women	Black Women	
No work	10.2	6.1	13.0	12.2	9.1	Single	42.7	37.9	52.5	25.2	51.6	
Part time only	7.3	7.6	3.1	8.1	10.2	Partner	21.8	16.7	23.8	24.5	21.7	
Full time only	66.4	73.5	72.2	60.8	60.8	Married	35.5	45.5	23.8	50.3	26.6	
Full time and part time	16.1	12.9	11.7	18.9	19.9	-	-	-	-	-	-	
(N)	(628)	(132)	(162)	(148)	(186)	(N)	(623)	(132)	(160)	(147)	(184)	

Source: Authors' compilation.
Note: Percentages except subsample sizes in parentheses.

Even though most stratification research keys on personal circumstances, status is transmitted family to family also. In this volume, we gauge the study participants' SES standing as young adults both ways. Today more than half of first marriages are preceded by cohabitation and more than half of African Americans remain never married through their early thirties (Settersten and Ray 2010, 31). Mindful of these realities, we use both spouse and partner attributes to determine family socioeconomic standing. Transitory unions of less than three months are excluded.

The groundwork now has been laid for locating the sample and their families in socioeconomic space. As for their birth families, we developed two measures of their standing at age twenty-eight: a continuous interval status ranking and, for descriptive purposes, a categorical classification.[35] The latter is used in table 6.8, which reports level of schooling completed, occupational status, and annual earnings for each of the three SES destinations (lower, middle, and higher) and by gender and race (overall and for those of lower-SES destinations).[36]

The overall averages in the last row have been reported already, organized in the previous section around primary occupations: years of schooling average just under thirteen, SEI job status 33 (clerks, sales, account collectors, and the like), and median earnings, here $28,700, just about at the average for young workers in Baltimore at the time.[37] The right panel again shows their partners a close match on all three measures. Family earnings, though, is new. At $39,800, it is well above the sample's solo earnings, but also well below the sum of the panel members' and their partners' separate earnings. That is because there are many families of one, for whom family and personal earnings are the same. In partnership households, the median combined earnings is $57,000, which would be still higher if calculated only for families with two earners.

The three status groupings signify relative standing, which the averages in table 6.8 help anchor concretely. Knowing that the 28 percent classified as lower SES average 10.9 years of schooling, earn below $16,000, and have an occupational status of 23 establishes what it means to be lower SES or, equivalently, urban disadvantaged.[38] At the other extreme, for the 22 percent of the panel classified as higher SES, years of schooling is just a shade below bachelor's (15.3), they earn almost three times the lower-SES average, and their SEI score of 49.7 locates them in comfortably middle-class and higher occupations: senior account manager, accountant, senior loan officer, social worker, special education teacher, reference librarian, mortgage broker, and police officer or detective.

Table 6.8   SES Destinations: Lower, Middle, and Higher, by Race-Gender

Race-Gender	BSSYP Panel Member			BSSYP Spouse-Partner			Family
	Years Education	Occupational Status (SEI)	Median Earnings ($1,000s)	Years Education	Occupational Status (SEI)	Median Earnings ($1,000s)	Median Earnings ($1,000s)
White men (N)	12.5 (132)	34.3 (123)	34.2 (124)	13.1 (81)	35.3 (51)	26.0 (61)	42.0 (125)
Black men (N)	12.7 (162)	30.7 (139)	26.8 (139)	13.0 (76)	34.2 (65)	29.0 (57)	34.8 (144)
White women (N)	13.2 (148)	34.6 (129)	27.8 (129)	13.1 (109)	35.4 (92)	37.7 (97)	48.0 (143)
Black women (N)	13.0 (186)	32.8 (164)	24.9 (167)	12.7 (89)	33.4 (69)	31.5 (73)	31.2 (173)
Destination SES							
Lower SES (N)	10.9 (178)	23.0 (142)	15.9 (144)	11.9 (101)	28.4 (73)	25.5 (73)	23.7 (161)
White men (N)	10.2 (30)	23.7 (27)	23.5 (27)	11.6 (19)	27.2 (8)	18.0 (11)	28.8 (28)
Black men (N)	11.0 (45)	21.5 (37)	15.5 (36)	12.3 (19)	27.8 (17)	17.3 (11)	17.6 (40)
White women (N)	11.2 (51)	23.8 (38)	17.7 (39)	11.8 (40)	28.5 (32)	33.3 (34)	39.0 (47)
Black women (N)	11.0 (52)	23.2 (40)	14.9 (42)	11.9 (23)	29.2 (16)	27.0 (17)	19.5 (46)
Middle SES (N)	12.9 (312)	30.2 (280)	29.4 (280)	12.4 (162)	36.7 (126)	31.7 (143)	38.9 (263)
Higher SES (N)	15.3 (138)	49.7 (133)	44.4 (135)	15.4 (96)	46.4 (85)	39.8 (72)	65.0 (139)
Overall (N)	12.9 (628)	33.0 (555)	28.7 (559)	13.0 (355)	34.6 (277)	31.6 (288)	39.8 (585)

Source: Authors' compilation.
Note: Standing at age twenty-eight.

By construction, half the sample falls into the middle-SES category, and by design its profile is midway between the extremes. Their schooling average is 12.9 years, exactly as intended. Their earnings center at the midpoint of the distribution. Last, with an SEI average of 30.2, they work as warehouse managers, administrative assistants, debt collectors, bookkeepers, secretaries, plumbers, forklift mechanics, and research assistants. These distinctions across status levels are large and meaningful, just as we saw in chapter 3 for the parents.[39]

Also as seen previously, the sample's personal standing aligns so well with that of their partners' as to be practically interchangeable. Still, a second earner in the family matters for the economic profile. Those ranked higher SES realize the largest increase in absolute dollars, with family earnings at $65,000, 46 percent above their personal average of $44,400; for SES destinations at the middle level, the increase is 32 percent; and for those at the lower level, it is 49 percent.

Whether these households with upwardly adjusted earnings are correspondingly better off is a separate matter. A spouse or partner in the picture means extra dollars to cover expenses for at least two adults and often children. The lowest median family earnings in the sample is $14,800 (not shown in the tables) for lower-SES single mothers, 60 percent of whom are poor by 2005 standards.[40] This puts them almost $9,000 below the lower-SES family median of $23,700.

For education and job status, differences across lines of race and gender are not large. Although white men rank lowest on education and white women highest on job status, the larger disparities in table 6.8 involve earnings. The personal earnings gap across the extremes, white men against African American women, is almost $10,000, but whether this gap involves a career woman on her own or a single mother with two children makes a big difference. So does having two earners in the family. The median earnings of African American women parenting alone (37 percent of African American women) is $20,700, for white women parenting with a spouse-partner (53.1 percent of whites) is more than double, $57,000 (not shown in tables).

Importantly, most of what appears to be a race difference in family earnings traces to family type: for the 9.5 percent of white women parenting alone, household earnings average $28,300; for the 41 percent of African American women with partners and children, the average is $52,000. The family type difference among both whites ($28,500) and blacks ($31,300) is uncomfortably large, but poses a greater challenge for African American women because so many more of them are parenting alone (not shown in the tables).

Comparisons by gender and race among those of lower SES are much the same as overall, although at appreciably lower levels of schooling, job status, and earnings. Lower-SES white men have the lowest school-ing average and comfortably the highest earnings; lower-SES white women have relatively low personal earnings, but they are the ben-eficiaries of high spousal earnings and their family earnings is high-est of the four lower-SES race-sex groups. The contrast against African American women's earnings stands out especially, as their personal earnings ($14,900) and family earnings ($19,500) are both low.

The family earnings disparity comparing black and white women of lower SES traces to two considerations, one obvious and one hinted at table 6.7. First the obvious: at $33,300 versus $27,000, white spousal-partner earnings are considerably higher. The second consideration has come up already, and here we see one of its tangible implications. Lower-SES African American women are much more likely to be with-out a spouse or partner at age twenty-eight: of the fifty-two lower-SES African American women in table 6.7, just seventeen (33 percent) are paired with spouse-partner earnings data; by contrast, thirty-four of fifty-one (65 percent) of lower-SES white women are in unions.[41]

The distinction between status attained personally and status defined around family is not often addressed in mobility research, but these comparisons make clear that family counts, and can count for a great deal. Year 2000 Census data reveal a like pattern, and for the same rea-son (Attewell et al. 2004, 15). For example, among high school graduates nationally, black and white women's personal earnings were practically identical at around $13,000, whereas white family earnings averaged almost $20,000 above African American ($58,000 versus $30,000). Why is this? Fewer African American women than white were married or in partnerships (40 percent versus 75 percent), which means that fewer of them realize the benefits of a second earner in the household.

Looking Ahead

The Long Shadow is a study of intergenerational mobility centered on the life prospects of the urban disadvantaged. Chapters 2, 3, and 4 sketched family circumstances growing up, the origins side of intergenerational mobility. This chapter reviews the destinations side. Many of the sample rank low on conventional measures of socioeconomic standing, but others completed college and moved into solidly middle-class and professional occupations with high earnings. Those in family unions benefit tangibly from a second earner in the household. Some of these differences in adult well-being involve race and gender; differences are also large along lines of family socioeconomic background. The next step is to explore how it is that these ties across generations are maintained.

We begin in the next chapter by examining patterns of socioeconomic mobility and immobility in the sample, but we have already learned that not many of Baltimore's lower-SES youth advance in life on the strength of strong educational credentials. A mere handful finished college, yet not all those counted among the urban disadvantaged growing up were similarly disadvantaged as young adults. Large differences between personal and family earnings among the urban disadvantaged hint at a mobility dynamic outside schooling, one centered on the non-college workforce. This blue-collar attainment regime largely has gone unremarked in the literature, we think because working-class whites are not often encountered in studies of the urban disadvantaged. That oversight is taken up in chapter 8.

Chapter 7

Origins to Destinations Across Generations

S O, HOW far from the tree does the apple fall? In stratification terms, the question becomes how much social mobility there is across generations. In popular thought, the United States stands apart as the land of opportunity where, through hard work and perhaps a bit of good fortune, anyone can rise to the top. As Joseph Stiglitz points out in the *New York Times Opinionator* blog, however, the truth is rather different ("Equal Opportunity, Our National Myth," February 16, 2013). National comparisons of intergenerational mobility centered on occupation, income, and wealth find that socioeconomic well-being in adulthood depends more on family circumstances in the United States than in many other mature economies (see, for example, Isaacs 2008), for example, "42 percent of Americans born to parents at the bottom rung of the income ladder . . . remain at the bottom as adults," nearly twice that of many European and Asian countries (Economic Mobility Project 2009, 2).

Where one lives also matters—"place" counts. In their Equality of Opportunity Project, Raj Chetty and his colleagues (www.equality-of-opportunity.org 2013) calculate parent-to-child income mobility for the hundred largest U.S. cities, concluding that "some areas [of the country] have rates of upward mobility comparable to the most mobile countries in the world, while others have lower rates of mobility than any developing country for which data are currently available." The latter puts us in poor company indeed. Their analyses compare the incomes of children born in 1980 and 1981 (close to the Youth Panel generation) at roughly age thirty against their parents' household incomes between 1996 and 2000 (their children's teenage years), an origins to destinations exercise much like the present volume. One of their measures, referred to as *absolute income mobility*, locates in the national income distribution children whose parents were in the 25th income percentile (approximately $30,000). Higher scores indicate better mobility prospects, and Baltimore, with a value of 39.2, ranks seventy-third of a hundred cities. For perspective, Salt Lake City (Utah) and Scranton (Pennsylvania) register the highest mobility chances (46.4 and 46.3), and Memphis (Tennessee) and Fayetteville (North Carolina) the lowest (34.4 and 35.2). Movement from low origins to high destinations is reflected in the percentage of children reaching the top 20 percent of the income distribution whose parents were in the bottom 20 percent. Baltimore, at 6.5, is roughly midpoint, the range nationally being 12.4 (Bakersfield, California) to 2.6 (Memphis, Tennessee).

The characteristics of place that distinguish cities with more favorable mobility prospects from those with less favorable prospects (potential explanatory factors in the authors' terms) include:

the size of the middle-class population (larger is better);

the extent of residential segregation by income (less is better);

school quality K–12—achievement test scores (higher is better), spending per pupil (higher is better), and the dropout rate (lower is better); and

the number of children raised by single parents (fewer is better).

Against such a risk factor profile, places like Baltimore do not fare well. These data are uncommon, and even if they are limited, to know such large regional differences exist in the opportunity for upward mobility is informative.[1]

Status Mobility and Immobility Across Generations

From a stratification perspective, we want to understand both immobility and mobility. For immobility, the issue is how status is inherited across generations. Not inheritance in the sense of offices or titles passing directly from parent to offspring, because that kind of inheritance is largely a thing of the past. Rather, it is how privilege in one generation passes through to the next, such that, on average, children born into higher-SES families manage to complete higher levels of schooling, get higher status jobs, and earn more than children from disadvantaged families. The mobility issue asks why some children advance and some fall back.

Two approaches are used to inform these questions. The first, mobility table analysis, interrogates the cross-classification of parents' status origins and children's status destinations; the second interrogates the correlation between parents' status levels and their children's attained status as adults by way of multivariate statistical analyses. The time frame of both is generational—parent to offspring. We begin with the tradition of mobility table analysis.

Origins to Destinations

Mobility tables locate persons in socioeconomic space using categorical placements. The earliest studies in this tradition examined occupational inheritance from father to son, distinguishing between white- and blue-collar occupations, sometimes adding farm origins as a third category (see, for example, Lipset and Bendix 1959). White-collar sons of blue-collar fathers are seen as upwardly mobile and blue-collar sons of white-collar fathers as downwardly mobile. Children in the same type of work as their fathers are said to be immobile, signifying occupational inheritance. The question typically is which pattern predominates. If it is movement up and down, the stratification system is said to be relatively open; if immobility predominates, the system is relatively rigid.

Our application of this approach classifies the birth families and the sample themselves as lower SES, middle SES, and higher SES. The two mobility cross-tabulations reported in table 7.1 are derived by arraying children's status levels against those of their parents. In the left panel, SES destinations are determined by personal levels of education, occupational status, and earnings; in the right panel, SES destinations are determined at the family level, with spouse and partners status attributes included (see chapter 6 and appendix B). The issue is how the sample's socioeconomic standing as young adults aligns with that of their birth families.

In table 7.1, status immobility is clear from examining patterns along the main diagonal. For personal status (left panel), almost half (296 = 130+88+78) of the sample find themselves at the same status as adults as they had been as children.[2] From the table marginals, however, only 200.4 (88.8+77.0+34.6) would be expected.[3] Additionally, opportunities for upward mobility are limited, especially for those of lower-SES origins. Movement up one level is about at expectation: lower to middle: 154 observed against 156.0 expected; middle to higher: 30 against 34.2 expected. Lower-SES background youth, however, are badly underrepresented at higher-SES destinations: 30 observed versus 69.2 expected.

The immobility and mobility extremes are particularly telling. Lower-SES background youth remain lower SES at 1.5 times expectation ($130/88.8 = 1.46$) and are represented among those of higher SES at less than 0.5 expectation ($30/69.2 = 0.43$). That is the legacy of urban disadvantage. The legacy of urban advantage is evident as well: higher-SES origin youth remain higher SES at more than twice expectation ($78/34.6 = 2.25$) and rarely drop to lower SES—just ten in all, at 0.23 expectation ($10/44.4$).

Table 7.1 Intergenerational Mobility

Origin Status Level		Destination Personal Status Level				Destination Family Status Level			
		Lower	Middle	Higher	(N)	Lower	Middle	Higher	(N)
Lower SES	observed count	130	154	30	(314)	141	140	33	(314)
	expected count	88.8	156.0	69.2		100.3	141.5	72.2	
Middle SES	observed count	37	88	30	(155)	40	81	34	(155)
	expected count	43.8	77.0	34.2		49.5	69.8	35.7	
Higher SES	observed count	10	69	78	(157)	19	61	77	(157)
	expected count	44.4	78.0	34.6		50.2	70.7	36.1	
(N)		(177)	(311)	(138)	(626)	(200)	(282)	(144)	(626)

Source: Authors' compilation.

As mentioned, the Economic Mobility Project (2009, 2) reports that 42 percent of children born into families at the bottom rung of the income ladder remain there as adults, a much higher percentage than in other countries. In the experience of the Youth Panel, the figure for lower-to-lower status inheritance is almost identical at 41.4 percent (130/314); higher-to-higher, however, exceeds even that: 49.7 percent (78/157). For economists, the persistence of privilege and disadvantage at the extremes of immobility reflects "stickiness" (Isaacs 2008); for us, it is a manifestation of the long shadow of family influence.

For family status, we see much the same. That almost half do not change status is well above expectation (299 versus 206.2 expected), and mobility across the extremes is rare. Only thirty-three of the sample move all the way up from lower to higher, less than half the 72.2 expected, and falling from higher to lower is rarer still, at 19 against an expectation of 50.2.

Throughout the sample, the mobility experience of blacks and whites, men and women are not dramatically different, but some details merit note. In comparisons not shown, women less often than men preserve high standing through their attainments at school and on the job. Spousal and partner families also evidence more high-end status maintenance and more mobility from lower and middle social origins to higher destinations. Two-earner income effects are embedded in the family socioeconomic composites, and so African American women, who are less often married or in partnerships, fare the worst of any group. In broad terms, this pattern follows national trends: women experience less upward mobility and more downward mobility than men do (see, for example, Mazumder 2008).

These mobility flows bring to light the extent of family privilege and family disadvantage, as well as of movement up and down the status order across generations, but to understand how family privilege and family disadvantage are maintained parent-to-child requires a different approach.

There are nine cells each in table 7.1. To pose additional questions just about how mobility differs by race and gender (two categories each) overlaid on SES, the tables expand to thirty-six cells, beyond what is practical with a sample of this size. As an alternative, multivariate modeling locates individuals along finely graded continua of socioeconomic standing. With status recast this way as a continuous metric, the correlations between SES origins and SES destinations are midrange; 0.49 at the personal level; 0.51 at the family level, allowing for both alignment (inheritance) and misalignment (mobility).[4] What remains is to investigate the source of these correlations.

The Blau-Duncan Basic Model
and Its Extensions

The status attainment approach to modeling intergenerational mobility took a giant step when Peter Blau's and Otis Duncan's *The American Occupational Structure* (1967) identified school performance as the critical link transmitting socioeconomic advantage and disadvantage across generations. Higher-SES children fare better in the world of adult work in large measure because they remain in school longer than their lower-SES counterparts, acquiring academic credentials that lead to higher status and more lucrative jobs.

Their foundational idea was to graft schooling onto a multivariate mode of analysis, reorienting mobility research away from global distinctions across occupational types (such as white-collar, blue-collar, farm). It was a good start, but preliminary. Because success in school is key, we naturally want to know why it is that school success varies according to children's family background. Research to inform the question has proceeded along two lines. The first examines the social psychological and interpersonal dynamics of schooling. How do parents, teachers, and peers influence children's goals for the future (educational and occupational aspirations), and how do students respond to their school performance as reflected in their test scores and report card grades (Sewell, Haller, and Ohlendorf 1970; Sewell, Haller, and Portes 1969; Sewell and Hauser 1980)?

The second line of research examines structural arrangements in schools that favor children of privilege over other children. Educational tracking is the main facet of school organization we address in this book. At the high school level, it takes the form of different curricular concentrations (college prep versus general and vocational), in the middle grades, of course-level distinctions (for example, honors versus regular math), and in the elementary grades, of grade retention or promotion and assignment to special education (see Alexander and Entwisle 1996; Entwisle, Alexander, and Olson 1997).

Whether children are placed high or low in the track level moves them along different educational paths, some toward higher and more economically valuable credentials (college degrees and certificates), others toward lower and less economically valuable ones (high school diploma or GED), or none at all (high school dropouts). For instance, students in a college preparatory program in high school are more likely to finish high school and attend college than youth in vocational or general tracks are. Educational tracking also tends to separate children along SES and ethnicity lines, and so is one of the ways that school organization contributes to educational stratification and an achievement gap across social lines (Mickelson 2005; Tyson 2011).

On the Passage of Time: Status Attainment as Development

Status attainment is a developmental process that unfolds over time. The resources for schooling that support children's development could be from first grade, middle school, or high school, and the same resource can be of more or less importance at different levels of schooling. For example, parent support could be most important in the early grades, when children's academic self-image is just beginning to coalesce, but over time, as children become more self-directive, the immediate influence of parent support might wane.

Schooling also has a temporal dimension. For many children, track placements persist across levels of schooling, with favorable placements at one level forecasting favorable placements at the next (Entwisle, Alexander, and Olson 2006, 2010a; Kerckhoff 1993). Persistence in structural placements across levels of schooling brings into focus the institutional underpinning to educational stratification, and that a long time frame is needed to capture both family and school developmental processes in their entirety.

A Life-Course Frame for Status Attainment

We are not the first to advocate for a developmental approach to the process of schooling. Working with British data, Alan Kerckhoff's *Diverging Pathways* (1993) traces how family privilege and family disadvantage are transmitted by educational tracking at each stage of schooling.[5] As children progress through school, family background influences school placements at the outset as well as later, first through infant school placements (roughly ages four to seven), then junior school placements (roughly our middle school grades), and then secondary school placements (roughly our high school).

The elaborate British credentialing system that governs the school to work transition has no exact counterpart in the United States, but does have parallels (Kerckhoff and Glennie 1999). For example, in the United States in 2011 among full-time workers age twenty-five and older, high school dropouts earned $471 weekly (on average), high school graduates $652, associate's degree holders $758, bachelor's graduates $1,066, those with a master's degree $1,300, and those with professional and doctoral degrees, $1,735 and $1,624 respectively. Unemployment rates track similarly, but reversed: 12.4 percent among high school dropouts in 2011, 8.3 percent among terminal high school graduates, 6.2 percent for those with associate's degrees, 4.5 percent for those with bachelor's degrees, and 3.5 percent or less among those with advanced degrees

(Bureau of Labor Statistics 2012). In the United States, as in Britain, educational credentials help open doors.

It is key that Kerckhoff traces children's educational trajectories back to their earliest schooling. At the outset, he observes that some children are put on a path leading to higher level, more valued occupational qualifications and other children are put on a path to lower level, less valued qualifications. Family status at the point children begin their school careers helps determine both the paths children take and their progress along the way. Advantages and disadvantages in this way cumulate as children advance in their schooling. For Kerckhoff, the imagery is diverging pathways; for us, it is the long shadow of family background.

Urban Disadvantage in Life-Course Perspective: A Conceptual Account

Figure 7.1 identifies the influences we examine as potentially transmitting family advantage and disadvantage from parent to child. The life-course framing follows progress through school and after: childhood, adolescence, early adulthood, and mature adulthood. Each stage involves a transition from one level of development to the next. In the beginning, it is from home child to school child; twenty plus years later, it is the transition to adulthood, captured through the milestone markers introduced in chapter 5. The time order potentially identifies causal priorities in development—for example, elementary school precedes middle school, so influences issuing from elementary school resources and experiences can affect middle school outcomes, but not the reverse.

The principle that doing well at school is one key to intergenerational mobility hardly needs testing, but when the process begins and the how of it are not as well established, especially for youth who grow up in disadvantaged urban circumstances. When risk factors for adverse status outcomes and protective factors for favorable outcomes are patterned across social lines, they promote status inheritance, yet the very same resources also can support mobility up and down the status hierarchy.

In trying to root out risks and resources, studies of the role of schooling in social mobility typically begin with the high school or middle school years, focused on dropout, grade failure, or the high school to college transition, but what happens in the upper grades adds onto an existing foundation, shaped by conditions at home before children begin school and at school during the early years. Neglecting that foundation misses much of consequence in setting children on different life paths.

Figure 7.1   Origins to Destinations in Life-Course Perspective

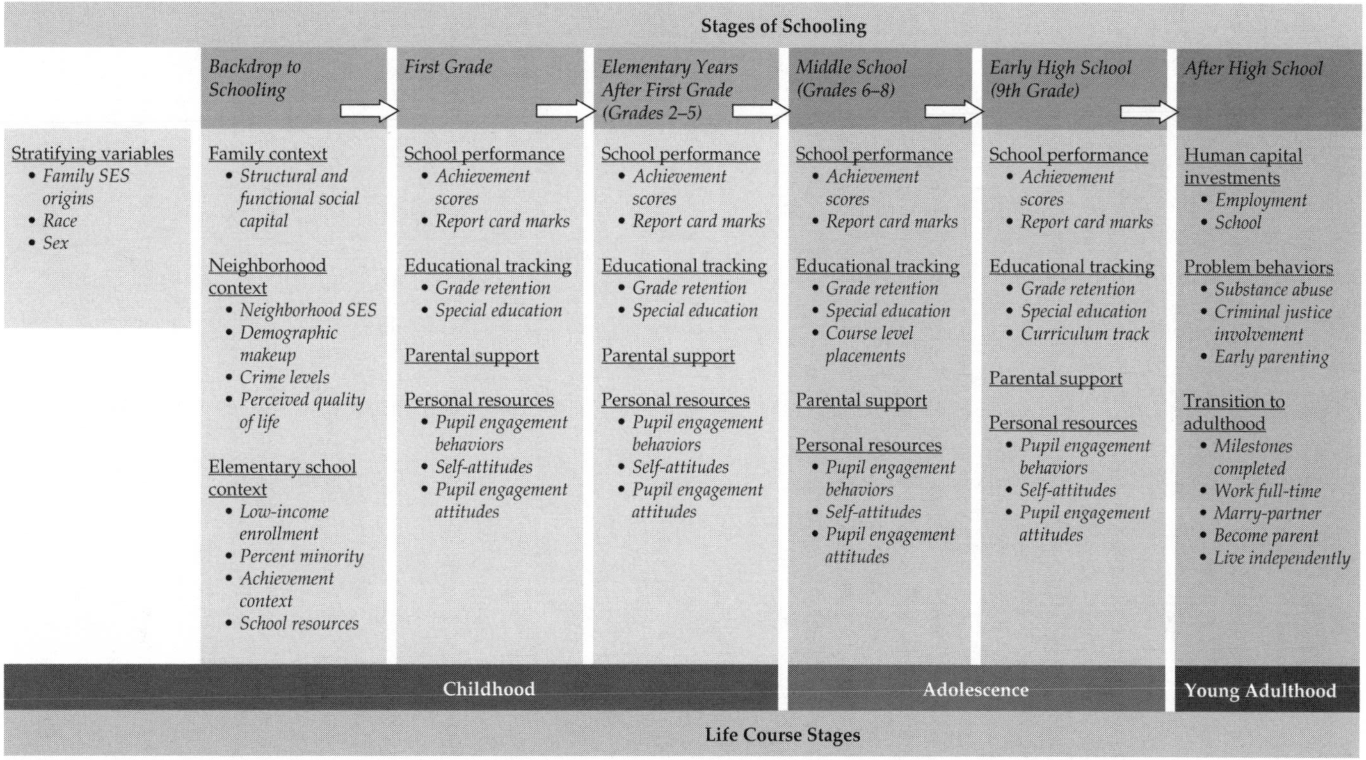

Stratifying variables
- *Family SES origins*
- *Race*
- *Sex*

Stages of Schooling

Backdrop to Schooling

Family context
- *Structural and functional social capital*

Neighborhood context
- *Neighborhood SES*
- *Demographic makeup*
- *Crime levels*
- *Perceived quality of life*

Elementary school context
- *Low-income enrollment*
- *Percent minority*
- *Achievement context*
- *School resources*

First Grade

School performance
- *Achievement scores*
- *Report card marks*

Educational tracking
- *Grade retention*
- *Special education*

Parental support

Personal resources
- *Pupil engagement behaviors*
- *Self-attitudes*
- *Pupil engagement attitudes*

Elementary Years After First Grade (Grades 2–5)

School performance
- *Achievement scores*
- *Report card marks*

Educational tracking
- *Grade retention*
- *Special education*

Parental support

Personal resources
- *Pupil engagement behaviors*
- *Self-attitudes*
- *Pupil engagement attitudes*

Middle School (Grades 6–8)

School performance
- *Achievement scores*
- *Report card marks*

Educational tracking
- *Grade retention*
- *Special education*
- *Course level placements*

Parental support

Personal resources
- *Pupil engagement behaviors*
- *Self-attitudes*
- *Pupil engagement attitudes*

Early High School (9th Grade)

School performance
- *Achievement scores*
- *Report card marks*

Educational tracking
- *Grade retention*
- *Special education*
- *Curriculum track*

Parental support

Personal resources
- *Pupil engagement behaviors*
- *Self-attitudes*
- *Pupil engagement attitudes*

After High School

Human capital investments
- *Employment*
- *School*

Problem behaviors
- *Substance abuse*
- *Criminal justice involvement*
- *Early parenting*

Transition to adulthood
- *Milestones completed*
- *Work full-time*
- *Marry-partner*
- *Become parent*
- *Live independently*

Life Course Stages

Childhood | Adolescence | Young Adulthood

Source: Authors' compilation.

The Backdrop to Schooling:
Family as First Educator

For understanding how family resources set children on life-long achieve-ment trajectories through school, we adapt James Coleman's and Thomas Hoffer's (1987) distinction between family-based structural and func-tional social capital. Structural social capital involves parents' pres-ence in children's lives, such as whether the father resides in the home. Functional social capital involves how parents help their children do well in school through the actions they take and the psychological support they provide.[6]

Examples of family structure include, for Coleman and Hoffer, fami-lies in which the mother is employed outside the home and single-parent households, both of which tend to reduce parental presence day-to-day and so impede effective parenting.[7] Our measure of structural capital includes more: whether the mother was a teenager at the birth of her first child, whether the first grade household included two parents, whether the mother was parenting alone at the time (with no other adults pres-ent), and whether the mother worked outside the home during the child's first grade year, all from first grade parent interviews. Each yes is coded 1 to denote a structural risk; otherwise 0. Our measure sums the four, and the maximum score is 4. Higher-SES households average 1.6 structural risks, lower-SES white households 1.4, and, lower-SES black households 2.1.

Functional social capital involves parent-child relationships. Examples include parents' monitoring of homework, providing books and com-puters, taking children to museums and science centers, and holding high expectations for children's success. This concept is not far different from Karl White's (1982, 470) "home atmosphere" construct, grounded in the family's cultural and intellectual activities, including parents' attitudes toward education and the goals they hold for their children, Annette Lareau's (2003) "concerted cultivation" parenting style, said to be characteristic of middle-class families (think soccer mom), and Frank Furstenberg and colleagues' (1999) "promotive strategies" used by low-income parents to insulate their children from the drag of poverty. When these kinds of parents' attitudes and actions differ across social lines, as is often the case, they are vehicles for the transmission of advantage and disadvantage through schooling.

There are many layers to family-based functional capital. For one, upper-income parents invest more in learning resources, and as income inequality has increased nationally, so has this disparity—the invest-ment difference comparing families at the top and bottom income quin-tiles has increased from 4.2 times in 1972–1973 to 6.7 times in 2005–2006

($8,872 versus $1,315) (Duncan and Murnane 2011, 11). Moreover, the difference is largest for enrichment activities, such as music lessons, travel, and summer camp (Kaushal, Magnuson, and Waldfogel 2011).

The investments that matter for children's development are not all counted in dollars though. From birth through age six, compared with children in higher-income families, low-income children spend approximately one and a half hours less time per week on literacy activities and cumulatively about 1,300 fewer hours out and about in what Meredith Phillips calls novel places, meaning not at home, school, or day care: "everyday family experiences of young children from different socioeconomic and racial backgrounds differ in ways that probably contribute to socioeconomic and racial disparities in academic success" (2011, 223). Differences are also huge across social lines in language exposure over the preschool years. Middle-class parents are more verbal generally, their vocabulary is richer and more expressive, and they are more supportive and less controlling in conversation with their children (see Hart and Risley 1995).

We measure weak functional social capital as a risk factor by summing five items: whether the parent expects an unsatisfactory or satisfactory mark in reading and math on the child's first report card in first grade (coded 1 as a risk factor, good and excellent high-mark expectations coded 0), whether the parent does not expect the child to attain any college (coded 1, versus 0 for an expectation of some college or higher), whether the child went to the library during the summer between first and second grade (no coded 1, yes 0), whether the family experienced a level of social stress during the first grade year above the panel-wide average (1 if above average), and whether the mother scored at risk on a six-item inventory of depressive mood (1 if at risk).[8] The last two are not behavioral like the others, but are relevant because high levels of stress and maternal depression impair effective parenting behavior (see, for example, McLoyd 1990).

Our coverage of stressful life events (Dohrenwend 2006), a component of the functional social capital composite, includes a family move, divorce, death, an adult entering the household, and an adult leaving the household, all coded 1 if the event occurred and 0 if not, asked of parents in fourth grade but referenced back to the first grade year. Higher-SES families have the lowest average (1.2), lower-SES whites are next (1.7), and lower-SES blacks the highest (2.3). As an example, 56 percent of lower-SES black families reported a death in the family during the child's first grade year compared with just 32 percent of lower-SES white families.

Our intent is to capture differences across social lines in parental resources relevant to the sample's schooling and socioeconomic attainment. For disadvantaged children, family stress levels tend to be higher and stressful events more numerous. Consider Anna's history. A white lower-SES woman, by age nineteen she had seen the death of at least six relatives and the birth of several out-of-wedlock children to her sisters; she herself had attempted suicide and suffered drug and alcohol abuse. Or consider Gail's and Chip's situations, as described in their words.

Gail, also white and lower SES growing up:

> Well, . . . um . . . back in eighty-three . . . eighty-three I think it was [her second grade year], my mom's . . . um . . . father died and . . . she really went . . . kind of lost it. Like she started drinkin' and then she went to drugs and so forth. . . . Um . . . probably cocaine. [And her father] . . . Well, he. . . . didn't really worry about it 'cause he was out runnin' around on her.

And this from Chip, an African American whose drug-dealing brother was gunned down in his sleep by thugs who invaded their house:

> It was a month or two months . . . that I would try to go [to school], but I would leave cause I . . . if I felt like I was . . . I had to cry, I would leave. I wouldn't cry in front of nobody. . . . And that's a hurtin' feelin' when you lose somebody that close.

Although the checklist stocktaking we use identifies meaningful differences across social lines, as illustrated by these statements, it misses the intensity of the stresses children experience in their family lives. To get at that requires a more nuanced approach, one beyond the reach of survey data.

The functional social capital risk scale is the sum of these stress tallies plus the other four measures mentioned, with negative family attributes scored high. Across social lines, the averages are lowest in higher-SES households (1.1), highest in lower-SES white households (2.9), and intermediate in lower-SES African American households (2.1). Among the Youth Panel, then, lower-SES white families embody somewhat higher levels of structural social capital but lower levels of functional social capital.[9]

The Institutional Backdrop: First Grade Neighborhood and School

Neighborhood and school are the institutional contexts beyond the family most relevant to young children's development. Typically differences across social lines in children's experience of them are large. High levels of poverty and unemployment are characteristic of lower-SES neighborhoods. Many also are plagued by violent crime, more so in poor black than in poor white communities (chapter 4). Neighborhood

distress is relevant in that it is associated with depressed school performance (see Leventhal and Brooks-Gunn 1998).

Achievement levels are low in the schools attended by lower-SES
children. Academic press typically is weak under such circumstances,
which means that many disadvantaged urban youth find themselves
enveloped in a triangle of disadvantage—at home, in their neighborhoods, and at school. Whether neighborhood and school contexts early
in life have consequences for adult socioeconomic prospects is evaluated in table 7.2.

For neighborhood context, we examined socioeconomic level, percentage female-headed households, crime levels (violent and property), and residents' perceptions of neighborhood quality. For school
context, we examined percentage low-income enrollment, percentage
African American enrollment, the school's academic profile, and tangible
resources (such as per pupil expenditures and average class size). This
was our starter set. Only those that proved consequential in preliminary
analyses are reported in table 7.2.

Along the Road: Schooling in
Life-Course Perspective

Some of the resources and experiences relevant to children's development are attitudes about self and school. As children become more self-
reflective, these resources would be expected to increase in importance.
Other resources located within the family also weigh on children's development. In figure 7.1, they are represented by parents' psychological support for their children's schooling, which preliminary analyses identified
to be the key component of functional social capital as measured here.

We also include measures of school performance (achievement scores
and report card marks), the experience of educational tracking (which
takes on different form at different levels of schooling), and children's
academic engagement (for example, educational goals and classroom
deportment), all assessed independently and in rough parallel at the
elementary, middle, and high school levels (see appendix B for detail).
This allows us to pose questions about potential critical periods in the
schooling process: Do the elementary years stand out as distinctively
important? Do resource advantages and disadvantages cumulate across
time in relation to family background?

Moving On: Development After High School

The transition out of high school into young adulthood is the stage of
life when the differentiation of life paths comes into clearest view, but
research in the status attainment tradition has little to say about these

Table 7.2   Origins to Destinations: Individual Socioeconomic Status (Standardized Regression Coefficients)

	Stage A	Stage B		Stage C				Stage D
	1	2	3	4	5	6	7	8
SES origins	.51**	.40**	.33**	.29**	.27**	.22**	.18**	.07
African American women[a]	-.08	-.09	-.05	-.07	-.08	-.10	-.11*	-.16**
African American men[a]	-.06	-.07	-.03	-.02	-.02	-.01	-.01	-.00
White women[a]	-.10	-.10	-.10	-.12*	-.13**	-.16**	-.15**	-.15**
Family functional social capital		-.22**	-.20**	-.12**	-.12**	-.11*	-.10*	-.08*
Neighborhood and school context			-.14*	-.12*	-.12*	-.12*	-.12*	-.06
First grade resources				.22**	.14*	.11	.12*	.11*
Grade 2 through 5 resources					.13*	-.02	-.07	-.02
Grade 6 through 8 resources						.27**	.12	.03
Ninth grade resources							.26**	.08
Months employed since high school								.09*
Months enrolled since high school								.33**
Problem behaviors								-.16**
Positive transition sequences								.11
Negative transition sequences								-.13**
Number of transition milestones								.10
R^2	.27	.30	.31	.35	.35	.38	.41	.58
N = 445								

Source: Authors' compilation.

Stage A: family background; stage B: institutional backdrop (family-school-neighborhood); stage C: stages of schooling; stage D: transition to adulthood after high school

[a]White men are the reference group.

*$p \leq .05$; **$p \leq .01$.

years beyond how educational level completed relates to occupational status and sometimes earnings. It is as though other experiences over the transition to adulthood, like brushes with the law and establishing a family, count for little, but we know that is not the case.

Today, cycling back and forth between school and work is common, and many are students and workers at the same time—for example, in 2003–2004, nearly eight of ten undergraduates in the United States held jobs (American Council on Education 2006). Also, whether the path through school and into the workplace is round about or straight through is socially patterned: interrupted schooling (Bozick and DeLuca 2005) and early labor market churning (Bureau of Labor Statistics 2010; Holzer and LaLonde 1999) are more characteristic of the disadvantaged.

Figure 7.1 covers development after high school in three domains: investments in human capital through postsecondary school enrollments and employment (chapter 6); navigation of the transition into adulthood by way of the milestone experiences of entering a marriage or a stable live-in partnership, becoming a parent, working full time, and living independently of parents (chapter 5); and problem behaviors, including substance use, encounters with the law, and precocious parenting.

The topic of problem behaviors is relevant because these behaviors, and what follows from them, address the consequences of taking a misstep en route to adulthood. The fallout from decisions made and actions taken in adolescence and early adulthood is potentially irreversible: becoming a single parent at an early age, for one (Maynard 1997); a juvenile arrest record, for another (Western 2006). By the same token, problem avoidance—postponing parenthood, avoiding substance abuse, avoiding criminality—also has consequences, especially for the urban disadvantaged, whose parents may be less able to shield them from adverse consequences. Problem behaviors in adolescence and early adulthood often come in waves; indeed, their bundling is so common that Richard Jessor (1993) refers to their co-occurrence as a syndrome. Accordingly, we examine them together.

Human capital investments over the years after high school and problem behaviors engaged in or avoided could be vehicles for overcoming or intensifying urban disadvantage, yet are seldom investigated. However, experiences during the after high school period of figure 7.1 are not strictly time aligned in relation to SES destinations or to one another (for example, drug and alcohol abuse can cause problems on the job, but also be caused by difficulties in the workplace or in family life). Figure 7.1's directional arrow imagery thus is a bit looser here than for the earlier life stages.

Modeling Pathways of Intergenerational Mobility: Unbundling Urban Disadvantage

With figure 7.1 as a guide, the results reported in table 7.2 represent our account of how the long shadow of family background plays forward in the lives of the Youth Panel children. It begins when they enter first grade and concludes with their SES at age twenty-eight. The model we use is additive—the simplest form possible. Starting from the left side of table 7.2, potential risk factors and resources are added column by column following the timeline in figure 7.1. Regression analysis yields estimates of the optimum weight to assign to each risk or resource in predicting SES destinations (for a nontechnical overview, see appendix B).

Modeling status attainment as done here differs in two ways from what is typical in studies of this genre: we model family mobility (table 7.3) as well as personal mobility; and we define status as a composite of level of schooling, occupational status, and earnings rather than as single outcomes. Our focus, then, is individual and family socioeconomic mobility across generations.

The initial value of 0.51 in table 7.2 expresses the strength of the relationship between SES origins and adult destination SES, adjusted for race and gender.[10] Note that each of the life paths from child to adult is represented separately. Parallel analyses are presented for individual SES (table 7.2), family SES (table 7.3), educational level (table 7.4), occupational status (table 7.5), individual earnings (table 7.6), and family earnings (table 7.7). The coefficients for family SES origins are large and significant throughout, whereas the paths for each race-sex group look much the same except for earnings. The table entries contrast the experience of white women, African American women, and African American men against that of white men, who are used as the reference group.[11] Comparing the race-sex coefficients for personal and family earnings in column 8 of tables 7.6 and 7.7, we see that for individual earnings African American women lag behind not just white men in column 8 (–0.35), but because their deficit relative to white men is larger than is that of others, also behind white women (–0.27) and African American men (–0.17). The pattern for family earnings is different: white women and African American men are about at parity with white men (with coefficients of –0.02 and –0.12 in column 8, the latter not significant), but African American women continue to lag behind (in column 8, –0.22).

A word is in order about these race-gender contrasts. Race and gender are fixed aspects of personal identity, but social categorizations as well. "African American" and "white" locate the sample in social space. In posing questions about what is distinctive about their life experiences, we also are tracing the developmental paths open to them, constrained by the social contexts within which they are embedded.

(*Text continues on p. 142.*)

Table 7.3   Origins to Destinations: Family Socioeconomic Status (Standardized Regression Coefficients)

	Stage A	Stage B			Stage C			Stage D
	1	2	3	4	5	6	7	8
SES origins	.53**	.44**	.37**	.33**	.31**	.25**	.22**	.10*
African American women[a]	-.03	-.04	-.00	-.02	-.03	-.05	-.06	-.11*
African American men[a]	-.04	-.05	-.02	.00	.00	.00	.01	.02
White women[a]	-.00	.00	-.00	-.02	-.04	-.06	-.05	-.06
Family functional social capital		-.19**	-.18**	-.11*	-.11*	-.10*	-.09	-.07
Neighborhood and school context			-.13*	-.12*	-.12*	-.12*	-.11*	-.06
First grade resources				.20**	.10	.08	.09	.08
Grade 2 through 5 resources					.15*	.03	-.02	.01
Grade 6 through 8 resources						.25**	.09	.01
Ninth grade resources							.27**	.07
Months employed since high school								.05
Months enrolled since high school								.37**
Problem behaviors								-.15**
Positive transition sequences								.16**
Negative transition sequences								-.12**
Number of transition milestones								.18**
R^2	.28	.31	.32	.35	.36	.38	.40	.59
N = 445								

Source: Authors' compilation.

Stage A: family background; stage B: institutional backdrop (family-school-neighborhood); stage C: stages of schooling; stage D: transition to adulthood after high school

[a]White men are the reference group.

*$p \leq .05$; **$p \leq .01$.

Table 7.4   Origins to Destinations: Years of Education (Standardized Regression Coefficients)

	Stage A	Stage B		Stage C				Stage D
	1	2	3	4	5	6	7	8
SES origins	.59**	.47**	.43**	.40**	.37**	.32**	.27**	.12**
African American women[a]	.16**	.15**	.17**	.15**	.15**	.12*	.10*	.04
African American men[a]	.08	.07	.10	.11*	.11*	.11*	.12*	.11**
White women[a]	.13*	.14**	.13**	.12*	.10*	.08	.09*	.07
Family functional social capital		-.23**	-.22**	-.15**	-.15**	-.14**	-.13**	-.08**
Neighborhood and school context			-.08	-.07	-.07	-.07	-.06	-.01
First grade resources				.20**	.11	.08	.10	.08
Grade 2 through 5 resources					.14*	.02	-.05	.01
Grade 6 through 8 resources						.25**	.03	-.05
Ninth grade resources							.36**	.17**
Months employed since high school								.00
Months enrolled since high school								.51**
Problem behaviors								-.11**
Positive transition sequences								.06
Negative transition sequences								-.13**
Number of transition milestones								.01
R^2	.34	.37	.38	.41	.41	.44	.48	.71

$N = 445$

Source: Authors' compilation.
Stage A: family background; stage B: institutional backdrop (family-school-neighborhood); stage C: stages of schooling; stage D: transition to adulthood after high school.
[a]White men are the reference group.
*$p \leq .05$; **$p \leq .01$.

Table 7.5   Origins to Destinations: Occupational Status (Standardized Regression Coefficients)

	Stage A	Stage B		Stage C				Stage D
	1	2	3	4	5	6	7	8
SES origins	.46**	.39**	.33**	.31**	.28**	.22**	.21**	.11
African American women[a]	.00	-.00	.03	.02	.01	-.01	-.02	-.09
African American men[a]	-.10	-.10	-.07	-.06	-.06	-.05	-.05	-.07
White women[a]	-.01	.00	-.01	-.02	-.04	-.06	-.05	-.09
Family functional social capital		-.14**	-.12*	-.08	-.07	-.06	-.06	-.03
Neighborhood and school context			-.11	-.11	-.11	-.11	-.10	-.06
First grade resources				.13*	.04	.01	.01	.01
Grade 2 through 5 resources					.14*	-.01	-.04	.02
Grade 6 through 8 resources						.30**	.22**	.15*
Ninth grade resources							.13	.01
Months employed since high school								.01
Months enrolled since high school								.31**
Problem behaviors								-.14**
Positive transition sequences								.02
Negative transition sequences								-.10
Number of transition milestones								-.00
R^2	.22	.23	.23	.24	.25	.29	.29	.39
N = 390								

Source: Authors' compilation.
Stage A: family background; stage B: institutional backdrop (family–school–neighborhood); stage C: stages of schooling; stage D: transition to adulthood after high school.
[a]White men are the reference group.
*$p \leq .05$; **$p \leq .01$.

Table 7.6 Origins to Destinations: Individual Earnings (Standardized Regression Coefficients)

	Stage A	Stage B		Stage C				Stage D
	1	2	3	4	5	6	7	8
SES origins	.16**	.10	.04	.02	.01	-.01	-.02	-.04
African American women[a]	-.34**	-.35**	-.32**	-.33**	-.33**	-.34**	-.34**	-.35**
African American men[a]	-.23**	-.24**	-.21**	-.20**	-.20**	-.20**	-.20**	-.17*
White women[a]	-.25**	-.24**	-.25**	-.26**	-.26**	-.27**	-.27**	-.27**
Family functional social capital		-.13*	-.12*	-.08	-.08	-.08	-.07	-.09
Neighborhood and school context			-.11	-.11	-.11	-.11	-.11	-.08
First grade resources				.11*	.10	.09	.09	.09
Grade 2 through 5 resources					.02	-.04	-.05	-.05
Grade 6 through 8 resources						.12	.08	.05
Ninth grade resources							.07	.00
Months employed since high school								.06
Months enrolled since high school								.00
Problem behaviors								-.12*
Positive transition sequences								.20*
Negative transition sequences								-.03
Number of transition milestones								.23**
R²	.10	.11	.11	.12	.12	.12	.12	.17
N = 395								

Source: Authors' compilation.
Stage A: family background; stage B: institutional backdrop (family-school-neighborhood); stage C: stages of schooling; stage D: transition to adulthood after high school.
[a]White men are the reference group.
*$p \leq .05$; **$p \leq .01$.

Table 7.7 Origins to Destinations: Family Earnings (Standardized Regression Coefficients)

	Stage A	Stage B		Stage C				Stage D
	1	2	3	4	5	6	7	8
SES origins	.19**	.12*	.09	.08	.06	.05	.04	.00
African American women[a]	-.20**	-.20**	-.19**	-.19**	-.20**	-.20**	-.21**	-.22**
African American men[a]	-.19**	-.19**	-.18**	-.17*	-.17*	-.17*	-.16*	-.12
White women[a]	.01	.02	.01	.01	-.01	-.01	-.01	-.02
Family functional social capital		-.13*	-.12*	-.09	-.09	-.09	-.08	-.10
Neighborhood and school context			-.06	-.06	-.05	-.05	-.05	-.02
First grade resources				.09	.02	.01	.01	.01
Grade 2 through 5 resources					.11	.08	.07	.05
Grade 6 through 8 resources						.06	-.00	-.01
Ninth grade resources							.10	-.01
Months employed since high school								.11*
Months enrolled since high school								.11
Problem behaviors								-.11*
Positive transition sequences								.26**
Negative transition sequences								-.01
Number of transition milestones								.46**
R^2	.08	.09	.09	.10	.10	.10	.10	.26
N = 414								

Source: Authors' compilation.
Stage A: family background; stage B: institutional backdrop (family-school-neighborhood); stage C: stages of schooling; stage D: transition to adulthood after high school.
[a]White men are the reference group.
*$p \leq .05$; **$p \leq .01$.

One of this book's contributions is to identify what is typical of disadvantaged African American and white boys and girls circa 1982 and of young African American and white men and women circa 2005. Race and gender bear on their mobility prospects by virtue of their group's location in the larger social structure, itself a function of relevant history and current circumstance. Mobility regimes for disadvantaged urban youth are not the same as those for average U.S. youth. Not only might outcomes differ, but also the means by which mobility is achieved.

Modeling the life progress of individuals, as here, provides a way to decompose the correlation between SES origins and SES destinations along lines of the developmental perspective depicted in figure 7.1. The decomposition tells us how socioeconomic advantage and disadvantage are conferred by one generation on the next in urban Baltimore between 1980 and 2005. This chapter centers on family advantage and disadvantage along the socioeconomic gradient. Advantage and disadvantage by race and gender, evident in tables 7.6 and 7.7, are deferred until chapter 8.

Status Attainment in Life-Course Perspective: An Empirical Account

We begin by reviewing the utility of our life-course development approach in broad sweep terms.[12] Across successive stages of the analysis, the value that attaches to SES origins predicting SES destinations drops from 0.51 in column 1 to 0.07 in column 8 (see table 7.2), a proportionate reduction of roughly 86 percent (and 81 percent for SES measured at the family level).[13] As well, the column 8 coefficient is too small to be considered statistically significant, and that for SES measured at the family (table 7.3) is significant, but, at 0.10, quite small. This means that when evaluated empirically, the account advanced in figure 7.1 affords an almost exhaustive interpretation of how, for the sample, disadvantage and advantage along the status gradient are maintained across generations.

This is one important insight. A second follows from the explanatory power contributed by the same intermediate-stage predictors (last row of table 7.2) above that traceable to SES origins, race, and gender. From the first stage to the last, explained variance more than doubles to 0.58.

The explanatory power attributable to SES origins, race and gender by themselves is considerable: at 0.27 in column 1 (see table 7.2), it represents almost half the total variance accounted for by the full model. The other half traces to the intermediate-stage predictors, "value added" that represents mobility up and down the status gradient. Hence, the same mechanisms that help perpetuate socioeconomic advantage and disadvantage across generations can be said also to contribute to mobility. As a concrete example, doing well in school is one way children of privilege maintain their privilege; it also is one way some of the urban disadvantaged move up.

Interpretation of these results as reflecting influence relies on three premises: things that are causally related will tend to covary, generally influence tracks forward in time rather than backward, and how we have phased in predictors is reasonable. For most of the measures in table 7.2, the time order and phasing in are aligned (for example, census data from 1980 precede the 1982 first grade interview data from parents and children, which precede the collection of data from second through fifth grade, and so on). This is one strength of a panel approach to studying development.

Development as Routed Through Intermediate-Stage Predictors

The most relevant details in table 7.2 beyond those already mentioned involve the intermediate-stage predictors and how they contribute over the years. We judge these using four considerations: the size their coefficients at first appearance, how their inclusion affects the size of the SES-origins coefficient, how their coefficients change when subsequent stage predictors are added, and how much additional explanatory power they provide. The first gauges that variable's distinctive importance as a risk or protective factor, the second its role in transmitting or mediating family background influence, the third the extent to which its influence is itself mediated by or routed through later stage mechanisms, and the fourth its contribution to intergenerational mobility beyond other measures already in the analysis.

Table 7.2 may be read either across rows or down columns. Changes across rows track the behavior of explanatory variables as measures are added to the analysis. So, for example, when the coefficient for family SES drops with the addition of resources in support of children's schooling, we conclude that higher-SES youth preserve their advantage over their lower-SES peers to that extent owing to their greater command of resources that contribute to doing well at school and later in life (a stronger academic profile, more robust parental support, more favorable track placements, or a superior personal profile of achievement-related attitudes and behaviors).

The column entries correspond to the life-course stages in figure 7.1. Each column amounts to an additive model and the models grow more inclusive across columns. Generally, a variable's maximum impact is its value when first introduced, and because all predictors are scaled in the same metric (standard deviation units), the table entries are directly comparable: larger numbers signify greater influence.

Note, though, that there is not a one-to-one correspondence between figure 7.1 and the results summarized in table 7.2. There are three reasons for this. First, some predictors that might have been kept distinct are combined. This holds for school resources at each stage, yielding one predictor per stage rather than many. Second, the measures of early neighborhood and school context are too highly intercorrelated to be kept distinct. Third, preliminary screening eliminated some measures thought to be relevant, but that proved not to be predictive when tested.[14]

The preliminary screening exercise was performed to center the final analysis on risk factors and resources that have the greatest bearing on socioeconomic prospects. In winnowing for relevance, we evaluated all six SES destination measures separately: the personal and family SES composites, education, occupational status, personal earnings, and family earnings. Our standard for retention was that a candidate explanatory measure be significantly predictive in at least two of six equations with SES origins, race, and sex controlled (like the equation in column 1 of table 7.2). As predictors, we evaluated each potential mechanism from figure 7.1 three ways: by itself, together with other predictors from the same stage of analysis but kept distinct, and, where appropriate, substituting composites constructed from them.

We conducted literally hundreds of analyses and deliberately set the bar low for retention, opting for inclusiveness over exclusiveness. Even so, many candidates fell short, including some about which much has been written. In the family domain, none of the measures of structural social capital, including teen parenting and family makeup (two parents versus other configurations), made the cut. From the neighborhood context set, property crime levels, residents' perceptions of quality of life, and the neighborhood's demographic makeup (percentage African American and concentration of single-parent households) are omitted. From school context, left out are the school's racial makeup (percentage African American) and tangible school resources, including expenditures per pupil, student-teacher ratio, and the availability of special programs.

At least two useful lessons can be learned from the results of this screening exercise: considerations that seem important intuitively or when evaluated in isolation may not prove to be important when tested against other relevant considerations; and to play a distinctive role in shaping life trajectories requires some considerable heft.

Urban Disadvantage in Life-Course Perspective

From column 1 to column 8 of table 7.2, the SES-origins coefficient predicting SES destinations drops from large and highly significant at the outset to small and not significant in the final estimation, in which all intermediate-stage predictors are controlled. The drop is steady, not precipitous, across the successive stages. Levels of explained variance also increase steadily, and almost all the coefficients attached to variables added at each stage are significant when first added.

This orderliness tells us three things immediately: first, many factors are implicated in the transmission of SES advantage and disadvantage across generations; second, there is no singularly dominant determinant; and, third, the same forces that carry forward advantage and disadvantage also contribute to mobility up and down.

Backdrop to Schooling: Family First (Column 2)   Parental resources within the family are examined first. The composite for within-family structural social capital, which includes single parenting among other considerations, did not survive screening for relevance and so is not included. However, functional social capital, the hands-on side of parenting, emerged as important for all six status outcome measures. In more detailed analyses, parents' attitudinal support for children's schooling was almost always implicated: parents' expectation for how well their child will do on the upcoming report card and whether they foresee college in their child's future. Family functional social capital thus here effectively reduces to parents' psychological support for their children's schooling, well-established in the literature as a valued resource (see, for example, Entwisle, Alexander, and Olson 1997; Yamamoto and Holloway 2010).

Functional social capital is coded as a risk factor, such that high values signify lower levels of functional capital. Its coefficient in table 7.2 is small but fully significant effect (−0.22) when first added to the analysis (table 7.2) and that it is negatively signed signifies that weak family support for children's schooling early in life depresses status attainment nearly a quarter century later. Moreover, at this stage the coefficient for SES origins drops from 0.51 to 0.40, so the parent-child relationship indeed counts, and it does so over the long haul. The risk here is having parents who are less sanguine about their children's academic success, an attitude more prevalent among, but not exclusive to, the urban disadvantaged.

It is important that this first assessment of parent expectations, having been elicited before the first report card in first grade, is properly considered part of the family backdrop to schooling. Such a class divide in parents' optimism absent feedback from school suggests world view differences across social lines in the nature of Pierre Bourdieu's habitus (1990; Swartz 1977). Here it is the sense that "schooling is not for the likes of us."

In the sample, almost 75 percent of higher-SES children expected they would finish college when we first posed the question to them in fourth grade and on every later occasion through the end of high school, versus just 23 percent of lower-SES youth (Bozick et al. 2010). Differences across social lines in schooling aspirations—initially those of parents and later those of children—are one of the ways the long shadow imprints itself on children's academic and personal development. This is one way stratification by family background is socially constructed: it is reinforced daily through life's experience and discernible on the very first occasion we are able to measure it.

Neighborhood and School as Backdrop to Children's Schooling (Column 3) Neighborhood and school context as a single composite appear next in table 7.2. The correlation between neighborhood SES (from census data) and school percentage low-income enrollment (from school records) is 0.90, close to the ceiling, so we cannot keep measures from the two contexts distinct as originally intended. For us this presents a technical problem.[15] For Baltimore's children it poses a practical one: those living in high-poverty communities also are clustered in schools that enroll mainly students of like background. John Logan (2002, 6), for example, reports that school and neighborhood segregation indices for Baltimore are high and practically identical: in the 1989–1990 school year, 76.3 and 79.1, respectively; a decade later, 79.0 and 74.3.[16]

That these segregation figures are so closely aligned is hardly coincidental: segregated neighborhoods create segregated schools. Although these calculations pertain to racial segregation, they have implications for children's poverty exposure. In 1999–2000, the poverty enrollment in Baltimore schools attended by African Americans was 42.4 percent (seventh highest of the fifty large cities covered in Logan's analysis); for whites, it was 19.6 percent. We saw much the same for the Youth Panel's schools (chapter 4).

Does any of this matter? Most decidedly so: as a risk factor, the school-neighborhood context composite from first grade is significant when first added in the third column of table 7.2, with a coefficient of −0.14.[17] The negative sign indicates that the riskier the childhood context, the lower the adult status level. Moreover, with it included the coefficient for family SES in table 7.2 drops from 0.40 in column 2 to 0.33 in the next column, indicating family influence carried forward through the character of children's neighborhoods and schools. More broadly, the institutional backdrop to children's development—family social capital, neighborhood, and school—together accounts for more than 33 percent of the influence of SES origins on SES destinations (1−0.33/0.51 = 0.35). Because family determines neighborhood and school, this risk exposure is one way family casts its long shadow.

The neighborhood-school context composite retains its size and significance through column 7 when academic resources from the elementary grades, middle school years, and high school all are entered. Neighborhood and school context thus are consequential beyond their relevance for access to resources in support of children's schooling from first grade through high school, including test scores, grades, and so forth.

This impact for the neighborhood-school nexus is impressive in light of all that was dropped in screening for relevance: for neighborhood context, property crime levels, residents' perceptions of quality of life, the neighborhood percentage African American, and the neighborhood concentration of single-parent households; for school context, the school's racial makeup (percentage African American) and tangible school resources, including expenditures per pupil, student-teacher ratio, and the availability of special programs. Conditions that stand out instead are school and neighborhood SES context, the level of neighborhood violent crime, and the school's academic profile.

It is noteworthy that socioeconomics—that is, poor neighborhoods and poor schools—are prominent in both settings. Long ago, the Coleman report (1966) concluded that family socioeconomic level plays a greater role in children's academic achievement than features of the schools children attend, but also that the socioeconomic makeup of a school's enrollment is the most consequential school quality factor. Research since reinforces the second point, with stronger school-SES effects than in Coleman's early research (Borman and Dowling 2010; Rumberger and Palardy 2005).

As regards neighborhood, Tama Leventhal and Jeanne Brooks-Gunn (2000, 315) conclude that significant effects of neighborhood SES are more numerous in the literature than effects for measures of racial-ethnic composition and residential stability (the three aspects of neighborhood context most often examined in this literature). They also note in passing that "school characteristics are shaped by the social and economic makeup of neighborhoods" (323). A passing comment for them, but for us a critical insight for understanding why it is that the urban disadvantaged so often find themselves enveloped in a web of disadvantage.

Development Across the School Years: First Grade into High School (Columns 4–7)   That the transition into first grade is a developmental milestone is one of the important insights from our work over the years (Entwisle and Alexander 1989, 1993; Entwisle, Alexander, and Olson 2003). It also explains why we separate the first grade year from the rest of elementary school. The time of school entry is a high hurdle for many children. First graders are obliged to acquire a new identity—that of school child as distinct from home child—in a setting where for the first time outside the home they are compared to other children. At home, they are judged against where they themselves were the previous year or their siblings; at school, it is against other children and absent the strong parent-child emotional bond. What counts is academic accomplishment and deportment, and it does not augur well that poor children lag behind by both standards at the very launch of their schooling (Lee and Burkam 2002). Minority children also suffer unfavorable stereotyped perceptions (Alexander, Entwisle, and Thompson 1987; Downey and Pribesh 2004).

After first grade, table 7.2 distinguishes three additional stages of schooling: the rest of the elementary school years (grades 2 through 5), the middle school years (grades 6 through 8), and the first year of high school. At each stage we add a set of resources of known relevance for children's schooling, keyed to that particular level of schooling and adjusted to be stage appropriate.[18] Coverage stops at ninth grade (the first year of high school in Baltimore) because dropout rates escalate quickly thereafter and resources cannot be assessed in parallel for the entire cohort. This is limiting, but the first year of high school sets the tone for what follows and students who stumble badly then rarely recover (Roderick and Camburn 1999; Neild 2009).

At each stage of schooling, tracking, measures of school performance, parental expectations, students' role fit and expectations together are significant when first introduced, add to the model's explanatory power, and reduce the size of the SES coefficient. Moreover, at each stage beyond the first, coefficients for resources from prior stages shrink, eventually all dropping to nonsignificance in column 8 except resources keyed to first grade.[19] Its coefficient drops almost by half, from 0.22 to 0.12, but remains significant, so whether one gets off on a good or poor footing initially at school echoes far into the future.

A history of accumulating advantages and disadvantages thus sets youth on divergent trajectories. Additionally, the underlying skill set, academic placements, and success orientations of parents and children become increasingly important as the transition out of high school nears (for example, resource coefficients from the middle grades and high school are larger than are those from the elementary grades). Years later, the yield from resources keyed to the early years eventually comes to fruition, but mostly routed indirectly through intermediate stages of development. This is the embodiment of Alan Kerckhoff's (1993) developmental model of structural deflections, but here realized in broader terms, given that parents' psychological supports and children's developing self-agency are not addressed in his research.

Across the sweep of children's schooling, these joint processes of stability and change count for a great deal. The SES coefficient drops from 0.33 in column 3 of table 7.2 to 0.18 in column 7 and explained variance increases by almost a third, from 0.31 to 0.41. Even more broadly, the institutional backdrop to schooling, together with school experiences from first grade into high school, account for almost 65 percent of the influence of socioeconomic origins on the adulthood SES (dropping from 0.51 to 0.18). We thus are well along in detailing the long shadow's reach by way of risks and resources from early in life, beginning with early childhood and extending into high school.

Development After High School (Column 8)   This last assessment extends coverage beyond high school, examining three domains of experience: investments in human capital by way of postsecondary schooling and employment, problem behaviors, and adulthood transition milestones. In young people's lives these strands of development play forward concurrently and interweave. Here we ask which stand out as distinctively consequential among the many issues considered.

Postsecondary schooling and employment are measured separately as the percentage of months invested in these two activities since leaving high school up to the MAS interview (age twenty-eight). Both stand out as consequential, with respective coefficients of 0.33 and 0.09 in table 7.2 (column 8). This equation also yields the largest single stage increase in explanatory power, from 0.41 to 0.58, and the largest proportionate decrease in the SES-origins coefficient, from 0.18 to 0.07 (the latter nonsignificant).

The value of investments in school makes sense. Continuing in school is the understood way to get ahead in the world of work, and though more time invested in school does not always yield more degrees or certificates, that is the tendency. The correlation between months of enrollment after high school and highest level of education attained at age twenty-eight (coded into years, 12 for a regular high school degree; 16 for a four-year degree) is 0.78.[20]

Schooling after high school also explains how ninth grade (and earlier) academic resources link to status destinations, because the coefficient for ninth grade resources shrinks by half or more when enrollment and employment after high school are added to the equation. In this way, cumulative disadvantage extends into the years after high school and magnifies: the correlation between months enrolled after high school and resources in support of children's schooling increases from 0.35 for the first grade composite, to 0.39 for the remaining years of elementary school, to 0.47 in the middle grades, to 0.56 in ninth grade. High school may be the launching pad, but the trajectory is rooted in children's earliest schooling.

Despite high rates of postsecondary attendance, the Youth Panel's urban disadvantaged earn few postsecondary degrees and their employment is intermittent, which means less accumulated work experience (chapter 6). It is, rather, the urban advantaged who benefit most from human capital investments in school and work, facilitated by their successes at school.[21] Because these assets for status attainment are accumulated over the years after high school, it is easy to think they originate in the transition to adulthood, but their foundation is set years before.

However, months of employment after high school are weak predictors even for earnings, where job seniority would be expected to pay off. Indeed, our entire explanatory framework offers little insight when it comes to earnings differences: just 17 percent total variance explained for personal earnings and 26 percent for family earnings, half or less that for the other measures of socioeconomic standing (tables 7.3 through 7.7). This is not altogether unexpected, however. For one thing, earnings tend to be less stable across years than are occupation and education, which means a single point in time estimate, as here, may be a poor barometer of long-term earnings prospects. Using Social Security Administration data, Bhashkar Mazumder (2005) reports father-to-son income elasticities (analogous to correlations) of 0.27 when father's earnings are averaged over two years, 0.47 when averaged over seven years, and 0.65 when averaged over sixteen.[22]

Another consideration is the age at which earnings are referenced. At age twenty-eight, the sample is short of its anticipated peak earnings. Samuel Bowles, Herbert Gintis, and Melissa Groves (2005, 6) report that the correlation between father's and son's earnings increases with age until the retirement years. Additionally, time on the job often yields little return in the low-wage, low-benefit jobs held by many of the urban disadvantaged. Age-earnings profiles in this sector of the economy tend to be relatively flat, whereas earnings increase across careers in the kinds of jobs held by more highly educated workers (Kalleberg and Sorensen 1979; Connolly and Gottschalk 2006). Although the starter jobs taken by highly skilled workers may not pay well initially, their salaries move up over time, so pay differentials by level of education increase with age (Bureau of Labor Statistics 2010). Comparisons at younger ages will understate these career advantages of the highly skilled and factors that would discriminate among earnings at older ages are less discriminating at younger ages. What is revealed in tables 7.6 and 7.7 is important nonetheless: differences in earnings by race and gender that favor white men over everyone else are large. Chapter 8 explores why this is the case.

As routes to self-advancement, success at school and on the job are, at least in theory, available to everyone. Problem behaviors likewise are subject to personal control—no one is forced to do drugs, binge drink, become a parent when young, or run afoul of the law. But many youth do engage in these behaviors, and though here too social patterning is evident, it is not altogether the patterning that might be supposed.

Figure 7.2   Problem Behaviors in Adulthood

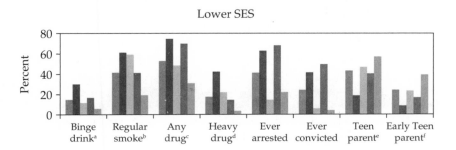

Lower SES

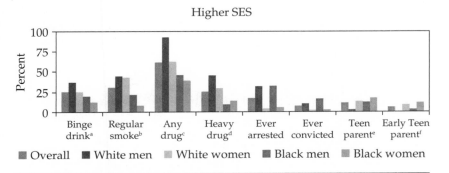

Higher SES

■ Overall   ■ White men   ■ White women   ■ Black men   ■ Black women

Source: Authors' compilation.
[a]Five or more drinks in last two weeks.
[b]Ever a regular smoker.
[c]Ever any drug use.
[d]Ever any drug use other than marijuana.
[e]First birth at age nineteen or younger.
[f]First birth at age seventeen or younger.

Of the ten problem behaviors evaluated in table 7.2, eight are displayed in figure 7.2.[23] Across the entire sample, the average number of problem behaviors acknowledged is 2.8 (of the ten): 3.2 among lower-SES youth and 2.4 among their higher-SES counterparts. Although the lower-SES average is higher overall, higher-SES white men have the highest reported levels of binge drinking, of any drug use, and of drug use other than marijuana, followed in each instance by lower-SES white men. In fact, within SES levels, white averages exceed the African American: 3.8 versus 2.9 for those of lower-SES origins; 3.0 versus 1.6 for those of higher origins.

This pattern hardly squares with the popular perception of lower-SES African Americans as the face of urban disadvantage, fueled by the media's racialized portrayal of inner-city drug abuse, dealing, and violence (see, for example, Alexander 2010). The white poor tend to be invisible as a class, and many implications follow, one being that they are less likely to be held back by unflattering stereotype, such as when looking for work.

For higher-SES whites, it is less a matter of invisibility than of social capital: their family privilege can buffer adverse consequences and hide their transgressions, with their drinking, drug use, and the like dismissed as "college hijinks" or "boys will be boys." The African American urban poor have neither advantage—they suffer guilt by imagined association and lack a protective family shield.

Even when problem profiles do conform to image, the twists can be interesting. Teen motherhood, for example, is rare among higher-SES youth, but common among lower-SES women, both African American and white. The context of lower-SES parenting differs by race, however: white women are much more likely to be parenting in a marriage or partnership (chapter 6); African American women more often become parents while in high school and parent outside a family union.

Another twist involves contact with the criminal justice system. Although almost 33 percent of higher-SES men, black and white, acknowledge an arrest, their conviction rates are low. That they are suggests that their arrests will not be as detrimental as those of lower-SES background youth, especially blacks, whose high arrest rates are accompanied by high rates of conviction and incarceration.

This brings us to consequences. The coefficient for problem behaviors in table 7.2 is small yet significant, and this holds also for the other status outcomes shown in tables 7.3 through 7.7.[24] However, for a risk factor or resource to transmit socioeconomic advantage and disadvantage across generations, it must be correlated with both origin status and destination status, and the larger the correlations, the more prominent its role. Although the problem behavior composite is significant in its consequences, its correlation with SES origins is small (−0.14), and much smaller than for the other modeled risks and resources in table 7.2. Problem behaviors thus do incur penalties, but not in a way that contributes to the transmission of socioeconomic advantage and disadvantage across generations.[25] There is an important exception though: in subgroup analyses, problem behaviors are significant only for African American men. We return to this result in chapter 8.

By age twenty-eight, half the sample had worked full time, entered into a marriage or partnership, lived apart from parents, been married or had a live-in partner, and become a parent (chapter 5). This Done All path was most characteristic of lower-SES origin youth, especially white

women. The other high prevalence patterns presented strikingly different sociodemographic profiles. The issue now is whether these different
pathways into adulthood lead to different socioeconomic destinations.

To pursue the question, we reduced the number of pathways to three,
using the Done All fast track into adulthood as the base of comparison:
Positive Transition Sequences combines transition patterns associated in
preliminary analyses with SES outcomes superior to the Done Alls (for
example, higher SES and earnings levels); *Negative Transition Sequences*
are transition patterns associated with inferior outcomes.[26] In column 8
of table 7.2, a significant positive coefficient means better (adjusted) outcomes, on average, than the Done Alls; a significant negative coefficient
means worse outcomes, on average. Table 7.2 also evaluates a tally of
milestones completed. It ranges from zero to four, but there is just one
zero—a rare case indeed.

Parenthood, it turns out, is common to all the negative transition
sequences (that is, those that depress socioeconomic prospects) and
delayed parenthood is common to the positive transition sequences.
That divide seems to implicate parenthood as the key consideration
for mobility, but parenthood per se does not depress SES destinations
because the Done Alls also are parents and they attain higher status
levels, on average, than those who take a negative transition path to
adulthood. The key, rather, is the context of parenthood, whether in a
union or as a single parent.

In table 7.2, only the *Negative Transition Sequence* is significant, and
it is associated also with depressed family SES at age twenty-eight
(table 7.3) and depressed education level (table 7.4). The coefficient
for the tally of transition milestones completed is positive (and significant) for family SES, indicating more is better.[27]

Precisely how the transition to adulthood is negotiated thus intersects
other domains of adult standing, but in different ways. Completing more
milestones is associated with enhanced earnings. Compared with those
who follow the Done All path into adulthood, the negative transition pattern depresses status attainment and level of schooling. None of the three,
though, predicts occupational status. Recalling that the Done Alls are
parents with partners and have worked full time, and those who took
one of the Negative paths to adulthood are parents never married or in
a partnership, two themes in this volume, and in the broader literature,
likely underlie these results: a two-earner benefit boosts earnings, whereas
solo parenting entails financial hardship and interferes with educational
attainment. These benefits and liabilities, moreover, accrue mainly to the
urban disadvantaged, who dominate the Done All and negative sequence
paths and, as seen, rarely get ahead through higher education.

The Long View

The last equations from tables 7.2 and 7.3 are informative from another vantage point. Column 8 is the last analysis anticipated under figure 7.1 and it is the most inclusive. Everything is there, from the backdrop-to-schooling conditions of family, neighborhood, and school, through children's journey through school from first grade into high school, culminating with an expansive set of experiences over the years after high school. In column 8 of both tables 7.2 and 7.3, near-term predictors from the years after high school dominate the results. Problem behavior avoidance, completing milestones to adulthood, and investments in school and work explain how the urban advantaged outpace the urban disadvantaged in adulthood, while influences from earlier in life amount to little—two small coefficients in table 7.2, one for family functional social capital and the other for first grade resources, and none in table 7.3.

Viewed in isolation, early development seems to count for little. There is no story of any consequence about the panel's early family life, or school and neighborhood context, or their early schooling. It is as though the life record that counts begins only over the years after high school. However, we did not limit the inquiry to the years after high school and so are not misled in this way. Instead, we know that risks and resources evaluated through ninth grade account for more than 50 percent of the influence of SES origins on SES destinations and increase explained variance by nearly 33 percent; and most of the modeled risk factors and protective resources contribute distinctively in both respects. The full expanse of these analyses thus instructs us that the long shadow of family background works through developmental processes that are long term and multifaceted, anchored in childhood conditions, then through adolescence, and continuing into young adulthood.

SES Background or Race and Gender as Disadvantage?

Thus far we have not had much to say about disadvantage centered on race and gender. When evaluated for their relevance in table 7.2, not a single significant difference is associated with either at the outset, and this holds also for socioeconomic attainment at the family level (table 7.3).[28] The empirics of this chapter best explain how family socioeconomic background passes through to the next generation, and the explanation holds in the main for blacks and whites, men and women when evaluated separately (not reported). The earnings gaps that privileges white men over others are exceptions. Their personal earnings are higher than those of all others (table 7.6), whereas at the family level, African American women's earnings continue to lag far behind.

We said at the outset that socioeconomic status as a construct is faithful to the understood meaning of socioeconomic standing and this chapter demonstrates its utility for understanding status mobility across generations. However, we also cautioned that locating persons and families in socioeconomic space by averaging across educational level, occupational status, and earnings can obscure important detail. The differences that emerge with earnings as the standard of adult attainment in fact hold the key to stratification along lines of race and gender.

The next chapter pursues this insight, advancing an account of urban advantage and disadvantage rather different from the status attainment through school paradigm vivid in this chapter. In chapter 8's alternative account, schooling is not the key to getting ahead and the beneficiaries are not the children of higher-SES families. The arena of contestation, rather, is the workplace, and working-class whites are the beneficiaries. It is an account of white privilege in what remains of Baltimore's old industrial economy.

Escaping Urban Disadvantage by Way of Out-Migration

Perhaps the key to moving up is to move out—of the city and its school system. That would be a much simpler explanation for status attainment and mobility than the one posited in figure 7.1 and it has surface plausibility. As reviewed in chapter 2, Baltimore's economy suffered immensely during the last decades of the twentieth century and conditions locally have been anything but opportune. The city's population loss also is relevant in that many of the Youth Panel children joined the out-migration: 40 percent left the city school system at some point and at age twenty-eight, 48 percent were living outside Baltimore. Most had moved to one of the surrounding counties, where as children they might have benefited from what are thought to be better schools and as adults from more robust economic conditions. In addition, as was the case city-wide, the movers were disproportionately higher SES.[29]

To test this alternative account, we revisited the analyses in tables 7.2 through 7.7, asking whether those who transferred out of the city's public schools or relocated outside the city were better off socioeconomically as young adults. We added two relevant measures to the final stage regressions: a 0–1 code identifying whether the last school attended was a Baltimore City public school (left city schools: 1 = yes); and a like code indicating residence in Baltimore City at the time of the age twenty-eight interview (left Baltimore: 1 = yes). These measures are less refined than we would like and most assuredly do not exhaust the issue. Timing, for example, is not considered. The move could have been early in life—after first grade—or later, after finishing college to take advantage of a good job opportunity. Nor do we know the destinations, though from the literature on residential mobility, for those of lower SES, their new communities and schools may not have been all that different from those left behind (see, for example, Rosenblatt and DeLuca 2012). The test is blunt, but to leave the city or its schools seem large steps, and we ask whether either kind of move made a tangible difference in adult well-being.

The answer is clear. In analyses not shown, none of the coefficients for leaving the city schools is significant, while relocating outside Baltimore does seem to matter, with significant positive coefficients for the two SES composites and both earnings measures (own and family). Those who relocated outside Baltimore thus were somewhat better off, but the coefficients are small (0.08 for table 7.2, 0.09 for table 7.3), and what is more important, including the exiting measures induced no changes of consequence in the results of this chapter.[30]

Discounting alternative explanations plays a large role in the logic of science (Stinchcombe 1987). These results are of interest in their own right, but also as a critical test of the long shadow's life-course developmental account of mobility prospects. Surviving this test cannot be said to prove the truth of that account, but that it has withstood a potentially fatal assault is reassuring.

= Chapter 8 =

Stratification by Race and Gender

To THIS point, our focus has been stratification along the socioeconomic gradient, largely governed by success at school. Conditions and experiences in the early years set the foundation; in the later years, the opportunities afforded by that success materialize or are closed off by its lack. Doing well in school surely is not the only path to upward mobility or status preservation at the high end, but in the modern era it is the one most deeply embedded in the national psyche and through labor market processes in social structure.

It therefore is limiting that so few of the Beginning School Study Youth Panel (BSSYP, or Youth Panel) urban disadvantaged complete college. Many do not even complete high school. For them, the path to upward mobility through school has little relevance. The previous chapter identifies some of the things that hold them back: their families are not well positioned to help them advance through schooling; they live in high poverty, and for some violent, neighborhoods; they attend high-poverty schools; their balance of school-based risk and protective factors is heavy on risk and short on protection; their employment in early adulthood is erratic or absent; and their attempts at postsecondary education, when they do enroll, mostly are unsuccessful.

Further, for many family responsibilities come into play: women shouldering the burdens of parenting alone and the Done Alls, whose family life includes parenting with a spouse or partner. There are many more Done All women, but they have attracted much less attention, probably because they pose no obvious social problem. Still, from a stratification perspective, their family life is just as relevant as that of single mothers because a second earner in the household, or a first earner with superior earnings prospects, makes a large difference for women's economic well-being.

Apart from these details of family structure, the status attainment framework used in chapter 7 sheds little light on stratification by race and gender: the socioeconomic destinations of black men, black women,

157

and white women all are at parity with those of white men (the compared with group) when equated statistically for family background in the first stage of the analysis. They emerged as significant only after phasing in controls for a variety of life-course experiences. This appearance of parity was not anticipated at the outset, yet such a conclusion has an impressive lineage in William Julius Wilson's (1978) "declining significance of race" thesis. Although advanced some thirty-five years ago, and controversial at the time (Morris 1996; Willie 1978), it nevertheless has currency still. For example, according to Robert Putnam, quoted in Garance Franke-Ruta (2012), ". . . what we are talking about [how people escape poverty] is now as least as much about class itself and not just about . . . race."

Wilson argued that class disadvantage and not racial disadvantage has become the major impediment to the advancement of African Americans in urban ghettos.[1] Chapter 7, though, brought to light a form of inequality hidden below the veneer of socioeconomic parity. Race and gender are integral to it and schooling incidental. It is inequality specific to earnings.

Intersectionality in Earnings Attainment

Thus far we have assessed the importance of race and gender versus socioeconomic status (SES) origins in generating social inequality using a mode of analysis that assumes the causes of inequality are additive in their consequences. The logic is to isolate effects of each potentially disadvantaging attribute apart from the others, but that separation misses consequences that trace to distinctive profiles of disadvantage: rather than inequality being partly this and partly that, perhaps it originates at their intersection (Warikoo and Carter 2009). The intersectionality perspective takes us to a very different account of urban disadvantage in the urban context, one in which race and gender jointly are central.

Taking white men as the frame of reference in the previous chapter and comparing them with white women, African American women, and African American men sheds light on this intersectionality by revealing white men's earnings advantage over others. Had we taken a different approach, contrasting the experience of African Americans against whites, on the one hand, and of women against men, on the other, those disparities would not have emerged as in table 7.2, and repeated in table 8.1. They would not because the earnings differences at issue are not simply a matter of race or of gender, but rather of race and gender jointly as bases of stratification. The disadvantage of women is not the same for whites and blacks, and that of African American men is more different still.

Table 8.1 Earnings, Personal and Family (Standardized Regression Coefficients)

	1[c]	2	3	4	5	6	7	8
Overall								
Personal earnings								
SES origins	.16**	.10	.04	.02	.01	-.01	-.02	-.04
Black women[a]	-.34**	-.35**	-.32**	-.33**	-.33**	-.34**	-.34**	-.35**
Black men[a]	-.23**	-.24**	-.21**	-.20**	-.20**	-.20**	-.20**	-.17*
White women[a]	-.25**	-.24**	-.25**	-.26**	-.26**	-.27**	-.27**	-.27**
Family earnings								
SES origins	.19	.12	.09	.08	.06	.05	.04	.00
Black women[a]	-.20**	-.20**	-.19**	-.19**	-.20**	-.20**	-.21**	-.22**
Black men[a]	-.19**	-.19**	-.18**	-.17*	-.17*	-.17*	-.16*	-.12
White women[a]	.01	.02	.01	.01	-.01	-.01	-.01	-.02
Lower SES[b]								
Personal earnings								
SES origins	.08	.06	.05	.04	.03	.02	.01	-.05
Black women[a]	-.55**	-.56**	-.53**	-.56**	-.57**	-.59**	-.59**	-.58**
Black men[a]	-.33**	-.33**	-.31**	-.29**	-.30**	-.30**	-.29**	-.24*
White women[a]	-.35**	-.35**	-.35**	-.38**	-.40**	-.42**	-.40**	-.45**
Family earnings								
SES origins	.17*	.13	.13	.11	.09	.09	.09	.02
Black women[a]	-.38**	-.40**	-.37**	-.39**	-.43**	-.43**	-.43**	-.40**
Black men[a]	-.25*	-.26**	-.25*	-.23*	-.25*	-.25*	-.24*	-.17
White women[a]	-.01	-.01	-.01	-.03	-.08	-.08	-.06	-.10

Source: Authors' compilation.

Note: Regression coefficients are from the full equations, as in table 7.2.

[a]White men are the reference category.

[b]Selecting on lower-SES origins based on the categorical measure reduces the variance of SES origins as a predictor, but there is sufficient variability to keep it in the regression analysis.

[c]Predictors are added as anticipated in figure 7.1: 1 = stratifying variables; 2 and 3 = family and neighborhood context; 4 through 7 = stages of schooling; 8 = transition to adulthood after high school.

*$p \leq .05$ **$p \leq .01$.

Table 8.1 revisits the personal and family earnings regressions from chapter 7, the only SES outcomes for which initial race-sex differences are significant. The upper panel repeats results for the entire sample from tables 7.6 and 7.7; the lower panel, which is new, is for those of lower-SES origins.[2] The entries are standardized coefficients. Comparing results in the upper and lower panels of table 8.1, almost every race-gender entry is substantially larger among those of lower SES than overall. That those of lower SES are included in the overall comparisons tells us that earnings differentials are most pronounced among the urban disadvantaged, adding a third dimension to the intersectionality that drives earnings inequality in the sample: race, gender, and status.

In terms of personal earnings, everyone lags behind white men, but in terms of earnings at the family level, only African American women and men do. The differences, moreover, are substantial. Lower-SES white women suffer a personal earnings shortfall against white men of $15,300 at the outset and of $19,300 in the last stage, after adjustment for intermediate-stage predictors.[3] At the family level, however, lower-SES white women are at parity with white men, even in column 1, because they are the beneficiaries of a second-earner gain that offsets their low personal earnings. Inasmuch as the recast comparison is white families against white families, this makes perfect sense.

This recast comparison matters much less for African Americans, though, because their earnings at the family level still fall short. However, African American men's family earnings deficit is accounted for in table 8.1. The table traces it to differences in experience over the years after high school (comparing columns 7 and 8), most noticeably their employment history and problem behaviors.[4] The pattern for lower-SES African American women is different. Their family earnings shortfall is large at the outset ($25,200) and hardly changes after adjustments ($26,700 in column 8).[5] For them, the life-course developmental framework that informs table 8.1 is largely irrelevant, including the transition to adulthood family milestone, which is "ever been in a union" rather than "currently." And too, the second earner gain accounts for less than half their personal earning deficit (−.55 SD originally and −.38 SD at the family level).[6] For white women, the comparison is like against like. Not so for African American women, whose family makeup leaves them at a disadvantage.

These striking differences in earnings attainment by race and gender prompt two questions. First, why do the family earnings of lower-SES white women exceed that of their African American counterparts? The answer is that lower-SES African American women are less likely to marry or partner, which means no two-earner advantage. Moreover, when African American women are in unions, their partners have lower earnings, on average, than the men with whom white women form unions.

But if marrying or partnering well is the key, then, second, what is it that gives the advantage to working-class white men? They clearly are not earning more on the strength of superior academic credentials, given that they acquire less schooling than others, not more. Rather, it is that they excel in the workplace.

The main route to higher earnings for lower-SES white men in the sample is their stronger work histories, their superior access to high-paying work in the skilled crafts, and their better quality jobs within that sector. Specifically, white men find more steady work than others do (for example, lower-SES white men were employed for 70 percent of the months since high school, African American men for 52 percent), their employment is more concentrated in the blue-collar industrial and construction trades (at age twenty-eight, 45 percent versus 15 percent), where earnings are much higher than in other lower-tier sectors of the economy, and within that sector, they secure more lucrative employment ($43,383 annually versus $21,569 for African American men).

This form of white working-class advantage is long standing in Baltimore, and probably in other places like Baltimore. Bernard Levenson and Mary McDill (1966) observed a similar 2:1 earnings advantage for the white auto-mechanic graduates of Baltimore vocational high schools in the late 1960s. More recently, Deirdre Royster (2003) documented similar employment advantages. Working-class whites in this volume are the latest generation to benefit from blocked opportunities for blacks in the skilled trades, barriers that extend back at least as far as the World War II mobilization (chapter 2). With income data only, Levenson and McDill could not pursue root causes, but Royster's interviews and on-site observations implicate guidance counselors, who steer whites to good jobs. "Connections and family are important," Royster concludes (2003, 164).[7]

Family connections are relevant in the sample also: when asked at age twenty-two about how they found their jobs, 58 percent of lower-SES white men mention family, 75 percent mention friends, and 40 percent report finding work on their own.[8] The corresponding figures for lower-SES African American men are 42 percent, 66 percent, and 68 percent. Whites get help from family and friends; blacks more often are obliged to fend for themselves (see table 8.2). Echoing Royster, family and connections indeed matter, and not just at the interior of family life.

Table 8.2   Working-Class Families and Social Capital: Help Finding
Work at Age Twenty-Two

	Whites	Blacks
Family[a]	58[b]	42
Friends	75	66
Self	40	68

Source: Authors' compilation.
Note: All numbers in percentages.
[a]The question is: who helped find the job?
[b]Percentages exceed 100 because multiple sources of help finding work were permitted.

Network Advantage and Disadvantage in the Job Search

Mark Granovetter (1974, 1983) was among the first to show the importance of network contacts in the job search. He distinguished strong ties (family and close intimates) from weak ties (casual acquaintances) and found weak ties to be more helpful because casual contacts are more numerous and add information beyond that available in closed systems of strong ties. Granovetter studied the job search strategies used by high-level technical workers, professionals, and managers, but research since then finds that the poor and near-poor are prone to rely on strong ties (1983, 212). Their strong networks may not be as advantageous, however. Often they entail obligations that drain assets (Swartz 2009) and the strong ties available to the urban disadvantaged may not include useful job contacts (Stack 1974). Too, even when their networks might prove useful, low-income African Americans may be reluctant to make job referrals for fear of adverse repercussions if the hire ends badly (Smith 2010).

White working-class privilege among the Baltimore sample comes about through access to good employment opportunities that are contextually and historically embedded, and that date back at least to the World War II mobilization, when the sample's parents and grandparents were coming of age. The booming industrial economy of that time created a blue-collar elite workforce, but though the collar was blue, in segregated Baltimore the beneficiaries were white.

Those days are long gone, but the legacy of that era continues to shape the lives of Baltimore's blue-collar children. The racial contrasts are striking: before leaving high school, 21 percent of whites but not a single African American worked in the construction crafts; at age twenty-two, the numbers were 30 percent and 8 percent; and at age twenty-eight, 45 percent and 15 percent.

Whites fare better on other benchmarks as well (see table 8.3). They find full-time work more quickly after high school and more are employed

Table 8.3   Vocational Development of Noncollege Men

	White Men	Black Men
Jobs during high school		
% quarters employed	33.0	20.0
% in crafts	21.0	0.0
Jobs after high school		
% Full-time job first quarter	51.6	34.8
% Full-time job first year	68.0	49.2
Earnings ($/hour) first full-time job	$7.04	$6.54
Age twenty-two employment		
% employed full time	70.7	54.9
% quarters employed full time, end	73.0	56
high school to age twenty-two		
% in crafts	30.0	8.0
Earnings ($/hour) full-time job	$10.30	$9.35
Age twenty-eight employment		
% employed full time	79.4	60.7
% quarters employed full time,	80	64
last twenty-four months		
% in crafts	45.0	15.0
Earnings ($/hour) full-time job	$20.34	$14.75
Earning from work, previous year	$41,648	$28,700
(N)[b]	(102)	(122)

Source: Authors' compilation.
[a]Did not attend four-year college.
[b]Figures given are the maximum Ns.

full time at ages twenty-two and twenty-eight. At every juncture and in every category of employment, whites have better jobs. In sales, for example, whites sell insurance, blacks sell shoes; in protective services, whites work in crime labs, blacks are security guards. The white earnings advantage also increases with time. That whites manage to secure more lucrative work at age twenty-eight is more than good fortune; they are, rather, the beneficiaries of a racial advantage that spans their entire vocational development as far back as their middle school summer jobs.

Todd's and Aaron's experiences capture the sense of this (see box 8.1). Both grew up in low-income West Side neighborhoods, Todd's segregated white, Aaron's segregated black. Neither followed the college path. Todd did start down that road, but preferred the physical labor he experienced on his summer job between high school and college. The opening was where his father worked, a small detail in his story, but a large one in his life and a detail absent from Aaron's account. At age twenty-eight, Aaron, like Todd, was working in what is left of Baltimore's old economy, but at the low end, making just $10 an hour as

---

**Box 8.1   Making It in the New Economy the
             Old-Fashioned Way: Two Tales**

Immediately after high school, Todd enrolled at a four-year college away from home, but the summer before enrolling he took a job at the transport company where his father worked. He drove a big-rig tractor trailer delivering freight and discovered that he liked the physically demanding work more than the desk work at school: "The more I thought about it, I was like, I like doing the physical labor. I don't want a job where I sit behind a desk, that'll drive me nuts, cause I don't like to sit still. . . . I love my job. I love what I do." Todd left college after one semester and returned to the trucking company. When we spoke with him a decade after high school, he was earning $50,000 per year and had built a rewarding blue-collar career without the benefit of college.

Aaron's biological father was an alcoholic drug-abuser who spent many years in prison; the cabbie uncle who raised him with his mother was killed in a robbery when Aaron was fifteen. Aaron was expelled from high school for bringing a butcher knife to school (for self-protection, he insists) but later completed high school by way of the GED. His history includes run-ins with the law (car theft and drug-related offenses) and struggles with alcoholism. Aaron too works in what's left of Baltimore's old economy, but making just $10 an hour as a construction laborer.

---

a construction laborer. When asked why love and respect for his mother was not enough to keep him out of trouble, he replied: "Nothing she could have did would have stopped me from being the person that I am. Because I'm not just a product of her, I'm a product of my environment too. And she was not . . . the only influence in my life."

Aaron's story includes problem encounters with the law, something common in the lives of the urban disadvantaged, black and white. Indeed, white and black working-class men in the Youth Panel have similar problem behavior profiles, the whites' arguably the more problematic. But what of consequences? The broader literature shows that a history of problem encounters with the law is a greater impediment for African Americans than for whites (for example, Pager 2007; Western 2006). In the regressions reported in chapter 7, problem behaviors depressed status attainment in the full panel analysis (the significant negative sign in table 7.2), but in subgroup analyses this holds only among lower-SES African American men.

To pursue that lead, we revisited the employment measures in table 8.3 separately for men with and without a history of incarceration and with and without high school diplomas. Comparison groups are too small to sustain formal analysis, but the pattern is striking: blacks suffer a larger penalty both as dropouts and for incarceration. For instance, 84 percent of white dropouts with no record of incarceration were employed full time at age twenty-two and had worked on average 80 percent of the months since high school; for those with a history of incarceration, the figures are 39 percent and 34 percent. Of black dropouts with no incarcerations, only 40 percent were employed full time and they had worked on average 48 percent of the months since high school. For those with a history of incarceration, the figures are 15 percent and 22 percent, about as low as one can imagine.

At age twenty-eight, with the incarceration histories updated and a longer interval for differences in employment to materialize, employment rates for blacks and whites who stay out of trouble are fairly similar. Not so for those who run afoul of the law. White high school dropouts with a criminal record were employed 56 percent of the months since age twenty-two, blacks 47 percent. At age twenty-eight, 54 percent of whites and 33 percent of blacks were employed full time, and the hourly draw of whites was double that of blacks, $20.00 versus $10.42.

To be young, black, and a dropout in today's economy is trebly disadvantaging, and a criminal record adds another strike. Many employers harbor stereotyped doubts about the work ethic and reliability of young African American men (Moss and Tilly 2001). Joleen Kirschenman and Kathryn Neckerman (1991, 185) document the "halo" that attaches to whiteness in this context. In their survey of inner-city firms in and around Chicago, employers often drew social class distinctions when discussing blacks and generalized from neighborhood of residence. Rarely did they do either when discussing whites: "Employers . . . talked about Cabrini Green or the Robert Taylor Homes, or referred to the South Side and the West Side as shorthand for black, but they were not likely to make those distinctions among whites and Hispanics" (Kirschenman and Neckerman 1991, 217). Prospective employers also are less likely to inquire about a criminal record for a white applicant (Holzer, Raphael, and Stoll 2004).

A like point is made by Philip Kasinitz and Jan Rosenberg (1996, 191), who studied hiring practices in Brooklyn's Red Hook waterfront neighborhood: "residents in the housing projects are excluded from many jobs . . . based on race, address, fear of criminality and employer's perceptions about work habits." When employers are reluctant to hire African Americans in the noncollege labor market, including the construction trades, lower-SES whites benefit.

Among Youth Panel men at age twenty-two with clean records and a high school diploma, blacks and whites have the same employment rate of 89 percent. Among dropouts, though, the white rate is twice the black: 84 percent versus 40 percent. Over the next six years, 5 percent of white dropouts acquire a criminal record against 40 percent of black dropouts. The challenges African Americans without a high school degree and with a spotty employment history encounter in finding steady, well-paid licit work no doubt contribute to these different life trajectories.

Social Capital in the Family and Workplace

Social capital as an attainment resource currently is much in favor. Indeed, James Coleman and Thomas Hoffer (1987) contend that children's academic development now is influenced more by family social capital resources than by traditional markers of socioeconomic advantage and disadvantage. Whether that balance holds is unclear, but Coleman and Hoffer are quite correct that parents of limited means can help their children perform well in school (see Elder et al. 1995; Furstenberg et al. 1999). But what of lower-SES children who do not excel in the classroom and cannot look to advance through higher education, are their parents bereft of useful social capital?

For *The Long Shadow*, family help accessing lucrative blue-collar employment is a substantial asset, and whites have an edge. In an earlier era, this bias was quite public, and no doubt considered normal: "many skilled trade unions perpetuated a father-son tradition recruiting new workers through family connection" (Sugrue 2004, 158). In 1946, all thirty-two apprentices of a local chapter of the International Brotherhood of Electrical Workers were sons or nephews of union members and 40 percent of Philadelphia plumbers had sons in the trade (Sugrue 2004). Those kinds of job exclusions in principle are long gone, but survive sub rosa. Returning to the Brooklyn waterfront, Kasinitz and Rosenberg (1996, 187) tell us that "industries typically hire primarily on the basis of referrals, often from the current workers." As one informant says, "'basically it's all word of mouth. We don't advertise at all'" (quoting an oil transport company executive).

In Baltimore it was, and remains, much the same. Deborah Rudacille (2010) tells how, during the boom years, employment at Beth Steel commonly was a family affair: "my aunt . . . went to work in the receiving office after graduating from . . . [high school] in 1956, joining her father, brother and mother on the Beth Steel payroll. . . . after 2 years in the Air Force, [her uncle] too found a job at the Point." The social capital that helped open doors was not limited to the work site. Karen Olson (2005) describes a bar culture outside the gates of Beth Steel that fostered worker solidarity off the job, "a masculine ritual that was obligatory for steelworkers." One of her informants captures the sense of it: "drinking together . . . created more harmony than the union hall did."

White Working-Class Neighborhood Advantage

Neighborhood is another bastion of white working-class advantage. As seen in chapter 4, Baltimore's blue-collar residential enclaves are effectively closed communities, set off from other neighborhoods by man-made or natural barriers. But it is not just their geography that keeps these neighborhoods closed. As recounted recently by a resident of Baltimore's Little Italy, "It's hard to find properties for sale here because we're still a word-of-mouth market—'I heard Rosa is selling her house.'"[9]

As documented here, Baltimore's lower-SES white neighborhoods also have much lower crime rates than lower-SES black neighborhoods do and are viewed by their residents as much more cohesive. It is hard to separate cause from effect, but the stronger sense of community evident in these white neighborhoods involves more than their physical isolation. Assaults on community life (chapter 4) have undermined the community infrastructure of Baltimore's black working class, including urban renewal projects and the scars of the urban disorder of the 1960s.

It is useful to be reminded that in even the most distressed black neighborhoods, the majority of residents are "decent folk" who live by the rules and strive to lead respectable lives (Anderson 2000), yet crime and the fear of it weakens conventional social capital in these communities. Strong role models may be in short supply, the institutional infrastructure is weak, and, of most immediate relevance, bridges to good job opportunities in the wider world are in short supply.

These conditions do not always split cleanly along lines of race, but that tendency is reinforced by unyielding racial segregation at the neighborhood level (Massey and Denton 1993). Baltimore's urban ecology burdens blacks more than whites in their daily interactions and social networks, fostering conditions ripe for drawing boundaries between insiders and outsiders:

> Geographical separation makes it easier for the majority of families to perceive the minority of public dependents as "the other"—as a moral threat . . . as well as an economic burden. The core of Baltimore City is shared by a greater than average proportion of abandoned wives, unwed mothers, the unemployed and the underemployed, the scared and the maimed, high school dropouts, alcoholics. . . . A further guarantee of the sense of "otherness" is that the core population is 84 percent black. (Olson 1976, 23)

Baltimore was neighborhood-centric in the mid-1970s when Olson was writing and remains so today. Thus, when prospective employers invoke *neighborhood* as code for *black*, it is not an association that augurs well. Lower-SES whites are concentrated in what remains of Baltimore's high-skill, high-pay, blue-collar workforce for two reasons: they have better access to useful social networks in family, their wider social circle, and their neighborhoods; they are also less burdened by stereotyped negative identities, including those attached to so-called problem behaviors.

White Privilege in Modern Guise

Our analysis shows that today's white privilege is embedded in "the way things work," a tougher and more subtle kind of disadvantage to counteract. As Eduardo Bonilla-Silva (1996, 470) puts it, "the racial practices and mechanisms that have kept blacks subordinated changed from overtly and eminently racist to covert and indirectly racist." Examples can be found in just about every sphere of life, including everyday commercial interactions (such as buying a car), hailing a taxicab, and dining out (Siegelman 1999). In one application of the audit methodology, testers with similar background profiles (such as age, education, and appearance) and bargaining scripts were sent to local car dealerships. After negotiations, the asking price for black men for the same vehicle was $1,600 above the price set for white men; for women, the difference was $400. In a paired tester study of taxicabs in the Washington, D.C., whites were about 11 percent more likely than blacks to get a cab and blacks waited 27 percent longer (5.7 minutes versus 4.5).

Racial discrimination in the housing and rental markets is documented in matched tester studies conducted by the U.S. Department of Housing and Urban Development (the 1977 Housing Market Practices Study, the 1989 Housing Discrimination Study and the Housing Discrimination Study 2000, summarized in Turner et al. 2002). Whites and blacks supplied with identical backgrounds visited real estate sales offices or responded to newspaper advertisements to inquire about rental properties or buying a home. In one study involving 4,600 paired tests in twenty-three cities, rental agents were found to engage in discriminatory practices in 22 percent of the cases, sales agents in 17 percent. Blacks sometimes were told that properties were unavailable when white seekers were shown the property; often blacks and whites were shown properties in, or steered to, different neighborhoods.

A study of banking practices in more than sixty U.S. cities finds much the same, African Americans being more than twice as likely as whites to be denied a home loan. In Chicago and Milwaukee, blacks were four times more likely to be turned down, and wealthy blacks were rejected twice as often as whites with similar assets (Bergquist 2001). African Americans face the greatest barriers when applying for credit to live in high-income white neighborhoods (Holloway and Wyly 2001).

Employment is the domain of most immediate relevance (see, for example, Bendick, Jackson, and Reinoso 1994). With the same level of labor market experience, credentials, and overall quality of resume, applicants with white-sounding names (such as Emily Walsh or Brendan Baker) received 50 percent more callbacks than applicants with black-sounding names (such as Lakisha Washington or Jamal Jones). In fact, applicants with black names and high-quality résumés received no more callbacks than whites with low-quality résumés (Bertrand and Mullainathan 2004).

Race also affects which applicants receive job offers. In a matched pair study conducted by the Fair Employment Council, one in four employers was found to discriminate in hiring (Job Opportunities Task Force 2003; Annie E. Casey Foundation 2001). Forty-seven percent of white job candidates who were interviewed received job offers against 11 percent of blacks. White job applicants were offered higher starting salaries and more often advised of other job openings with better pay and benefits. Extending this line of research, Devah Pager (2007) finds that for black applicants in the low-wage labor market, a criminal record is more detrimental than for white applicants (for more detail see Gosa and Alexander 2007; Pager and Shepherd 2008).

In the sample, as elsewhere, the surface impression is that the significance of race has declined, but lower-SES white men are a privileged class of workers. Their work might not appeal to those in the high-tech, highly credentialed professional workforce, but that world has little relevance for them. In their world, lower-SES white men are helped through superior on-the-job and off-the-job contacts, a highly gendered division of labor, and employer preferences for whites over blacks in the noncollege labor market. These advantages do not convert to high socioeconomic standing overall but show up instead in the paycheck. School is incidental. This is an account of white male privilege in the workplace, though white women also benefit, derivatively as wives and partners.

Women, Work, and Mobility Through Marriage

The gender divide in employment across job sectors is pronounced, and women's work is concentrated in the characteristically low-wage pink-collar sales, clerical, and service sectors (chapter 6). Clerical and services account for 66 percent of African American women's full-time employment and 53 percent of white women's, and neither group has much presence in the high-pay skilled construction crafts. With this backdrop, it hardly surprises that women's earnings lag behind men's, and more so among the urban disadvantaged than overall.

A history of gendered exclusion and current conditions continue to channel disadvantaged women into low-wage work. Although some achieve higher earnings through marriage and partnering, many are cut off from both routes to material well-being. The experience among the sample in this respect is the national picture in microcosm: the feminization of poverty, driven by increases in never-married and single parenting. Growth in the number and percentage of female-headed households are estimated to account for between 11 percent and 41 percent of the rise in income inequality nationally (McLanahan and Percheski 2008, 259). The implications for upward mobility are unmistakable: "If having two earners is critical to the economic success of many of today's families, then this decline [in marriage rates], by depriving many families of a second earner, has reduced economic mobility" (Isaacs 2008, 3). Additionally, "for women, there is an additional route to upward mobility beyond earning a good income: marrying well" (5).

Many women today, however, do not marry well, or even at all. Among those with a high school education or less, 30 percent more blacks than whites are single mothers, a disparity seen as far back as 1980 (McLanahan and Percheski 2008, 259). Between 1980 and 2009, the percentage of births to unmarried women more than doubled, from 20 percent of all births to more than 40 percent (Autor and Wasserman 2013, 33). This plays out in two ways to undercut African American women's economic well-being: at age twenty-eight, fewer are in unions (25 percent versus 52 percent of white women) and more are mothering alone (37 percent, including 45 percent of lower-SES African American women, versus 10 percent, of whites). The depressed earnings that follow is seen nationally as well (Attewell et al. 2004).

Almost half the sample follow the fast track into adulthood (chapter 5). By age twenty-eight, they have "done it all"—married or partnered, become parents, worked full time, and lived apart from their parents. This profile applies to 66 percent of lower-SES white women, but also to 50 percent of lower-SES African Americans, so these differences in family life are quantitative, not qualitative. Still, parenting alone is a burden borne disproportionately by African American women: just 5.1 percent of the sample are parenting alone and living on their own, but lower-SES African American women make up 47 percent of that total and lower-SES white women only 6 percent.

Women of lower-SES origins value children. For many, parenting is central to who they are (for example, Edin and Kefalas 2005), but owing to a depleted pool of desirable marriage prospects, few are disposed to hold off parenthood in the hope of finding a reliable partner. According to Wilson (1978), concentrated poverty leaves many inner-city neighborhoods distressed and the marriage-age men in them scarred by high rates of incarceration, poor employment prospects, and—when they are working—low wages (Autor and Wasserman 2013, 20–21). Consider this: in 2003, 25 percent of African American men ages twenty to thirty-four did not work at any time during the year. Even worse, for those in central cities without a high school diploma or GED, the figure was 44.4 percent (Sum et al. 2004). The consequences are clear: "All the studies show that male unemployment or underemployment has a large negative effect on union formation and stability" (McLanahan and Percheski 2008, 262).

High rates of arrest and incarceration also factor into the equation. Kerwin Charles and Ming Ching Luoh (2010) estimate that a 1 percent increase in the male incarceration rate reduces the probability of women's ever marrying by 1 percent, and the deterrent effect is strongest for women with low levels of schooling (high school or less). In 1970, fewer than 5 percent of black men ages twenty-five to thirty-nine with a high school degree were in prison; in 2010, the figure was 26 percent (Autor and Wasserman 2013, 31), and of those without a degree, 37.1 percent in 2008 (Pew Charitable Trusts 2010, 8).

Limited job prospects and incarceration as deterrents to marriage are hardly separable: young men drawn into the criminal justice system—be it by way of arrest, conviction, or incarceration—face impaired economic prospects (Pew Charitable Trusts 2010; Schmitt, Warner, and Gupta 2010). It is disproportionately African American men with low levels of schooling who suffer this "perfect storm" (Smeeding, Garfinkel, and Mincy 2011, 8–9), which has predictable implications for their partners and children.[10]

The ecology of neighborhood life also likely contributes to African American women's depressed marriage rates, though this is harder to document. As children, lower-SES blacks and whites in the Baltimore sample lived in neighborhoods practically indistinguishable across a range of census criteria, but in other respects their communities were worlds apart: poor black neighborhoods had much higher crime rates and much weaker social cohesion. Many residents in such neighborhoods insulate themselves by withdrawing from public space into the safety of the home. Given lower neighborhood crime rates and stronger community cohesion, it likely is easier for lower-SES whites to establish network ties useful in the workplace, and perhaps even more intimate ties—life partners are not found exclusively in high school biology labs and college mixers.

Summary

The vast difference in the economic well-being of lower-SES white and black women in the Youth Panel traces to three considerations. First, these women, black and white, earn much less on average than do men owing to persistent patterns of workforce gender segregation. Second, as young adults, more white women than African American women are married or living in partnerships, which provides for a second earner in the household. Third, for those in unions, the spouses or partners of white women earn appreciably more than those of African American women. The second and third considerations point to characteristic differences in family life that close the circle of white privilege: when lower-SES white men earn more, their partners benefit.

Consider this insight from E. J. Dionne (2013) in a column on recent advances in the legalization of same-sex marriage: "Well-off Americans are far more likely to be in stable marriages than are the less affluent. This creates a damaging social cycle—economic inequality is breeding family instability even as family instability is breeding economic inequality." Although not all of America's less affluent are trapped in this downward spiral, Dionne has the tendency exactly right. In other parts of the country, the context might be high-poverty Native American or (some) Hispanic communities, but in Baltimore, low-income African American women are most vulnerable.

═ Chapter 9 ═

Life-Course Perspective of Urban Disadvantage

T HIS BOOK is about the reproduction of social advantage and disadvantage across generations in the experience of typical Baltimore youth, anchored in their childhood and extending into their late twenties. For most, their socioeconomic status as adults is about what it was when they were children, but their sense of their lives today is not simply a matter of how far they have gone through school or their workplace success. For disadvantaged youth growing up in a city with one of the nation's highest homicide rates (*The Atlantic* 2011), the clichéd "life, liberty and pursuit of happiness" is not to be taken for granted.

"I think I'm successful now, because I'm happy, you know. I don't have a lot of money, you know. You know, I live paycheck to paycheck, but I'm happy. Because I come home every day to the person I want to be with, you know. I pick up the phone, my parents are still there if I need to talk to them, or if I want to talk to them. . . . I'm happy, I'm comfortable." [Ken]

"I think my parents are successful. I mean, they're not rich or anything, but . . . They were successful as far as, like, raising all those children, you know. And, you know, even though we did, like, some things, you know, nobody did anything real major, and we all, we all still alive, you know. All of us, still alive." [Dilan]

That at least twenty-six of the Beginning School Study Youth Panel (BSSYP, or Youth Panel) never made it to age twenty-eight is context for Ken's and Dilan's standards of success.[1] To "be happy" and to be "still alive" are sentiments that came up often in our discussions, including from Floyd, as recounted in the first chapter. High socioeconomic standing defined around accomplishment on the job and at school is not requisite for a fulfilling life. It is useful to be reminded of that, yet the issues addressed in this volume also have resonance for members of the Youth Panel. We know because they told us so.

Table 9.1   Reflections on Life's Trajectory

SES Family Origin	SES Family Destination	% "Life Much Better"[a]	Satisfaction Level[b]
Lower (N)		65 (309)	2.9 (313)
	Lower (N)	52 (137)	2.7 (140)
	Mid-Level (N)	74 (139)	3.0 (140)
	Higher (N)	81 (33)	3.2 (33)
Higher (N)		81 (150)	3.1 (153)
	Lower (N)	67 (18)	2.3 (19)
	Mid-Level (N)	68 (57)	3.0 (59)
	Higher (N)	93 (75)	3.5 (75)
Overall (N)[c]		70 (608)	3.0 (616)

Source: Authors' compilation.
[a]Item: How much better or worse has your life been getting since high school?
Response options: much worse; hasn't changed much; much better.
[b]Item: How satisfied are you with the way your life has gone since high school?
Response options: 1, very dissatisfied; 2, somewhat dissatisfied; 3, somewhat satisfied; 4, very satisfied.
[c]Overall includes middle SES group.

When they were age twenty-eight, we asked them, "How much better has your life been getting since high school?" (see table 9.1). Among those of lower socioeconomic status (SES), the percentage replying "Much Better" is highest, at 81 percent, among those who rose to higher-SES destinations. For those at a middle status destination, the figure is 74 percent, and for those who remained urban disadvantaged across generations, 52 percent. The upwardly mobile realize they have advanced and feel better about their circumstances, yet most of those stably disadvantaged across generations also view their lives as improved, seeing, correctly, that there is more to life than SES standing and SES mobility.

The pattern is much the same at the other end of the origins distribution. Of those urban advantaged at the outset, 93 percent who maintained their higher standing reply "Much Better"; among those who slipped to middle- and lower-status destinations, the figures are 68 percent and 67 percent. Here too, status privilege preserved across generations wins out, but most of the downwardly mobile also respond favorably.

A second question asked, "How satisfied are you with the way your life has gone since high school?" Answers were coded 1 (very unsatisfied) to 4 (very satisfied). The overall sample average is 3.0, somewhat satisfied, but the downwardly mobile (2.3) and those intergenerationally stable at the lower end (2.7) are least satisfied with how their lives have unfolded; those upwardly mobile from lower-SES origins to higher (3.2) and intergenerationally stable at the higher end (3.5) are most satisfied.[2]

This orderliness is striking: the sense of well-being among the sample as young adults is tempered by their place in the status hierarchy and their mobility histories. Although our agenda is also theirs, whether they could articulate the mechanisms behind these moves up and down the social ladder with the same clarity is dubious. To understand the what, the how, and the why of their mobility experience, *The Long Shadow* has probed conditions and experiences behind the panel's divergent life paths.

Status Attainment Through School and Other Means

Until now, relatively little research on disadvantaged youth has focused on the early life course, yet we see that the reproduction of disadvantage can be forecast with some fidelity even before children reach age six. For children already behind academically at the start of first grade, following the recommended path to fulfill the American Dream will not be easy: to get a good education as the way to realize their potential. Even so, most accept the truth of that prescription, likely not realizing how rare it is for children "like them" to move up this way: 59 percent of lower-SES boys in the sample were held back in first grade, fewer than half completed school with a regular high school diploma or above (49.6 percent), and less than 5 percent earned an associate's or bachelor's degree. Despite all this, the notion that school is the way to get ahead in life is so widely diffused that at age twenty-eight more than 80 percent of the sample expected to get more education. Indeed, many tried to advance through school, but most of the urban disadvantaged among them fell short.

The analysis in chapter 7 identified numerous risk factors and resources that contribute to mobility up and down the status hierarchy. They are potential means to advancement in that disadvantaged children who have strong family support, avoid debilitating neighborhood and school conditions, have access to resources that help them do well in school, and do their part by building on those resources and excelling academically, are likely to move up. But how many of the urban disadvantaged profit from such a propitious developmental history and how far along the SES gradient does this uncommonly favorable set of circumstances carry them? The answers, it seems, are "not many" and "not far." In the sample, the urban disadvantaged who advance to the next stage of life with postsecondary credentials of any sort are a tiny fraction of the total. For the rest, the promise of upward mobility through educational success has proven to be an empty one.

With much attention centered on school reform as the way out of poverty and the interior elements of our analytic framework demonstrably important, can we not do better? Unfortunately, it is hard to be optimistic. Against calls for universal preschool (Badger 2013) and evidence that high-quality preschool can make a tangible difference in poor children's lives (Barnett 2008), we learn that 2012 was the worst year in a decade for preschool funding, state appropriations dropping from $4,284 per enrolled child in 2011 to $3,841 in 2012 (Holt 2013). More broadly, federal spending in support of children declined altogether between 2010 and 2011, cuts that hit K–12 funding especially hard (Isaacs et al. 2012).[3]

Dollars in and of themselves are not transformative, but dollars wisely spent can be. People of means understand that and act on that understanding, investing much more in their children's enrichment than low-income parents do (Duncan and Murnane 2011; Kaushal, Magnuson, and Waldfogel 2011). If there is to be greater balance against highly educated and higher-income parents' resources, it will have to come from public investments, but K–12 educational expenditures favor children in higher-income communities over lower (Arroyo 2008) and tuition subsidies are more generous in selective colleges and universities than in schools catering to needy students (Carnevale and Strohl 2010). This is backdrop to Sean Reardon's observation that "Whatever we've been doing in our schools, it hasn't reduced educational inequality between children from upper- and lower-income families. . . . we should take a lesson from the rich and invest much more heavily as a society in our children's educational opportunities from the day they are born" ("No Rich Child Left Behind," *New York Times*, April 27, 2013, p. SR1).

Transmission of Advantage by Way of Family

Reardon, we suspect, intends "from the day they are born" to be taken literally. The urban disadvantaged find themselves on the short side of stratified inequalities long before they cross the threshold on the first day of school (see, for example, Farkas and Beron 2004; Hart and Risley 1995). Over time, those stratified origins conditions carry them to stratified destinations. Rodgers and Hammerstein's folk wisdom in their musical *South Pacific* has it exactly right:

> You've got to be taught before it's too late,
> Before you are six or seven or eight.

These lyrics about racial prejudice hold just as well for the broader idea of learning (and finding) one's place in the social order. As noted, almost 75 percent of the higher-SES children in the sample expected to finish college when first asked in fourth grade and on every later occasion through twelfth grade. Fewer than 25 percent of lower-SES background youth were similarly sanguine (Bozick et al. 2010).

Schooling aspirations are one way the long shadow channels children along different life paths. For the sample, first grade is when school enters the picture, and school makes a difference. Children are in both school and family during the school year, but during the summer months, when school is closed, their learning is wholly dependent on family and experiences outside school that flow from family. The literature on the seasonality of learning establishes that children from disadvantaged families come close to keeping up academically when school is in session, but do not advance over the long summer break when the school's resources are cut off (Entwisle, Alexander, and Olson 1997; Downey, von Hippel, and Broh 2004; Heyns 1978).

Schooling in that sense promotes greater equality. Disadvantaged children's learning the kinds of skills tapped by standardized achievement tests, at least during the foundational early grades, depends more on school than higher-SES children's learning does. For them, the early school curriculum matches the home curriculum. Still, specific resources and experiences that are advantageous for children's schooling tend to mirror family advantage. This web of advantaging resources is not easily parsed. We have not attempted to do so, but from many studies, including our own, we know that parents' support for children's schooling, children's academic engagement and attitudes, children's achievement test scores and report card marks, and structural or track placements in school all tend to follow SES lines. This volume adds evidence that their relevance for socioeconomic destinations in adulthood extends as far back as first grade.

Some of the most powerful of these resources are situated in the family, as in parents' expectations for their children's school performance (psychological capital); others are within the child (achievement aspirations, work habits, and attitudes). Still others are institutional, such as the school's academic climate, socioeconomic mix, and educational tracking. Children of privilege not only perform better in school than disadvantaged children do, they also benefit from educationally advantageous structural placements. Being easily observed and appearing to be meritocratic, that visibility has the effect of both preserving and legitimating the high standing attained by children of privilege and the low standing of those less well off.

This process of cumulative advantage-disadvantage spans the entire timeline of children's academic careers. Youth of privileged family circumstances start out ahead in first grade and their family advantage helps smooth their path all along the way. As David Baker and David

Stevenson (1986, 165) put it, "Parents must do a series of small [and not so small] things to assist their child toward maximum educational attainment." Higher-SES parents are good role models and effective advocates of their children's interests. They seek out safe neighborhoods, good schools, and favorable program placements within those schools. No one of these acts is itself determinant, but together they help move higher-SES children along the path to success. By contrast, lower-SES children labor under the burden of cumulative disadvantage imposed by their location in the SES hierarchy. Their parents want them to succeed in school and after, but most lack the means to help them do so.

It is much the same with the role of school in children's development. There is no simple or single solution to children's academic challenges. Rather, small influences cumulate to produce large and lasting consequences. The best preschools, for example, provide a short-term boost that leads to improved achievement that lasts several years, reduces the risk of grade retention, and increases parents' satisfaction with their children's school performance (see, for example, Barnett 2008). Martin Woodhead (1988, 447–48) outlined the process some twenty-five years ago: "If during the early grades these children were seen as smarter and more adjusted to the demands of the school, this could have been sufficient to trigger a more positive cycle of achievement and expectation . . . [and] carry the child through the later grades long after the original cognitive benefits had washed out." In other words, the school's and parents' responses to preschooled children when their achievement is temporarily elevated yields long-term benefits, including reduced odds of high school dropout and welfare dependency and enhanced odds of employment (Barnett and Belfield 2006; Schweinhart and Weikart 1997; Ou and Reynolds 2006).

The small-scale intervention projects that support these conclusions have high internal validity—that is, the lasting benefits that are conferred by a high-quality preschool experience appear to be quite real—but those potential benefits too often bypass poor children. They are less likely than middle-class children are to attend high-quality center-based preschools (Huston and Bentley 2010) and the potential benefits of a strong preschool experience are not realized when poor children later transition to high poverty, under-resourced elementary schools (Lee and Loeb 1995).

We believe that help at strategic points could boost prospects for more of the urban disadvantaged to get ahead through school. For disadvantaged children, however, the school improvement agenda typically is served à la carte or piecemeal. Many reforms have been tried and some of them hold great promise, but as a society we have yet to implement those reforms systematically in concert and with a sustained commitment. Our suggestions for the list pre-K through high school include:

a serious assault on the residential isolation that relegates many urban disadvantaged children to hypersegregated, hyperpoverty neighborhoods (Schwartz 2010);

quality preschools and related parent involvement initiatives (Haskins and Rouse 2005);

smaller classes (Krueger and Whitmore 2002) and possibly smaller schools (Bryk et al. 2010; Toch 2010);[4]

high-quality, engaging summer school and after-school programs (Borman and Boulay 2004);

highly qualified, well-prepared, well-supported, and committed teachers (Ferguson 1998; Hanushek 2004; Darling-Hammond 2010);

high academic standards paired with strong curricula (Ravitch 2010);

the supports that make high academic standards attainable (Bryk, Lee, and Holland 1993);

meaningful school integration across SES levels (Kahlenberg 2001);

a classroom environment that respects children's background and builds on their strengths (Boykin 1986); and

an it-takes-a-village mindset that addresses children's and their parents' needs beyond the classroom (Quane and Wilson 2011).

The Years After High School: College for Some

The years after high school play out the legacy of earlier disparities. Among the Baltimore sample, for raising occupational status, the large jump is between high school and the associate's degree (table 9.2). For increasing earnings, it is between the associate's and bachelor's degrees. Investments in schooling short of college, however, yield little return: those with general educational development (GED) certificates fare little better than high school dropouts, and those with certificates and licenses fare little better than terminal high school graduates.

The most certain route to higher socioeconomic standing is higher education. Months of enrollment since high school in a degree-granting institution trump all else, and by a considerable margin. Ironically, though investing in college apparently yields the greatest payoff for those whose background profile does not forecast college completion (Brand and Xie 2010; Hout 2012), children of advantaged background have the advantage in college completion—it is a large advantage at that, and it is they who claim a disproportionate share of the benefit.

Table 9.2   Occupational Status and Earnings

	Occupational Status (SEI)			Median Earnings ($1,000s)[d]		
	Overall	Whites	Blacks	Overall	Whites	Blacks
High school dropout	26.1	27.8	24.4	23.4	26.0	18.1
GED	26.5	26.7	26.3	24.0	29.5	21.5
High school graduate	30.9	30.3	31.4	29.6	30.0	28.0
Certificate-license	29.5	30.9	28.9	26.7	26.0	26.8
Associate's degree	38.1	40.4[a]	36.9	25.0	30.0[a]	23.0
Bachelor's degree	46.7	46.0	47.6	37.5	40.0	37.0
Master's degree	55.5	54.8	—[c]	40.0	40.0	—[c]
Doctoral or professional degree	74.0	72.8[b]	—[c]	52.5	50.0[b]	—[c]
(N)	(555)	(252)	(303)	(559)	(253)	(306)

Source: Authors' compilation.
Note: At age twenty-eight. Other than sample size, figures are percentages.
[a]Based on six observations.
[b]Based on five observations.
[c]Percentage not reported, based on fewer than five observations.
[d]Zero earnings are excluded.

The urban disadvantaged mostly enter adulthood without strong academic credentials. By age twenty-two, most dropouts in the sample, disproportionately lower-SES men, had come to regret their decision to leave school, and the majority, as nationally (Barton 2005), tried to do something about it. Some returned to school for a regular high school diploma, but most—90 percent—achieved high school certification by way of the GED. It is impressive that so many dropouts avail themselves of second chance opportunities, but the GED does not pay off as well as a regular high school diploma (Entwisle, Alexander, and Olson 2004; Cameron and Heckman 1993) and very few dropouts, whether permanent or recovered, make it to college.

Martha Bailey and Susan Dynarski (2011) review the remarkable expansion of postsecondary access between 1920 and 2000. They find that baccalaureate enrollments and completions both increased impressively, but also that the gap between them increased as well, with the disadvantaged, as in the sample, most prone to stop short: "Even if rates of college entry were miraculously equalized across income groups, existing differences in persistence would still produce large gaps in college completion" (Bailey and Dynarski 2011, 128). One reason is that low-income and disadvantaged minority youth who make it to college face distributional disadvantages: they disproportionately enroll in two-year colleges and less selective four-year colleges, where levels of noncompletion are scandalously high and public investments are much lower (Carnevale and Strohl 2010).

Most of the urban disadvantaged who finished high school with a regular diploma do continue in school, but their failed attempts at higher education outnumber their successes and the successes mostly are in certificate and licensure programs, which benefit them little. For many of them, overcoming academic challenge is not the only hurdle and may not be the most formidable one. First-generation, low-income college students often are workers first and students second and have family responsibilities. They might work hard to cobble together finances for a semester or two, and then stop out for a time when the money runs out or when family obligations intrude—a parent or sibling in need, a child sick. Tami, from chapter 7, exemplifies their challenges. At age twenty-eight, she was still without her associate's degree despite three enrollment spells. Multiply her experience manyfold and we can understand why so few of the urban disadvantaged are able to take the fast track through college. Many lower-SES college-goers invest years, often many years, in pursuit of a college degree with little to show for their sacrifices.

To the extent that school policy and practice can help smooth the path, a good starter set would include more generous targeted financial aid (preferably grants over loans, perhaps with a public service payback option) and stronger support systems and integration practices to draw commuter students into campus life (Bozick 2007; Tinto 1994). Women, especially, need child care. All need better transfer policies, more off-hour classes (evenings and weekends), and more flexible schedules. Two-year colleges do many of these things already (Brock 2010; Goldrick-Rab and Roksa 2008), but need to do them better and like initiatives are needed at four-year institutions.

Helping young people do what they already are disposed to do in the realm of schooling certainly holds greater promise than trying to persuade them to do things they are not disposed to do, like waiting to parent. A shortfall of schooling, however, is not the only impediment to getting ahead. Impediments to employment loom large as well.

Employment as a Developmental Resource

Like minority adults (Tienda and Stier 1996), minority teens in Baltimore experience more frequent episodes of joblessness than white teens do. The slower and less regular rates at which African American youth enter the labor market before leaving school may lead to deficits in human capital overlooked by studies that address only labor force activity after high school (Ahituv et al. 1994) and even cause problems in the adult labor market that are now attributed to school deficits. The inability of minorities to work regularly as teens could lead to labor market disadvantages in the same way that experience deficits create disadvantage in the labor market for adults (Clogg, Eliason, and Wahl 1990).

Employment in high school boosts the odds of later employment for men of both races, a circumstance that provides a strong rationale for taking steps to ensure more work for high school students who are not college bound, especially African Americans (Entwisle, Alexander, and Olson 2010b). Mentoring programs (Holzer 2009; Sara Neufield and John Fritze, "City Funds Sought for Peer Education," *Baltimore Sun,* April 26, 2008) and so-called career academies (Kemple and Scott-Clayton 2004) are promising examples of programs already in use.

For disadvantaged youth, who often are responsible for their own support and that of others, finding work quickly is critical. Stretching out the time making the transition from school to work is a luxury they cannot afford, but typically they get little or no help from their high schools (Bishop 1989; Kerckhoff 2003). For middle-class youth, a gap year or two after college will not depreciate the value of their educational credentials. Not so for the disadvantaged. Employers tend to assume that men from less affluent backgrounds need work, so a failure to work signals a lack of motivation, poor work ethic, or even lack of ability. Idleness builds negative capital—it erodes the value of these men's educational credentials and other assets.

For these reasons and others, it is troublesome that lower-SES African American men register rates of idleness so much higher than their white counterparts. Although not usually thought of in these terms, this workplace employment gap trajectory is much like the test score–achievement gap trajectory seen in school achievement—a fan pattern, starting small and expanding over time. The labor market disability of young African American men over the adult transition has multiple sources, including problem encounters with the law, employer bias, segregated neighborhoods, unremitting poverty, and family instability. We suspect the single most effective countermeasure would be quality jobs starting in adolescence.

Contingencies Along the Path to Adulthood

How life unfolds after high school—continuing in school, holding a job, marrying or partnering, becoming a parent, a focus on family rather than career, avoidance of substance use and problem encounters with the law—may be thought of as discrete events, but from a life-course perspective it is how they come together that situates young adults in social space, including socioeconomic space. Problem behaviors potentially are obstacles in both school and labor market, especially for the African American urban disadvantaged. White men, of both lower and higher SES, evidence problem behavior profiles much like those of African Americans, but less often suffer adverse consequences. Likewise, most lower-SES white women in the sample become parents at an early age, but more often parent in unions, and so to some extent are shielded from the economic hardship many African American women face. For the Baltimore study, these issues come into play largely through the exclusion of black men from high-quality blue-collar jobs, which brings us to the second path for getting ahead seen in this volume.

A Different Kind of Advantage: Blue-Collar Earnings Attainment

Another widely held success narrative centers on race: most Americans "believe that a black person today has the same chance of getting a job as an equally qualified white person" (Pager and Shepherd 2008, 186). This account spans at least three decades (Wilson 2010, 204–5), but for reasons that trace back even longer, it does not hold for prospects in the noncollege labor market.

The exclusion of blacks from high-skill, high-wage employment is rooted in Jim Crow and resistance to integration and is sustained through tradition, word-of-mouth network hiring, and employer attitudes. Also, although disinvestment and job loss have affected neighborhoods throughout the city, Baltimore's black neighborhoods have suffered more from urban renewal displacement, the scars left behind by the urban riots of the 1960s, and residential instability associated with single-parent poverty. This confluence of forces has left low-income black neighborhoods weakened, fractured, and more vulnerable to predatory crime. Of most immediate relevance, network ties useful for finding work are less abundant in these poor neighborhoods; also, when neighborhood residence is used by employers as a screen for applicants, it is low-income African Americans who lose out.

This history is backdrop to the advantage white working-class parents have over African American parents in helping their children find good jobs, that is, strong ties through kin and friendship networks, as well as weak ties (such as friends of friends or supervisors on the job). Learning of job openings from a friend, neighbor, or patron of the corner bar are manifestations of parental social capital that surface as soon as teens start looking for work.[5] It also comes about through the gatekeeper behavior of high school guidance counselors who favor their white technical high school graduates over African American students (Royster 2003) and through the behavior of employers who favor white applicants over equally qualified black applicants (Pager, Western, and Bonikowski 2009).

We have seen that more lower-SES black men in Baltimore are obliged to find work on their own and their employment histories are spotty. When they do work, it is more often in the low-wage laborer and service sectors. The contrast with lower-SES white men is telling. Despite a broadly similar problem behavior profile, whites are able to access well-paid jobs in the construction trades, a benefit outside the status attainment-through-schooling paradigm.

These advantages also are gendered because lower-SES white and black women also lack access to well-paid work. Recent employment breakthroughs by college-educated women in management and the professions hold little relevance for disadvantaged women, who remain concentrated in the low-wage service, clerical, and retail sectors. But lower-SES white women have one advantage that their African American counterparts do not: spouses and partners with higher earnings. Lower-SES white women are at parity with lower-SES white men in terms of family earnings, not so lower-SES African American women, fewer of whom marry or enter into stable partnerships, which means no two-earner family boost.

Mitigating Blue-Collar Attainment Disadvantage

Schooling plays a large role in perpetuating socioeconomic privilege across generations for even modestly higher-SES youth, but white working-class privilege is sustained across generations by a very different set of forces. Ensuring that working-class blacks have jobs of the same quality as working-class whites poses large challenges. The feminization of poverty is another burden, one that weighs especially on African American women and their children. Policies to encourage marriage and delay childbearing (such as the Bush administration's Healthy Marriage Initiative) do not have an especially distinguished record of success and the safety net for single mothers in the United States is weak (for background, see Rector and Pardue 2004).[6] Absent a deeper pool of African American men with good employment opportunities, the prospects for fundamental change seem poor.

A stronger social safety net can mitigate the economic hardship associated with single parenting (see, for example, Rainwater and Smeeding 2004), but the family and workplace, unlike school, are largely private spheres, beyond the reach of aggressive public policy. Effective school reform as the means to help lift the urban disadvantaged will not be easy, but counteracting the largely informal practices that privilege white men in the noncollege labor market and white women in the family sphere may prove to be even more daunting.

Two Attainment Regimes, Not One

The Long Shadow tells the story of the Baltimore-based Beginning School Study Youth Panel, a probability sample of typical urban youth who came of age over the last decades of the twentieth century and into the first decade of the twenty-first. Our account begins in childhood and extends well into their adult lives. The presence of disadvantaged whites in the sample, a group usually absent from studies of urban disadvantage, adds valuable perspective. As in most cases, this story has two sides. We believe that identifying and encouraging practices that lead to positive life outcomes for the urban disadvantaged offers more hope for improvement than emphasizing what is wrong. The urban disadvantaged are not all poor black women having babies out of wedlock, or predatory black men, and it does them a disservice to write as though they are.

Under one mobility regime, parental resources, including the functional social capital they bring to bear on children's upbringing, the quality of their children's schools and neighborhoods, resources in support of schooling at every stage, and how lives unfold over the years after high school together make up a convincing account of how the sample's social origins impinge on their social destinations. Constraints on mobility and supports for mobility often are two sides of the same coin, but disproportionalities also come into play: higher-SES children benefit from a cumulative developmental advantage in school that is grounded in family advantage; for those of lower-SES origins, the same developmental dynamic is shaded toward cumulative disadvantage.

The second mobility regime involves a lower-SES pathway to higher earnings that selects on race (white over African American) and gender (men over women). Access to what remains of Baltimore's old industrial economy is the foundation of this white working-class privilege. This pathway also privileges whites over blacks at the family level through combined family earnings, a side of stratification missed in the more customary person-level status attainment perspective.

It is well understood that middle-class and professional parents have social capital resources to deploy in support of their children's status attainment. Their resources have value in school, and perhaps too in the high-wage labor market for college graduates through network advantages. Working-class parents also have reserves of social capital, however. By helping open doors to good employment opportunities, its value is in the workplace, not the school.

Concluding Thoughts

Taking a life-course developmental perspective helps illuminate how family background plays forward in the lives of the urban disadvantaged, but such development is context bound. The life trajectories revealed in this volume are bound by time (the twenty-five years of fieldwork) and place (deindustrialized Baltimore). Contexts matter. First are the nation, state, and city, as captured in Baltimore's industrial boom and bust during and after World War II, with implications for the resources available to the sample's parents and to themselves. Second is the family, which determines patterns of daily life that help children develop. Time and place can be dissected as an analytic convenience, but people's lives have an holistic integrity not reducible to relationships among a set of empirical measurements, not even the ambitious set of this volume.

The quotes and biographical call-out text boxes throughout this volume make clear the complexities of life that elude capture through survey questioning. Nevertheless, our attempt to respect that holistic integrity has illuminated some of the powerful social forces that moved the Youth Panel participants as children, youth, and young adults along different life paths. Although it is not representative of the country as a whole, or even other urban areas, the Baltimore picture we have sketched is probably broadly characteristic of conditions that prevailed in many of the economically stressed cities of the East Coast and Midwest at the turn of the twenty-first century. Among such cities, two considerations make Baltimore distinctive, but for our purposes strategic. First is the depth of the challenges posed by deindustrialization and white flight, as reviewed in chapter 2. Second is that Baltimore houses many poor whites living side by side with, but separate from, poor African Americans, which brought to light the to-date largely submerged blue-collar attainment regime that privileges working-class whites.

The BSSYP research design is uncommon among local studies. Anchored in a strong sampling plan, its duration and closely spaced data-gathering directly from the principals involved (the sample, their parents, teachers, and school records) has made it possible to map the panel's developmental milestones in real time, and the size and composition of the panel allow close inspection of developmental differences across social lines—by family SES and, among the urban disadvantaged specifically, by race and gender.

Examining this one city and this sampling of its children in depth has allowed us to contextualize the process of status attainment among a segment of youth whose life experience usually is hidden from view. Through descriptive detail on family structure and function, school and neighborhood conditions, and the sample's personal experience, and with Baltimore as backdrop, we sought to capture some of the texture that distinguishes disadvantaged children's circumstances growing up from those of children in more advantaged families and communities, as well as differences in life experience among the urban disadvantaged. Although the family and neighborhood socioeconomic disadvantage that Baltimore's lower-SES blacks and whites experience is much the same, the other resources they access are quite different.

The analytic mode introduced in later chapters demonstrated that these separate details of the children's lives in fact are not separate at all. Quite the contrary, they come together across the developmental life course in ways that construct distinctive patterns of socioeconomic attainment. Parts of the account had to be surmised, but enough of it is evident that the totality seems fairly robust: the socioeconomic journey from their origins as children to their destinations as young adults has been governed by two attainment regimes, not one. Status attainment through school privileges the urban advantaged, whereas the blue-collar regime privileges the white urban disadvantaged, men in the workplace and women through family.

What ultimately determines well-being in adulthood is how young people negotiate the transition to adulthood, which is rooted in resources present all the way back to first grade (and from other literatures, before first grade). We see that children are launched onto stable trajectories very early in life, for many reasons. First, the SES of their schools aligns with that of their neighborhoods, and both trace back to the SES of their parents. This configuration has the children of the urban advantaged trebly advantaged and their lower SES counterparts trebly disadvantaged across the social contexts that bear on their development, and this before they even make it to school. Second, parents' plans for their children are in place long before high school, and these plans are strong determinants of their children's school performance and goals in life. A parent's outlook has implications for reproduction across social lines because parents' ideas about their children's future reflect their own social structural locations. In addition, the foundational school curriculum in the early years is cumulative. Not surprisingly, then, when children of the Baltimore Youth Panel grow up with parents who have less than a high school education, their school careers tend to be foreshortened. A few do move up by way of college, but just a few. For the rest, their SES as adults reflects theirs as children.

Had we only examined investments in human capital after high school, adult family lives, and problem behavior profiles, it would have been easy to think those an adequate accounting of SES destinations. Anchoring the adult transition to earlier transitions, though, makes it clear that how the sample fare over the years after high school continues a story begun long before anybody was having babies, doing drugs, leaving school, or entering the workforce. How far, then, does the apple fall from the tree? Disembodied across-generation correlations of socio-economic standing or earnings inform the question on average, but at the biographical level of people embedded in social context, the proper answer is: as far as their life-course development takes them.

Appendix A

Voices of the Beginning School Study Youth Panel

Chapter 1

Mae—black woman—lower SES (page 2) Mae grew up in a low-income neighborhood on Baltimore's West Side. She had trouble in school academically and behaviorally. She lived alternatively with her mother, then one grandparent, and then another grandparent. Mae graduated from an alternative high school on time, enrolled in but did not finish a cosmetology program, and was still enrolled in an associate's degree program for early childhood development at a local community college. She was unemployed, a mother of four, and living with a partner when last we spoke.

Floyd—black man—lower SES (page 7) Floyd grew up in a low-income neighborhood on Baltimore's West Side. He graduated from high school on time and worked toward a criminal justice certificate at a local community college because his SAT scores kept him from attending his first and second choice colleges. Family responsibilities prevented him from completing the program. Floyd had been working for five years as a corrections officer at our last interview.

Alice—white woman—lower SES (page 10) Alice, from the west side, graduated high school a year late and enrolled in a certificate program, but a pregnancy prevented her from completing the certificate. When last contacted, Alice and her husband were celebrating seven years of marriage. They and their three children were living in a house belonging to a friend.

Clyde—white man—higher SES (page 11) Although higher SES in our family background classification, Clyde was raised by a grandmother in a poor inner-city neighborhood. He dropped out of school in the twelfth grade and got his GED several years later. Both Clyde and his wife were working full time at salaried positions at our last interview. In hindsight, Clyde regretted being influenced by peer pressure and not dedicating himself to his schoolwork.

Frank—black man—lower SES (page 13) Frank and his two siblings grew up in a single-parent home headed by a strong, devoted mother. She was a nurse and had two years of college. All three children finished high school. Frank has been continuously employed since high school and admits that he never really thought

189

about college until recently, but would find it difficult to go back to school and maintain his warehouse work schedule. He had three children and was sharing custody with their two different mothers. He was living in his mother's home with his mother, grandmother, and one brother when we last spoke.

Chapter 3

Kim—black woman—lower SES (page 38)   Kim grew up in a poor Baltimore neighborhood with her high school–educated mother, her nongraduate father, and three siblings. When we last spoke with Kim in 2000, she was a single mother of three, suffering from occasional bouts of depression, studying for the GED, living with her parents, and working nights cleaning office buildings.

Maceo—black man—middle SES (page 43)   Maceo had a complicated family situation while growing up, never knowing his real father but experiencing several stepfathers and moving between households often. Both his parents did finish high school. Maceo's highest level of education is his GED. When we last talked, Maceo was unemployed, living with his sister after being released from several years of incarceration.

Karen—white woman—middle SES (page 44)   Karen's mother was a high school graduate and worked as a cosmetologist while raising her only child. Karen began attending a four-year college part time in the fall after graduating from high school. She later transferred to a community college, completing forty-two credits before withdrawing because of pregnancy. When we last spoke, she had been married for six years, had one child, and was working part time at the same government agency where she has been employed since her senior year of high school.

Geraldine—black woman—lower SES (page 47)   Geraldine said that life in her parents' household was unstable. Her father, a high school graduate, had been in the military and her mom had not finished high school. When she began living with her grandmother, she described that neighborhood as a ghetto, but admits she needed the structure her grandmother provided. When we spoke, Geraldine was engaged to be married and pursuing a doctoral degree. She was working in curriculum development and as an acting assistant principal.

Gail—white woman—lower SES (page 47)   Gail had a chaotic childhood, moving back and forth between her parents' and grandparents' homes. Her mother and father argued a lot, her mother used drugs, her brothers were incarcerated, and a sister had turned to prostitution. Gail dropped out in tenth grade when she was pregnant with her first child, a second child followed the next year. When we last spoke with her, Gail was separated, working as a waitress, and renting an apartment with her mother and two young children.

Bess—black woman—lower SES (page 48)   Bess grew up in a chaotic household environment, moving back and forth between her grandparents' home and wherever her mother was living at a particular period. Like her father, Bess dropped out of school. Her mother did have some college education, but struggled with alcoholism. When we last spoke with Bess in 2005, she was working full time at a convenience store and living with the father of the two youngest of her four children. They had been living in their own apartment since 2003. Bess reported that they had a very good relationship.

Bruce—white man—middle SES (page 48)   Bruce grew up in a two-parent household, and both parents were high school graduates. Bruce also finished high school, although a year behind his cohort, and had several college experiences, including two semesters at a state college and a semester or two at community colleges. In 2004, Bruce and his wife of five and half years had one child and were expecting their second. They both were employed.

Chapter 4

Peter—black man—lower SES (page 50)   Peter grew up in a rough neighborhood, where many of his childhood friends are dead or in jail. He described himself as a troublemaker as a child, but went on to say that it was a "good thing he had good parents to keep him on that straight road." Neither of his parents finished high school. Peter did finish—on time—despite multiple suspensions. When we last spoke in 2004, Peter had one run-in with the law and was on probation. He was unemployed, living with his parents. He had two children by different mothers; neither child lived with him.

Ken—white man—lower SES (page 50)   Ken attended parochial middle and high schools. Like his mother, Ken completed high school. He enrolled in community college, but after completing thirty-six credits, withdrew because of financial difficulties. In 2005 he was living with his wife of three years and their infant daughter in their own home. Both he and his wife were employed.

Alice—white woman—lower SES (page 53)   See earlier description in chapter 1 section.

Aubrey—white man—lower SES (page 61)   Both Aubrey's parents were high school graduates. Aubrey proudly told us that he, too, graduated high school, never failing a class, never failing a year. He did not, however, pursue postsecondary education. When we last spoke, he described his parents as loving and involved. Aubrey was working at the same warehouse supervisory position that he had held since high school. He was married and living with his wife in a house that they own. He had one child from a previous relationship, whom he saw every other weekend.

Mae—black woman—lower SES (page 61)   See earlier description in chapter 1 section.

Joe—black man—middle SES (page 61)   Joe grew up in a tough southwest Baltimore neighborhood. He described the block where he lived in different terms, however, as a block where people owned and cared for their homes and families stuck together. His parents, both high school graduates, were employed, and involved in Joe's life. He lost his father, though, at thirteen. Joe got involved with drugs, and during eleventh grade was incarcerated. He never returned to school. At age twenty-eight, Joe was working a minimum-wage janitorial job and living with his mother.

Sona—black woman—lower SES (page 64)   Like her mother, Sona graduated from high school. She enrolled in community college the following year and finished two semesters toward her associate's degree. Financial difficulties prevented her from finishing. Sona had been a self-employed shop owner for a year and a half when we last spoke with her. At the time, she had one daughter whom she was raising on her own.

Floyd—black man—lower SES (page 64)   See earlier description in chapter 1 section.

Terry—black man—middle SES (page 64)   Terry's early years with his two siblings seemed idyllic—two working, involved, and loving parents, both high school graduates—until his mother fell prey to the drug activity invading the neighborhood. With help from other family, he was able to graduate high school on time. Terry pursued a bachelor's degree but was unable to finish due to health problems. He and his partner were living in a subsidized apartment with their infant daughter. They both were employed; Terry was working full time in a labor-intensive job.

Chapter 5

Bedelia—white woman—lower SES (page 75)   Bedelia grew up in a northeast Baltimore neighborhood. Her parents, neither of whom graduated high school, divorced when she was in the third grade. Life was quite chaotic, with custody battles, many moves among several relatives, and threats from her father of confinement to a place for uncontrollable teens after she got in a fistfight with her stepmother. Bedelia dropped out of high school in the tenth grade and was never able to achieve her GED. Using drugs and in a relationship with an abusive boyfriend, her life has been difficult. When we last spoke with Bedelia in 2005, she was a mother for the first time, was unemployed, and had lived with a partner for two years.

Karen—white woman—middle SES (page 80)   See earlier description in chapter 3 section.

Phil—white man—lower SES (page 82)   Both parents graduated from high school. Phil graduated high school on time. Health problems prevented him from pursuing his college and military plans. He ended up in well-paid construction work but continued to have problems with substance abuse and brushes with the law. He and his girlfriend lost their apartment and, with their baby, moved in with his parents.

Bess—black woman—lower SES (page 88)   See earlier description in chapter 3 section.

Chapter 6

Ricardo—white man—lower SES (page 98)   Ricardo dropped out of school after completing eleventh grade, sometimes taking his classes in a detention center or jail. He was incarcerated when we last spoke, and Ricardo told us he had gotten his GED. He had never married and reported that he had no children.

Brendon—black man—lower SES (page 98)   Brendan's mother did not finish high school. He grew up with his grandmother as guardian, who had an eighth grade education. We last spoke with Brendan while he was incarcerated; his highest level of education was also eighth grade. He never married, but had four children, all with the same mother.

Tami—white woman—lower-SES (page 101)   Tami's father had a trade school degree, her mother a GED. Tami lived in the same blue-collar Baltimore neighborhood growing up. She had a baby in high school, but graduated on time in the top 10 percent of her class. After high school, Tami completed two semesters toward an associate's degree at a local community college. She later completed a semester of law classes at a different community college. After marrying and relocating, she withdrew from school in 2004. Still without an associate's degree at twenty-eight, her goal is a doctoral degree, but she expects to make it only as far as a bachelor's.

Chapter 7

Anna—white woman—lower SES (page 132)   Anna's life was fraught with complications on multiple fronts—asthma as a child, causing her to miss lots of school, depression, drug use, alcoholism and depression within her family. Neither of her parents finished high school. Anna left school in the middle of eighth grade, got a GED and enrolled in a certificate program, but was unable to finish. At the time of our last interview, she was working part time as a cashier at a retail store and living with her husband and four children.

Gail—white woman—lower SES (page 132)   See earlier description in chapter 3 section.

Chip—black man—lower SES (page 132)   Chip had health issues as a child—asthma and vision problems. Financial difficulties kept him from getting glasses, affecting his grades and his attention span in school. He grew up in a two-parent, two-income household, where one parent finished high school, the other did not. Chip eventually got his GED. He was incarcerated at our last interview, where he was taking some college courses, working toward a certificate. He had one child.

Chapter 8

Todd—white man—middle SES (page 164)   Todd's father finished high school and his mother had a GED. Immediately after high school, Todd enrolled at a four-year college. He left college after one semester and returned to the trucking company he had worked for the summer before college. When we spoke with him at age twenty-eight, he was earning $50,000 per year and had built a rewarding blue-collar career without the benefit of college.

Aaron—black man—middle SES (page 164)   Aaron grew up in a single-parent household. He had finished the eleventh grade when he dropped out of the alternative school he had been attending. He got his GED and spent one semester at a trade school, but did not finish the program. Like his father, Aaron has had some trouble with the law. He is the father of a son he does not see often because of disputes with the birth mother. Aaron was living with his girlfriend and getting financial help from his mother when things get tight. At the time, he was working as a construction laborer.

Chapter 9

Ken—white man—lower SES (page 173)   See earlier description in chapter 4 section.

Dilan—black man—lower SES (page 173)   Dilan grew up in a two-parent household, the youngest of five children. Neither of Dilan's parents finished high school. He earned a GED after dropping out in the twelfth grade. He went on to pursue a community college degree on three separate occasions, withdrawing each time for either financial reasons or simply lacking a clear sense of goals. When we last spoke, Dilan had been working at the same health-care facility for seven years, now as a salaried employee. He never married, but had two children and was living with the oldest in a rental apartment.

Floyd—black man—lower SES (pages 173)   See earlier description in chapter 1 section.

Tami—white woman—lower SES (page 181)   See earlier description in chapter 6 section.

= Appendix B =

Measurement Details
and Technical Issues

T HIS APPENDIX provides detail on the Beginning School Study Youth Panel
(BSSYP or Youth Panel) research design and elaborates on the measurement of key constructs not covered adequately in the text. We also provide a nontechnical overview of multiple regression analysis, the statistical
technique used in chapter 7.

Youth Panel Sample and Research Design

The Youth Panel is a prospective longitudinal study of children's academic
and social development beginning in first grade and continuing through high
school graduation and beyond. Data collection began in 1982 and concluded
in 2005–2006 when 80 percent of the original group was interviewed at ages
twenty-eight and twenty-nine. In tracking the sample's progress through school
we count time two ways, by grade or by year. All were in first grade in the fall
of 1982, the project's first year, but repeaters fall behind. In this volume, grade
refers to the modal grade of enrollment.

In 1982, a two-stage probability sample of children beginning first grade in
the Baltimore City public schools (BCPS) was selected for study. Probability
sampling is difficult to implement, but provides internal validity lacking in
other study designs (Michael and O'Muircheartaigh 2008). First, a random
sample of twenty schools was selected from a list of public elementary schools
in the city, stratified by racial mix (six predominantly African American, six
white, eight integrated) and by socioeconomic status (fourteen inner-city
or working class and six middle class). The African American enrollment
averaged 99.5 percent in the six African American schools, 6 percent in the
white schools, and 48 percent in the eight integrated schools (ranging from
17 percent to 87 percent). Second, within each school, students were randomly
sampled from the previous spring's kindergarten enrollment, supplemented
by fall class rosters to pick up new entrants. Over the summer, parents were
visited in their homes to obtain permission for their child's participation.
Three percent declined.

The final sample consists of 790 students beginning first grade for the first
time (nonrepeaters) in the fall of 1982. The city public school system then was

about 77 percent African American (U.S. Bureau of the Census 1983), but to sustain comparisons across social lines, the Youth Panel oversampled whites. At baseline, 55 percent of students were African American. Parents' educational levels averaged 11.9, with a standard deviation of 2.6. Broken down by race, African American parents had a slightly higher mean level of education than whites (12.1 years versus 11.7), but whites were overrepresented at the high and low ends of the distribution: for example, among white and African American mothers, 14.7 percent versus 10.3 percent college graduates; 43.7 percent versus 33.9 percent high school dropouts. Sixty-seven percent of the families received free or reduced price meals at school, 77 percent of African Americans and 53 percent of whites. Overall, 56 percent of the sample lived in two-parent households at the beginning of first grade, 70 percent of whites and 44 percent of African Americans.

Data Collection Procedures

Beginning in the summer and fall of 1982, data were collected by face-to-face interviews with students and parents. Teachers responded to questionnaires and school records were examined for data on marks, test scores, and the like. In later years most parent questionnaires were answered by mail or by phone, but students were interviewed face to face.

Parents were surveyed in the summer or early fall annually from year 1 through year 11 with the exception of year 5. Parent and student fall interviews always took place before the end of the first marking period and spring interviews took place between the third and fourth (final) marking periods. The timing of student and parent questionnaires ensured that measurement of parents' and children's mark expectations preceded receipt of report cards.

Students were interviewed in the fall of 1982 and spring of 1983, and fall and spring of the following year (1983–1984). They were then interviewed twice in their fourth and sixth years (1985–1986, 1987–1988), the sixth year being the first year of middle school for most. Those who were delayed making the elementary to middle school transition were interviewed twice in year 7. For the others, an abbreviated interview was conducted in the spring of year 7. Thereafter, spring interviews were conducted annually through year 13.[1]

Teachers filled out three questionnaires in each of the first two years. In the other years when students were interviewed through year 9, teachers filled out one questionnaire per year. Parents were interviewed up to eleven times between first grade and eleventh grade, and teachers up to nine times between first grade and ninth grade. Additionally, school records from Baltimore, as well as schools outside the city system to which members of the sample transferred, cover report card marks and deportment ratings, achievement test results, promotion histories, and disciplinary problems. In the third and fifth years, there were no student interviews or questionnaires. Data from school records were collected every year, however, including years 3 and 5. Only parents were interviewed in year 3. None of the interview cycles attained 100 percent coverage, but in most years the yields were quite satisfactory, averaging 77 percent across the entire set of participant interviews.

Sample Attrition

Students in the Baltimore City public schools are highly mobile. Data on school moves, both within-year and between-year transfers, were obtained from BCPS records. By the end of the project's fifth year, the children had dispersed from the original twenty schools, 80 percent to 112 schools within the system and the remainder to an unknown number of schools outside the system.

Over the period of the study, follow-up practices changed. During the project's first three years, resources permitted only students who remained in the original twenty schools to be followed. Beginning in year 4, tracking was extended to all of Baltimore, re-enrolling "lost cases" back into the study and, where possible, backfilling school record data.

At the beginning of year 6 (fall 1987), 490 of the original 790 students (62 percent) remained in Baltimore City schools and were still enrolled in the study. Those who left the sample were disproportionately white and of higher educational and economic family background (see table B.1). In the original sample, 55 percent were African American, 67 percent were eligible for meal subsidy, and the mean parent education level was 11.9 years; in the year 6 sample, 67 percent were African American, 74 percent were eligible for meal subsidy, and the mean parent education level was 11.6 years.

Beginning in year 7, the fall of 1988, an effort was initiated to re-enroll those who had earlier dropped out of the study. By the end of year 13 (spring 1995), this continuing effort to re-enroll students had located 663 (84 percent) of the original 790 participants.

The original probability sample compares well with the sample still active after thirteen years. Few differences emerge between these two groups on key variables measured in the fall of 1982 (see table B.1), either in terms of means or standard deviations. For example, both groups have nearly identical scores (281 and 282) on the reading comprehension subtest of the California Achievement Test (CAT) administered in the fall of 1982, when all students began first grade. Similarly, both the original sample and the year 13 sample are 55 percent African American. The proportion on meal subsidy differs by only 2 percent (67 percent versus 65 percent). The number of years of parental education was also very close, 11.9 for the original sample versus 12 for the year 13 sample.

Although the year 13 sample closely matches the original sample, the 127 students who were lost from the sample do differ significantly from those retained in the panel. For example, they underrepresent girls (37 percent versus 53 percent), have parents with lower levels of education (11.4 years versus 12), are more often on meal subsidy (76 percent versus 65 percent), and have lower beginning math scores (284 versus 294) (see table B.1).

The Young Adult and Mature Adult Surveys

The data archive includes two after high school surveys fielded at ages twenty-one and twenty-two (the Young Adult Survey, or YAS) and twenty-eight or twenty-nine (the Mature Adult Survey, or MAS), both with 80 percent coverage

Table B.1 Attrition Analysis

	Original Sample			Year 6 Sample			Year 13 Sample			t-test	Not in Year 13 Sample		
	Mean	SD	N	Mean	SD	N	Mean	SD	N		Mean	SD	N
California Achievement Test scores													
Reading, fall year 1	281	41.0	675	279	39.3	437	282	42.4	573		278	31.4	102
Reading, fall year 3	386	55.7	589	381	54.6	448	388	55.8	519	*	372	53.2	70
Math, fall year 1	293	32.0	693	290	30.8	447	294	32.5	586	*	284	26.9	107
Math, fall year 3	380	41.7	590	376	39.7	449	382	42.1	519	*	362	34.1	71
Reading mark, year 1 quarter 1	1.88	.71	702	1.81	.71	452	1.91	.71	591	*	1.75	.67	111
Math mark, year 1 quarter 1	2.24	.84	702	2.17	.87	452	2.27	.84	591	+	2.11	.82	111
Proportion African American	.55	.50	790	.67	.47	490	.55	.50	663		.51	.50	127
Proportion girls	.51	.50	790	.52	.50	490	.53	.50	663	*	.37	.48	127
Proportion mother alone[a]	.20	.04	754	.22	.42	466	.19	.39	638		.25	.43	116
Proportion two parents[a]	.56	.50	754	.52	.50	466	.57	.50	638		.49	.50	116

	Mean	SD	N	Mean	SD	N	Mean	SD	N		Mean	SD	N
Proportion mother or other adult[a]	.21	.41	754	.21	.41	466	.21	.40	638		.22	.41	116
Proportion meal subsidy, year 3	.67	.47	701	.74	.44	481	.65	.48	597	*	.76	.43	104
Occupational prestige scores (TSEI2)													
Mother's job	31.9	15.8	610	29.9	14.5	427	32.4	16.1	553	*	27.5	12.4	57
Father's job	33.3	18.1	518	29.8	15.2	343	33.6	18.2	475		30.0	16.6	43
Parent's education	11.9	2.59	753	11.6	2.44	464	12.0	2.62	636	*	11.4	2.40	117
Parent's ability estimate, year 1	3.65	.84	754	3.64	.85	467	3.67	.84	638		3.56	.87	116
Parent's expectations for student's marks													
Reading, year 1	2.67	.76	751	2.65	.74	465	2.71	.74	635	*	2.50	.84	116
Math, year 1	2.72	.72	749	2.65	.70	464	2.75	.70	632	*	2.56	.80	117

Source: Authors' compilation.
Note: Year 13 sample contains 663, 84 percent of the original sample. T-tests compare year 13 sample with those not in year 13 sample.
[a]In 4 percent of cases, mother was absent.
*$p \le .05$; +$p \le .10$.

of the original group.[2] Included among the 162 MAS nonrespondents are twenty-six known deceased, most of whom came to light when we tried to secure an interview or in response to our annual birthday card mailings. Seventeen of the twenty-six are African American men and five are African American women. Of the dozen for whom the cause of death is known, six died violently, one in a confrontation with the police.

Respondent tracking is a large challenge in panel research, and those challenges magnify with a low-income target population. Considering that the Youth Panel is overwhelmingly low-income urban, the 80 percent retention achieved for the YAS and MAS surveys (the latter over a quarter century) is quite credible. No doubt it helped that our relationship with the sample is long-standing and generally positive. We secured phone numbers and addresses of family members and close friends during every interview and between interviews in annual tracking updates. We also did annual birthday card mailings. Those returned as undeliverable were used to identify bad addresses, which we then would try to update through calls or visits to family and friends and, in the later years, on-line searches.

MAS and YAS coverage no doubt overrepresent those easiest to reach, but when we compare the original sample against those interviewed in the MAS and the YAS, the three groups are virtually identical. The upper portion of table B.2 covers sociodemographics, including race-ethnicity, gender, family type, family SES, and mother's and father's education. The lower portion reports some of the schooling data used in this volume, including standardized achievement scores from first grade, retention-promotion history through ninth grade, high school curriculum concentration, and dropout status, items that span the early years, the middle grades, and high school.

Despite sometimes large swings in case coverage, practically all the percentages and proportions are within a point or two of one another. For example, the proportion low income in first grade is 0.66 in the original sample (N = 713), 0.65 in the YAS sample (N = 574) and 0.66 in the MAS sample (N = 572). Father's education, for which coverage is spotty all along, averages 12.2 years in the original sample (N = 529), 12.4 years in the YAS (N = 443), and 12.3 years in MAS (N = 441). The academic measures likewise are similar: for example, 42 percent are known to have dropped out of high school at some point; the YAS and MAS figures are 40 percent and 41 percent, respectively.

Those lost are disproportionately of low socioeconomic background. Also, the lost cases began first grade with somewhat lower achievement scores and include a higher percentage of school dropouts: 48 percent of MAS nonrespondents and 51 percent of YAS nonrespondents, against 42 percent overall. Still, the overall thrust of our many checks is that the panel coverage achieved through year 13 and in the YAS and the MAS approximates well the makeup of the original sample.

Measuring Socioeconomic Origins

The Long Shadow is about how family socioeconomic status (SES) background impinges on socioeconomic standing in early adulthood. Data sources and procedures for locating the sample and their families in socioeconomic space are

Table B.2   Panel Attrition

	Original Sample (N = 790)			Young Adult Survey Sample (N = 631)			Mature Adult Survey Sample (N = 628)		
	Mean	SD	N	Mean	SD	N	Mean	SD	N
Proportion men	.49	.50	790	.47	.50	631	.47	.50	628
Proportion African American	.55	.50	790	.57	.50	631	.55	.50	628
Family SES composite	-.04	.80	787	-.01	.82	630	-.02	.82	626
Father's years of education	12.19	2.73	529	12.37	2.76	443	12.27	2.81	441
Mother's years of education	11.67	2.55	750	11.83	2.59	602	11.76	2.60	595
Proportion low income, first grade	.66	.47	713	.65	.48	574	.66	.48	572
Proportion two-parent family, year 1	.56	.50	754	.57	.50	602	.56	.50	597
Proportion high school dropout (ever)	.42	.49	728	.40	.49	623	.41	.49	606
Proportion retained at least once years 1 through 9	.51	.50	782	.50	.50	630	.51	.50	625
Fall first grade achievement, reading CAT	280.62	40.81	691	281.53	42.21	564	281.33	42.20	560
Fall first grade achievement, math CAT	292.49	31.94	708	293.84	32.82	574	293.48	32.99	571
Proportion high school vocational curriculum	.19	.39	657	.19	.40	561	.18	.39	556
Proportion college prep curriculum CAT	.30	.46	657	.31	.46	561	.30	.46	556

Source: Authors' compilation.

described in the sections that follow. Five measures are used to gauge SES origins: family income level, mother's educational level, father's educational level, mother's occupational status, and father's occupational status.

Family Income: Meal Subsidy Status

Beginning in year 3 (1984–1985), school records provided information regarding eligibility for participation in the federal meal subsidy program. Children were eligible for free or reduced price meals based on family income and size. For example, in July 1, 1984, a family of four with a yearly income of $13,260 was eligible for full subsidy; one with an income of $18,870 was eligible for partial subsidy. The first figure is 1.30 times the 1984 federal poverty level and the second is 1.85 times. These income figures are revised annually by the federal government. The meal subsidy program participation rate of Youth Panel students closely matches the overall meal subsidy rate for all Baltimore City children. For example, during year 5 (1986–1987), 68.7 percent of the panel qualified for subsidized school lunches, and the overall participation rate for Baltimore City elementary schools was 66.8 percent (Baltimore City Public Schools 1988).

Parent Education

During the first year of the study, parent education data were collected for the parent respondent, usually the mother (86 percent). Beginning in the spring of 1984, we asked about the education level of both coresident parents. Using pooled parent education data over the first eight years of the study and favoring the earliest response, the mean years of education completed by mothers (95 percent coverage) is 11.7 years, by fathers (67 percent coverage) 12.2 years.

Parent Employment and Occupation

Beginning in year 1, parents were asked whether they were employed, for how many hours, and whether another wage earner was in the household. Specific information on parent occupation was gathered for both mother and father (if both lived with the student) beginning in year 2. Beginning in year 9, parental occupation was asked of parents who had any regular contact with the student. Parent responses were classified according to 1970 Census occupational codes, and these codes were used to assign occupational status scores (Featherman and Stevens 1982).

Pooling data over the first nine years (again, using the earliest response available), information is available on mother's occupation for 610 students and on father's occupation for 518 students. No provision is made for occupational changes over this span of years.

Composite Socioeconomic Origins Status Measures

A metric composite of socioeconomic status was derived from the five SES indicators, first converting them to Z scores (that is, with mean zero and standard deviation of 1.0) and then averaging the Z scores, using as many of the five measures as available. Panel coverage is almost complete, and scores are computed for 787 of the 790. All five indicators are available for just under 70 percent of the panel, two or more for over 95 percent. The composite's alpha reliability based on the set of five items is 0.87 (N = 386).

A three-category ranking of family SES was derived from the metric composite for use in descriptive analyses: lower, middle, and higher. The cutting points, though largely judgmental, provide good separation across all five of the underlying indicators. Mother's education averages 10.0 years for the lower-SES group, 12.0 years for the middle group, and 14.6 years for the upper group; percentages participating in the meal subsidy program are 94.6, 54.1, and 12.9. Roughly half the sample falls into the lower category and a fourth fall in each of the other two categories.

Measuring Socioeconomic Destinations

Our measures of socioeconomic standing in adulthood include levels of education, occupational status, and annual earnings. We monitor both the panel members' individual status and their family status. Family status adds education, occupational status, and annual earnings information for spouses and cohabiting partners.

Years of Schooling

In both the YAS and MAS, panel members reported their high school completion status (diploma, GED, dropout) and all postsecondary enrollments. For each school attended, they reported the type of program (certificate, licensure, degree), length of enrollment, and whether they completed the program. From this information, we determined the highest level of enrollment, the highest postsecondary credential earned, and the time enrolled in each program. Data on educational attainment are available for the entire MAS sample.

Years of Education Completed combines information on highest educational credential earned with data on the number of quarters of postsecondary enrollment. High school dropouts are credited with the last grade of high school completed, scaled as years of education (see table B.3). A high school credential is scored 12, a certificate from a proprietary technical or vocational program 13, an associate's degree 14, a bachelor's degree 16, and advanced degrees 18. High school dropouts who earn certificates are coded 13, crediting their postsecondary training. Dropouts from certificate programs are coded 12 or last grade completed if high school dropouts. Dropouts from associate's degree programs with three or more quarters of associate's degree enrollment are coded 13, those with less than three-quarters twelve or the last grade completed. Dropouts from bachelor's programs are coded 13 if they completed two years or fewer of college. If they completed more than two years, they are coded 14.5. Associate's and bachelor's enrollment are counted as more than two years unless the direction of attendance was from bachelor's to associate's enrollment. This sequence is coded as 14.5 if at least eight quarters are bachelor's enrollments. In five cases, total associate's and bachelor's enrollment is more than two years but

Table B.3   Years of Education Completed

Years of Schooling	Frequency	Percent	Cumulative Percent
7.00 Seventh grade	2	.3	.3
8.00 Eighth grade	17	2.7	3.0
9.00 Ninth grade	23	3.7	6.7
10.00 Tenth grade	35	5.6	12.3
11.00 Eleventh grade	16	2.5	14.8
12.00 High school diploma or GED	181	28.8	43.6
13.00 Certificate or some college	197	31.4	75.0
14.00 Associate's degree	8	1.3	76.3
14.50 More than two years college	48	7.6	83.9
16.00 Bachelor's degree	81	12.9	96.8
18.00 Graduate or professional degree	20	3.2	100.0
Total	628	100.0	

Source: Authors' compilation.

the sequence of attendance is from bachelor's to associate's and bachelor's enrollment is less than eight quarters—these are coded 13.

Workplace Destination and Earnings

Data on employment and occupation come from retrospective accounts of employment history. To exclude casual, intermittent labor, panel members reported full-time or part-time jobs of at least three months' duration. Data for each job include job type, duration, and earnings.

Occupational Type. In assessing workplace destinations, occupational type and occupational status refer to jobs held at the time of the MAS (age twenty-eight) or the most recent job if that job occurred within twenty-four months preceding the MAS interview (the twenty-four month screen is to gauge the panel's current socioeconomic standing). Information pertains to full-time jobs if the panel member held a full-time job, otherwise part-time jobs. Job data are available for 88 percent of the MAS sample. The 1990 Census occupational classification is used to code the type of job held at the time of the MAS or within twenty-four months of the interview.

Occupational Status. The 1990 Census occupational classification for jobs held at MAS or within twenty-four months of the MAS are transformed into occupational status rankings using Robert Hauser and John Warren's (1997) socioeconomic index (SEI). This index is constructed around 1990 Census reports of the income and educational levels of occupational incumbents nationally. An occupational status score for the job currently held (or held within last twenty-four months) is available for 88 percent (555) of the MAS sample.

Personal Earnings. Earnings are measured by two sources, both referenced to the previous calendar year. The primary source is from the question, "How much did you earn from all your jobs before taxes and other deductions in the previous year (2003 or 2004)? Include wages, salary, tips, bonuses, overtime, and income from self-employment. Also include paid apprenticeships, assistantships, or internships while you were a student." For respondents with no or low earnings (under $10,000), a secondary source (level of earnings for the most recent job held during last twenty-four months before the MAS) was used if this yielded higher annual earnings.[3] This secondary source comes from reports of wages and salaries earned in specific jobs as recounted in a retrospective work history. Respondents had the choice of reporting their earnings as hourly rate, annual salary, or monthly income. We converted the wage and monthly earnings responses into an annual salary equivalent using the standard of 2,080 hours per year. The final personal earnings measure is available for 89 percent (559) of the MAS sample.

Socioeconomic Status of Spouse or Partner

The MAS asked respondents to report the education level, occupation, and earnings of current spouses or partners. These data were transformed into measures similar to those for individual panel members. We screened out partnerships of less than three months' duration.

Spouse-Partner Education. Respondents were asked "How far has spouse or partner gone in school?" These data were coded as years of education. Educational attainment for a spouse or partner is available for 53 percent (355) of the MAS sample.

Spouse-Partner Occupation. Respondents were asked whether their spouse or partner was currently employed, and if so, what kind of job they had. These responses are coded into 1990 Census occupational classifications, and then transformed into occupational status rankings using the 1990 SEI. Spouse-partner occupational status rankings are available for 47 percent (294) of the MAS sample.

Spouse-Partner Earnings. Data on earnings come from responses to the question "How much did your spouse or partner earn from (his or her) jobs before taxes and other deductions during the past year? Include wages, salary, tips, bonuses, overtime, and income from self-employment. Also include paid apprenticeships, assistantships, or internships while (he or she) was a student." Spouse-partner earnings from employment are available for 48 percent (303) of the MAS sample.

Family Earnings

Data for personal earnings and spouse-partner earnings are summed to get overall family earnings for the past year. For those without a spouse-partner or those whose spouse-partner had no earnings, personal earnings and family earnings are the same. Altogether, family earnings data are available for 93 percent (585) of the MAS sample. For 51 percent of cases, these earnings are from only the Youth Panel member; for 45 percent they are from self and spouse-partner combined; for 4 percent they are from only the spouse-partner.

Composite Socioeconomic Standing in Adulthood

The measures of educational attainment, occupational status, and earnings outlined were used to construct composite measures of socioeconomic standing for the sample, their partners, and their families. As a first step, all indicators were scaled to a common metric by conversion to Z scores (that is, with mean of 0 and standard deviation of 1).

Individual SES Composite. The Z scores for years of education, occupational status, and annual earnings are averaged to produce a standardized individual SES composite score. All three components are present in 88 percent of cases; in only 10 percent did we rely on only one measure (years of education). The composite's alpha reliability for the set of three items is 0.67 (N = 552).

We also developed a three-category classification of the individual SES composite. Educational level was used to determine the cut points. The mean level of education is 12.9 years; 60 percent of the panel had twelve or thirteen years of schooling. The intention was to have the majority of the sample clustered in the middle category and to have the level of education for this group average between twelve and thirteen years. To accomplish this, we used break points ±.5 SD around the overall scale mean of zero. The resulting personal SES classification included 50 percent in the midrange category, 28 percent lower SES, and 22 percent higher SES.

Family SES Composite. The family SES composite is the average of Z scores for individual level education and occupational status, spouse-partner education and occupational status, and the combined family earnings. All five components are present for just 40 percent of cases, but for 93 percent of cases at least 3 items are present. The family SES composite's alpha reliability for the set of five items is 0.81 (N = 249).

We also developed a three-category classification of the family SES composite. Again, we used break points ±0.5 SD around the overall scale mean of zero. The family SES classification has 41 percent in the midrange category, 35 percent lower SES, and 24 percent higher SES.

Resources in Support of Children's Schooling

Another set of composite measures was developed for resources in support of children's schooling. In this instance, the motivation was to keep the analysis and presentation tractable. Separate resource composites were developed for the first grade year, the rest of elementary school, the middle grade years and the first year of high school, ninth grade. Measures at each stage were first standardized and then averaged to construct stage-specific composites.

As resources for children's schooling, we include four items: measures of school performance; curricular placements and other forms of educational tracking (for example, grade retention and assignment to special education); parents' thinking about their children's academic prospects; and child-centered constructs—self-attitudes in the student role and academic engagement. Our earlier studies establish the relevance of these resources measured in first grade for high school dropout (Alexander, Entwisle, and Horsey 1997; Alexander, Entwisle, and Kabanni 2001) and, for some, level of education completed at age twenty-two (Entwisle, Alexander, and Olson 2005). Most also evidence large differences across social lines, which makes them candidates for carrying forward socioeconomic advantage and disadvantage.

Preliminary analyses for this volume confirm that their importance extends as well to socioeconomic attainments in adulthood—when assessed individually, every one of them was significant. However, rather than try to prioritize among stage-specific resources and risk factors, as in some of our previous studies (for example, Alexander, Entwisle, and Kabanni 2001), at each stage we combine them into a single composite measure. For example, our earlier research establishes that weak school performance elevates risk of grade retention and that grade retention, in turn, compromises later performance, eventually elevating the risk of dropout. However, such exercises invariably hinge on assumptions that require careful probing and can be quite involved. Instead, we focus on the developmental question, asking whether particular stages of schooling stand out as distinctively important. For those that do, we know it is owing to a multiplicity of valued resources. The specific measures are described next.

School Performance

California Achievement Test Scores (1979) are the average of fall and spring reading comprehension and math concepts–reasoning subtests after converting scale scores to standard scores. Averages are calculated within years for first grade and year 9 and averaged across years to determine children's standing over years 2 through 5 (the remainder of elementary school) and over years 6 through 8 (the middle school years). The BCPS stopped fall testing after year 6, so for years 7 and 8 only spring scores are available. After year 8, the BCPS discontinued use of the CAT battery, but beginning in the spring of year 9 and continuing for roughly eighteen months the study made special arrangements to have the CAT test administered. These scores are referenced back to spring of year 9 using a linear interpolation.

Report Card Marks, from school records, are measured each year as the average of reading and math marks from all four quarters (1 = failing; 13 = A+). Beginning in year 6, English and science marks also are included. Report card marks were combined across years in the same way as with the CAT achievement data.

Educational Tracking

Receipt of Special Education Services is derived from BCPS records: 1 = received some services during the period; 0 = no services. School record data for these measures are not available for children who transferred out of the BCPS system.

Grade Retention information is mainly from school records, supplemented by retrospective student and parent reports from years 10 through 12 to identify retentions outside the BCPS and to correct some mistakes in school records. 1 = retained during the period; 0 = not retained.

Course Level Placements in sixth and ninth grade are determined from school records. High-level English, math, and science courses are those classified as advanced academic or honors. Low-level courses are those classified as remedial, which includes reading in sixth grade. Foreign language courses at any level are considered high in both grades.

High School Program in ninth grade (1 = college preparatory; 0 = other) is determined, in the first instance, by the character of the student's high school (for example, citywide academic; citywide vocational-technical). For those attending comprehensive zoned schools, self-reports are used.

Parental Support[4]

Parent Attitudes are constructed from four items:

the average of mark expectations for the upcoming report card in math and reading, and, beginning in middle school, English and science also (coded from 1 to 13, with 1 = failing; 13 = A+);

conduct expectations for the upcoming report card (usually dichotomized, with 1 = satisfactory; 0 = needs improvement—the distinctions used in the BCPS during the primary grades);

parents' sense of their children's ability to do school work relative to others in the school (coded from 1 to 5, with 5 = much better; 1 = much worse); and

parents' expectation for their children's eventual level of school attainment (from 1 = not finish high school to 6 = more than college).

These items are available for parents in years 1, 2, 3, 4, 6, 7, 8, 9, and 10. Parent attitude scores are constructed each year as the average of the measures available, after conversion to standard scores. Alpha reliabilities calculated year by year on the four items range between 0.61 and 0.71, except in first grade (0.43). These annual constructions then are averaged across years to derive measures that span several years. To fill out coverage in year 9, when just 463 parents were surveyed (as against 651 in year 10), data from year 10 are used for parents not interviewed the previous year. However, to avoid problems of endogeneity, no substitution is made for children who dropped out between the two surveys. This approach increases year 9 case coverage on the parent attitude scale from 441 to 613.

Personal Resources

Children's *Self-Attitudes* are constructed from four sources:

the average of mark expectations for the upcoming report card in math and reading, and, beginning in middle school, English and science also (coded from 1 to 13, with 1 = failing; 13 = A+);

conduct expectations for the upcoming report card (usually dichotomized, with 1 = satisfactory; 0 = needs improvement—the distinctions used in the BCPS in the primary grades);

self-expectation for eventual level of school attainment (1 = not finish high school; 6 = more than college); and

a measure of academic self-image, having three components:

children's self-rating of their smartness relative to others in the school (4 = one of the smartest; 1 = not as smart as most kids);

a five-item scale that rates self-ability in different academic areas (for example, "How good are you at" math, reading, being a good student, learning new things quickly, and writing-handwriting, with response options ranging from 5 = very good to 1 = very bad);

a six-item self-rating of academic competence developed by Susan Harter (1982), for example, "Some kids feel they are very good at their school-work, others feel. . . . Is this very true for you or sort of true for you?"

Educational expectations, the Harter scale, and the smartness item were not elicited in first grade, nor were educational expectations asked in year 2. The "How good are you at" questions were not asked in year 9. Otherwise, all sources are available each year students were interviewed (years 1, 2, 4, 6, 7, 8, 9), with questions sometimes repeated fall and spring. Student self-attitude scores are constructed each year as the average of the measures available, after conversion to standard scores. These then are averaged across years. Alpha reliabilities for the academic self-image component of the self-attitudes composite average 0.70 and range from 0.60 in first grade to 0.84 in year 9. Reliabilities for the self-attitudes constructions themselves (based on three or four items) are low in years 1, 2, and 4 (averaging 0.44), but average 0.65 over years 6 through 9 (alpha reliabilities would be higher if calculated using the elements of the self-image scale separately).

The measures used to construct *Engagement Attitude* and *Engagement Behavior* scales change over time. The final constructions were guided, on an occasion-by-occasion basis, by psychometric analyses that most years screened out numerous candidate items. Alpha reliabilities for the final *Engagement Attitude* scales range from 0.58 in first grade to 0.76 in year 7 (averaging 0.67); for *Engagement Behaviors* the range is from 0.74 in year 8 to 0.86 in year 6 (averaging 0.81).

Engagement Behavior for the elementary years is constructed from math and English-reading teachers' ratings (on a scale of 1 to 6) of *Externalizing Behaviors* (seven items, with scores reflected, for example, teases, fights) and of *Classroom Adaptability* (four items, for example, is enthusiastic, creative), report card ratings of student work habits (five items, for example, works independently; completes assignments), and report card ratings of conduct. The measure for year 6 combines report card information on absences, work habits, and conduct (the last only for children still in elementary school in year 6), student reports of time spent on homework, and teacher ratings of externalizing and adaptability behaviors. In years 8 and 9, questions asked of students and parents about problems at school (six of students, three of parents; for example, "I was sent to the office because I was misbehaving") and of students about cutting school and cutting class are added to the year 6 measures, but work habit ratings are dropped (these are not included on report cards in the middle grades) and conduct ratings are reported by teachers rather than taken from report cards. Items are standardized and averaged within years. Measures that span years are constructed as the average of these averages.

Engagement Attitudes for years 1 and 2 are the average of four school satisfaction items, repeated fall and spring: "Would you say schoolwork is usually pretty dull or pretty interesting?" (interesting = 1; dull = 0); "If you could go to any school you wanted to, would you pick this school or some other school?" (this school = 1; other school = 0); "Do you like school a lot (coded 2), think it's just OK (coded 1), or not like it much at all (coded 0)?"; "Do you like [your teacher] a lot (coded 2); think he or she is just OK (coded 1), or not like him or her much at all (coded 0)?" In year 4, responses to six items asked of students about why they study (for example, because it is interesting; because you like to solve hard problems) and three items about motivation for doing schoolwork (to get good grades; to please parents) are combined with the four satisfaction questions. After year 4, the teacher question from the satisfaction set and the study-schoolwork questions were replaced, but other items were added. In years 6, 7, and 8, these include questions asked of teachers and parents about whether the study child "hates going to school." In year 9, seven self-ratings of the importance of school-related issues (for example, finishing high school; doing well in school; being good at math) are included. Response options that reflect favorably on school commitment are scored high throughout. To rate engagement attitudes, items are standardized and averaged within years. Measures that span years are constructed as the average of these averages.

Multiple Regression

Chapter 7 uses regression analysis to quantify how it is that the intergenerational correlation of socioeconomic standing in our sample data is maintained through the intervening mechanisms posited by our conceptualization, as displayed in figure 7.1. Correlational analyses make no distinction between independent and dependent variables, but the regression framework is predictive and, as used here, explanatory: figure 7.1 is a theory of process; table 7.2 conveys its implications when evaluated empirically.

Results are reported as standardized coefficients, meaning that all variables in the analysis, whatever their original measurement properties, have been normalized to distributions with an average value of 0 and standard deviation of 1.[5] Our interest in this volume is to illuminate the role of socioeconomic origins and the stratifying identities of race and gender in the perpetuation of urban disadvantage across generations—how large are their influences and what are the mechanisms through which they work?

A perennial challenge is to sort among potential disadvantaging attributes, race and gender and SES origins being obvious candidates. What makes this challenging is that disadvantaging attributes in stratification systems often overlap: for example, people of color and women are overrepresented among the poor. Advantaging attributes likewise tend to overlap: poverty rates are lower among whites than among members of disadvantaged minority groups and white men earn more on average than do white women. So, is it race, sex, or

SES that matters? It is a riddle with no easy or certain solution, but it is testable as a "could it be?" proposition.

The goal is to enhance credibility of the effect interpretation by evaluating, and discounting, alternative interpretations or possibilities. Arthur Stinchcombe (1987) calls these critical tests. Some of the alternatives may be self-evidently false, and are rejectable on those grounds. In this volume, we know that grown children's status levels in adulthood cannot influence their parents' status levels when they were growing up because influence does not extend backward in time. Much interpretation in the social sciences relies on that principle.

Other alternative interpretations or possibilities may not be dismissed so readily. Regression analysis used in an explanatory mode attempts to approximate the ceteris paribus logic of interpretation of the classical experimental design, but equating comparisons through statistical means rather than by random assignment to experimental and control groups. Random assignment is a more powerful tool, because at least in theory it equates the comparisons on everything that might be relevant, whereas statistical modeling equates only on variables included in the analysis, and even then the equating may not be perfect.[6]

With respect to family SES, race, and gender, the intent is to compare outcomes across groups that are identical in terms of the values of measured variables other than the focal one of the moment. Controlling for race means that we inspect the relationship between SES origins and SES destinations separately for blacks and whites, as though we had subdivided the sample along lines of race (the separation is statistical, not literal).

The logic of interpretation is that if the SES difference is present and of similar magnitude among African Americans and whites separately, then racial differences in SES destinations cannot account for the effect of social origins on social destinations. That is because within the population of African Americans there are no black-white differences, and the same holds for an analysis conducted just among whites. It is in this sense that the analysis holds constant race as an explanatory variable.

For gender and other differences controlled in the analysis, it is the same: there are no gender differences within the separate populations of women and men. Knowing that effects of social origins on destinations are not standing in for, or capturing, advantages and disadvantages issuing from race or gender passes two critical tests. Avoiding such misattribution is not conclusive, but it does help build the case that the SES-origins coefficients reflect real influence.

The same general approach is used to inform all the possible influences on socioeconomic destinations implied by figure 7.1. Consider, for example, the proposition that children from families of higher socioeconomic standing are advantaged at school because they benefit from stronger family support or advantageous educational track placements. If family resources and structural placements operate as supposed, they will be correlated with both family background (higher-SES families afford better access to useful resources) and SES destinations in adulthood (by supporting success at school, these resources give higher-SES children a workplace advantage later in life). If those conditions maintain, then adjusting statistically for these patterns of correlation or covariation will reduce the value of the original origins-destinations correlation.

In technical terms, the recalculated coefficient is a partial coefficient, and the effects of the control variables are partialled out. To illustrate, suppose the origins—destination coefficient shrinks from its original value of 0.51 to 0.25 when resources for schooling are controlled. It then can be said that differences in school resources account for about half the value of the original estimated effect, because that is the reduction when socioeconomic comparisons are made among children with like resource profiles. Given that resources are equated statistically, the remaining influence of SES origins on destinations must trace to other considerations.

Descriptively that is unarguably accurate, but whether the exercise is more than a statistical accounting is more problematic. That hinges on how well and comprehensively the relevant resources are measured (do the measures capture the essence of what is intended?) and our confidence in thinking of them as resources for schooling.

Generalizing from Sample to Population

The Youth Panel is a probability sample of 790 children who began first grade in twenty Baltimore City public elementary schools in 1982. Their story is of interest because it affords a window on the experience of children "like them" throughout Baltimore City at about the same time, and, in a looser sense, of children in cities like Baltimore throughout the nation. At issue is the generalization from sample to population, made possible by the project's original probability sampling. There are many single-city or single-site studies of youth development, but few anchored in probability sampling from a well-defined population. The Youth Panel's representativeness is evident at several points in this volume—for example, in the close agreement between the sample's 1980 neighborhood crime and sociodemographic profiles and the corresponding profiles citywide; also, in 2005 Census earnings data for young adults in Baltimore, which average close to the Youth Panel value.

Sampling theory, which presumes representativeness, is used to determine the likelihood that associations observed in our sample data also characterize the population to which we wish to generalize. In our notation (for example, table 7.2), two asterisks indicate that an association of that magnitude or larger would be expected in a sample this size in fewer than one in a hundred such samples if the association at issue were zero in the population (referred to as the 0.01 level of significance). A single asterisk uses a looser standard—one in twenty samples, or 5 percent of the time.

These are tests of statistical significance against the so-called null hypothesis that the population relationship is zero. At these levels of significance, the probability of getting an estimated coefficient of the magnitude reported (or larger) by chance is so remote that, following convention, we conclude the association holds not just in the observed sample, which we can see, but also in the population from which the sample was drawn. The population associations might not be the same size as those estimated, but the sample estimates encourage confidence that the relationships are not zero in the population. In shorthand, we say that the relationship or effect is significant, or not.

═══ Notes ═══

Chapter 1

1. Academic accounts tend to be somewhat more circumspect in their language, but concur that the word *underclass* "says more about behavior than income" (Ricketts and Sawhill 1988, 318).

2. The creative team behind *The Corner*, David Simon and Edward Burns, followed its success with two hugely popular television programs also set in Baltimore: *Homicide* and *The Wire*.

3. See "About the Book," *Random House*, http://www.randomhouse.com/book/167536/the-corner-by-david-simon-and-edward-burns (accessed November 18, 2013).

4. The labor force census count includes those looking for work as well as those employed. For that reason, labor force participation rates, as here, usually are higher than employment rates.

5. Needy children qualify for free meals at 1.3 times the poverty level and for reduced price meals at 1.85 times (adjusted for family size) under the National School Lunch and School Breakfast Programs. The 90 percent figure is for the entire school, based on school records.

6. It might be suspected these self-reports understate hard drug use, but any such underreporting likely is minor. We have been involved with these youth over many years. They know us well and seem remarkably candid.

7. In several instances, more than one family member was mentioned.

8. The only notable difference in these comparisons is the number of families headed by women: 51.8 percent in the black communities, 37.8 percent in the white. It is a difference of some consequence, as we will see later.

9. For blacks, the corresponding figures are 5.4 million, representing 36.9 percent of the African American population and an increase of 74 percent from 1969.

10. Although the earnings prospects of young college graduates have slipped during the recent recession (see, for example, Shierholz 2013), a college degree remains a wise investment (see Bureau of Labor Statistics 2012).

213

11. This is according to Claudia Goldin and Lawrence Katz (2008), who look back as far as is practically doable, to around 1915.

12. These figures are for sixteen to twenty-four-year-olds not enrolled in school.

13. Most births outside of marriage are to young women, but among African Americans the prevalence remains high into older ages, not dropping below 90 percent until ages twenty through twenty-four. Among whites, it dips below 90 percent at age eighteen (Martin et al. 2012, 45).

14. To sustain black-white comparisons, we oversampled schools with large white enrollments: the Youth Panel is 55 percent African American; the African American enrollment citywide was 77 percent (U.S. Bureau of the Census 1983).

15. Ninety-seven percent of the randomly selected children were successfully recruited into the project (that is, parental consent for their participation was obtained), as were 100 percent of the schools (though subsequently, one school was replaced when a parent objected to the project).

16. Citywide comparisons with the Youth Panel throughout the volume attest to the representativeness of the initial sampling. Sample retention over the panel's twenty-five-year span has been highly successful: 80 percent of the original group are covered in the project's two surveys after high school (appendix B).

17. Both after high school surveys achieved 80 percent coverage of the original group, though not the same 80 percent. Joint coverage for the two interviews is 71 percent. The first was on paper, the second computerized.

18. The totals ranged from 99.7 percent in the fall of first grade to 52 percent in the spring of year 8 (fall interview coverage that year was 77 percent).

19. Members of the panel all began first grade in the fall of 1982, but their progress through school was highly uneven. Many repeated one or more grades and many were assigned to ungraded special education classes. In year 9, most were in ninth grade, but some were in seventh or eighth grade and others already had dropped out. Hence, when we say ninth grade or some other grade, it is approximate, a convenient shorthand.

20. Low-income children tend to move frequently, and after five years (the typical elementary school grade span in Baltimore), panel participants had spread to more than a hundred schools within the city system and a fifth had transferred out, either to private schools or to public schools in one of the nearby counties.

21. Our chapter in that volume is a useful source for additional background on the Youth Panel.

22. Attributed to Gerhard Lenski in *Power and Privilege* (1966).

23. Elements of it are detectable across scattered literatures, but the pieces rarely come together. Jay MacLeod's (2008) account of working-class white and black gang members living in a Boston public housing project and

Deirdre Royster's (2003) study of the white and black graduates of one of Baltimore's vocational high schools are conspicuous exceptions, as are Kathryn Edin's inquiries into the family life of the urban poor (Edin and Kefalas 2005; Edin and Nelson 2013).

Chapter 2

1. The great migration of African Americans out of the South is well known, but white migrants outnumbered black by almost two to one. According to the 1980 census, 4.2 million "blacks and others" and 7.6 million whites born in the South were then living outside the South (Gregory 1995, 112).

2. These two Baltimore vocational high schools were segregated at the time.

3. Royster's (2003) study of black and white graduates of Baltimore's Glendale High (a pseudonym) suggests not much has changed over the ensuing thirty-odd years.

4. The corresponding percentages working as laborers were 15 percent white and 25 percent black.

5. Rebecca Blank (2009) is correct, but access to jobs also is a problem. In Baltimore, as elsewhere (for example, Wilson 1997), many low wage, low benefit jobs have relocated outside the city.

6. According to Ralph Taylor (2001, 365–66), the largest absolute declines in quality of life measures were registered during the decade of the seventies, while conditions relative the surrounding counties deteriorated most markedly during the eighties and into the nineties.

7. During this time, the black enrollment also declined, by a much smaller 26 percent.

8. It warrants note that the county's minority enrollment was more diverse than the city's, with 17.4 percent mixed race, Asian, Latino, or Native American. In Baltimore City, those groups were 6 percent of the total enrollment (Ayscue et al. 2013, 51).

9. In the 1982–1983 school year, the meal subsidy rate in the city's elementary schools averaged 68 percent, ranging from 11 percent to 100 percent (Baltimore City Schools 1988).

10. In Maryland, school districts are coterminus with counties. Maryland is one of four states where counties are the governing municipal units responsible for schools, roads, police, health, voting, and so on.

11. More recently, the charter school movement has been attracting activist parents into city schools and the landscape just sketched could well be changing.

Chapter 3

1. Whether the child is a son or a daughter has little bearing on the birth family's material conditions and other mobility resources. For that reason,

our consideration of gender is deferred until later, when we take up possible consequences of family resources and other issues for which gender is integral—for example, the transition to adulthood, patterns of educational attainment, and prospects in the workplace.

2. James Heckman (2008, 320) also reminds us that the early-late divide is an oversimplification, arguing instead for a "balanced approach" that builds on the gains accomplished through early interventions like high quality preschool: "If early investments are followed up with later interventions optimally, outcomes can be considerably improved."

3. Greg Duncan and Jeanne Brooks-Gunn also note that family conditions reemerge after adolescence as significant for educational attainment, income, and mental health.

4. When the Youth Panel was starting first grade, neighborhood and school overlapped. Over the years since, school choice has become more prevalent, and in Baltimore all schools today are nominally schools of choice. That policy shift could weaken the link between neighborhood and school. Parents remain in control, but with decisions about school now presumably deliberately made.

5. Measurement details are provided in appendix B.

6. Although data for midrank families are not reported, in practically every instance their profile falls squarely between the lower and higher groups—SES is very much a gradient or ranking.

7. The range for the Youth Panel parents is 14.71 to 88.37 for mothers; 15.97 to 88.42 for fathers.

8. For fathers, first grade coverage is thin, as we asked education and occupation only of the parent respondent, 85 percent of whom were mothers (in later interviews we asked about the other parent if coresident). When first grade data on fathers are unavailable, the second grade report is used.

9. Because data coverage for fathers is spotty, we report employment for all available years.

10. From time diaries, Suzanne Bianchi, John Robinson, and Melissa Milkie (2006) report that college-educated mothers, despite being more often employed outside the home, nevertheless invest considerably more time in enrichment activities with their children than do less highly educated mothers.

11. These are the percentages residing in neighborhoods with poverty rates of 40 percent and above. Levels of concentrated poverty in metropolitan areas declined sharply between 1990 and 2000 (for example, Jargowsky 2003), but that reversed during the ensuing decade (Kneebone, Nadeau, and Berube 2011). In 2009, 16 percent of Baltimore's poor lived in extreme poverty neighborhoods, although half the residents of those neighborhoods were not poor (Kneebone, Nadeau, and Berube 2011, 24).

12. In higher-income white neighborhoods, children were less likely to attend public schools. Citywide in 1980, the correlation between neighborhood

white mean income and the percentage of school-age children in the neighborhood attending public schools was –0.53 (Baltimore City Department of Planning 1983).

13. Hypersegregated schools in the literature are racially homogeneous at a level of 90 percent or greater.

14. These figures are calculated from information provided by the school system's Department of Research and Evaluation.

15. The majority of black births have been to unwed mothers since the mid-1970s; among whites, the highest figure through 1999 was 26.7 percent (Ventura and Bachrach 2000, 31).

16. The percentage of nonmarital births among whites has continued to rise. It stood at 33.3 percent in 2006, and among African Americans at 70.2 percent (Martin et al. 2009, 54).

17. This future, in Murray's estimation, was perilously close. He thought 25 percent the tipping point. When illegitimacy rates are beyond that level, he argued, underclass maladies spike sharply upward.

18. In the early 1990s, about the same percentage of white children (40 percent) as African American children (39 percent) of single mothers were in families with other adults (U.S. Bureau of the Census 1992), but 58 percent of African American families were headed by single mothers, versus 18 percent of white families.

19. Baltimore was a leader in providing the means for expectant mothers and mothers to stay in school. The Paquin School, founded in 1966 to serve those students, provided day care for infants on site, health care for mothers and children, and a warm reception to both.

20. Being never married is one reason for not being married in 1982. Others include the death of a spouse, divorce, and separation. Technically, separated couples are married, but the intent here is to characterize the home environment. Separated couples are living apart. Including them among the not married is shorthand for that.

21. The higher-SES figures are for black and white combined. Race differences among higher-SES families generally are smaller than among their lower-SES counterparts. That is one reason the two groups are combined. As examples, 3 percent and 17 percent of white and black higher-SES mothers were never married through 1982; 84 percent and 65 percent, respectively, were married at the time of the 1982 survey. The comparisons still favor whites, but by smaller margins than among lower-SES families.

Chapter 4

1. In table 4.1, a lower-SES child who attends school in a higher-income neighborhood will have higher-SES neighborhood values. When we refer in the text to higher- and lower-SES neighborhoods, we mean "neighborhoods that are typical of higher and lower SES children."

2. One other school, a combined elementary and middle, was a de facto middle-class magnet school in that many parents living outside its catchment area arranged access for their children. Most out-of-neighborhood students, white and African American, were middle class whose own neighborhood schools were perceived to be of lesser quality.

3. We are unable to monitor the duration of exposure to neighborhood poverty, but data at the national level reveal large differences by race. Using rates from the early through mid-1990s, Jeffrey Timberlake (2007) reports that the average African American child through age eighteen spent roughly half his or her lifetime in neighborhoods with poverty levels of 20 percent or greater; for white children, the corresponding exposure was just 5 percent. And this holds across generations as well: more than 70 percent of black children who grow up in the poorest quarter of neighborhoods nationally live in such neighborhoods as adults. For whites, the figure is 40 percent (Sharkey 2008).

4. Neighborhood crime data were acquired from the project *Crime Changes in Baltimore: 1970–1994* through the University of Michigan's ICPSR (we do not use the data from 1994, although they are available from the same source). They are from Baltimore City Police Department records as applied to Baltimore City Department of Planning designated neighborhoods, the same source used to organize the census data reported in table 4.1. Citywide crime statistics come from the Governor's Office of Crime Control and Prevention in Maryland (2013). It is noteworthy that the crime averages across all twenty neighborhoods track closely those for the entire city (Overall versus Baltimore City in table 4.2), another indication of the Youth Panel's representativeness.

5. Robbery, defined as the taking of property by force or the threat of force, appears in both because it embodies both.

6. The standard deviation is a measure of dispersion or variability in a distribution of scores. It has the stylized properties of the so-called normal or Z score distribution: an average value of 0 and a standard deviation of 1.

7. Four items: for example, "How much do you feel a sense of community with others in the neighborhood," and response options ranging from "not at all" to "a great deal"; and, "On a scale of 1 to 10, how would you rate your neighborhood as it is today?" 1 representing the worst possible neighborhood and 10 representing the best.

8. Eight items: for example, "For each item, tell me if it's a big problem, somewhat of a problem, or not a problem," followed by "vandalism," "bad elements moving in" and "crime"; and, "How would you feel about being out alone in your neighborhood [on your block] during the day [at night]," from "very safe" to "very unsafe."

9. Eight items: for example, "For each item, tell me if it's a big problem, somewhat of a problem, or not a problem," followed by "vacant housing," "people who don't keep up their property or yards," "people who say insulting things to or bother other people walking down the street," and "litter and trash in the streets."

10.   Seven items: for example, "Have you kept watch on a house or apartment while a neighbor was away, or has a neighbor done this for you?" and "Have you arranged with other people in your neighborhood to have newspapers or mail brought in while you or they were away?"; "Does your neighborhood have its own newspaper or newsletter"; "Do you have any friends who are not relatives living in the neighborhood?"

11.   Alpha reliabilities range from 0.88 to 0.97. All families in the same neighborhood are assigned the same item scores. Though the sample size for table 4.3 is 713, in fact there are just eighteen distinct values per item, repeated for each member of the sample in a particular neighborhood. This will tend to inflate reliability estimates.

12.   Across generations, African Americans are much more likely than are whites who grew up in poor neighborhoods to remain in poor neighborhoods as adults. For the poorest quarter of neighborhoods, the figures are 70 percent and 40 percent respectively (Sharkey 2008). Such continuity across generations in the experience of neighborhood poverty is found to depress children's school performance (Sharkey and Elwert 2011).

13.   Barbara Mikulski, Maryland's senior senator, helped lead the resistance. At the time, she was a social worker and community activist.

14.   Other accounts put the number displaced at 1,500 and another 1,500 relocated due to other projects under way around the same time (see Giguere 2009).

15.   Stephen Kiehl, "Neighborhood Sees $1.3 Billion Lifeline," *Baltimore Sun,* June 27, 2008, p. B1.

16.   The predominant grade organization at the time was K–5 (elementary school), 6–8 (middle school), and 9–12 (high school). *Take This School* does not cover combined elementary-middle schools, which excludes one of the original twenty. Three others are omitted for unknown reasons.

17.   Over the years since, nationally residential segregation by race has eased some (see, for example, Reardon et al. 2009), though segregation by income has increased (Reardon and Bischoff 2011).

18.   We also examined special education enrollments, but that issue is clouded by almost thirty years of litigation over the city's provision of special education services. The original lawsuit, not settled until 2010, traces to the period at issue here (Liz Bowie, "Judge Ends 26 Years of Special Education Oversight for City Schools," *Baltimore Sun,* March 8, 2010, p. 5). Additionally, special education rates evidence no clear patterning across school types, either citywide or for schools attended.

19.   Grade equivalent scores are calibrated to the expected level of performance for the school grade at the time of year the test is administered. So, for example, the expected score for second graders at the start of the school year is 2.0; at year's end, nine months later, it is 2.9.

20.   There also are race differences among lower-SES children. They favor whites, but by smaller margins: 0.3 GE in math, but just 0.1 GE in reading.

21. According to Carmen Arroyo (2008, 6–7), nationally the funding gap per student across the highest and lowest poverty districts in a state averaged $938 in 2005. Across districts with the highest and lowest concentrations of minority students, the gap was $877.

22. Today, all Baltimore schools are schools of choice, at least nominally so. However, because enrollment is roughly 90 percent African American and 80 percent low income, there are limits to the diversity that can be accomplished through within-district choice: were all of Baltimore's public schools maximally desegregated, every school would be *hypersegregated*, with an enrollment 90 percent African American, 8 percent white, and 2 percent other.

Chapter 5

1. The averages nationally among women were 25.3 years for a first birth (2010) and 26.6 years for a first marriage (2012). This reverses the historic pattern. College-educated women are an exception—for them just 12 percent of first births were outside marriage and their average age of first birth remains above their average age of first marriage (Hymowitz et al. 2013, 18). In 2006, nearly 40 percent of births were to unmarried women (Arroyo et al. 2013).

2. Studies that adjust for selection into teen parenthood (for example, attributes that increase the likelihood of becoming a teen parent) generally find fewer and less severe adverse consequences than less rigorously structured studies (for example, Hoffman 1998). Still, teen parenting makes it harder to finish high school with a regular diploma, rather than the GED, and has near-term, but possibly transitory, consequences for earnings and employment (Hotz, McElroy, and Sanders 1996).

3. Note, we are monitoring "ever married–cohabit" and "ever employed full time," not currently married–cohabiting or currently employed.

4. To screen out casual live-in pairings we exclude partnerships shorter than three months. Combining marriage and partnerships in the catchall *union* is not meant to equate cohabiting with marriage. Cohabitations, for example, tend to be much less stable: 39 percent of cohabiting couples with a child were no longer together five years later versus 13 percent of their married counterparts (Hymowitz et al. 2013, 10).

5. We are unable to distinguish drug use from distribution.

6. We say *deferred* because practically everyone expects to marry and have children someday, most between ages thirty and thirty-five.

7. The question was of the write-in variety, with replies coded and classified after the fact.

Chapter 6

1. Mothers' median age in the fall of 1982 was 29.4 years, almost identical to the panel's median age (28.8 years) when interviewed in 2005. However,

because the panel was sampled from a single school year, the age distribution is compressed relative to the parents': 70 percent were between 28.1 and 29.1 years at the time of the MAS; an eleven-year band (22.8 to 33.6 years) is needed to encompass a like percentage of the mothers.

2. Low-wage work tends to be characterized by relatively flat age-earnings or experience-earnings profiles, meaning that wages do not rise appreciably with experience (for example, Kalleberg and Sorensen 1979; Connolly and Gottschalk 2006). In 2011, almost 11 percent of working families fell below the poverty line and nearly 33 percent were low income, with earnings less than twice the poverty threshold (Roberts, Povich, and Mather 2012).

3. Individual dates are used for exiting high school, secured through retrospective calendars embedded in the two after high school interviews. The MAS interview asked for starting and ending dates of employment and enrollment spells; when memory failed, it asked for the year and season instead (fall, winter, and so on). The YAS interview used quarterly calendar grids, later converted to months. For employment, questioning referred to jobs held at least three months. The accuracy of recalled dates over many years is an obvious concern, and our procedures introduced two additional ones. First, any work or schooling during a given month or quarter is credited to that month or quarter—a week is counted the same as three full months. When seasons are used, the approximation to months is even cruder. Second, full-time and part-time schooling are not distinguished. Still, the relative differences evident in table 6.1 are informative, as any distortions should hold for everyone.

4. This accords with Sheldon Danziger and David Ratner (2010, 136), who report idleness rates of 21 percent for blacks and 12 percent for whites among young men ages sixteen to twenty-four in 2008.

5. Marta Tienda and Haya Steir (1991, 140) make a like point for low-income parents in Chicago: "Before concluding that parents who did not want jobs are shiftless, one needs to consider their reasons. Some 91 percent of those surveyed reported poor health or family responsibilities." The genuinely "shiftless" are uncommon.

6. The corresponding figures for white men of the same age are 1.8 percent and 12.0 percent.

7. Among African Americans, prison admissions for drug offenses increased from roughly twenty thousand in 1983 to almost a hundred thousand in 2001. Over this same period, white admissions increased from a baseline of just under 20,000—quite close to the African American figure—to around 45,000 (Pager 2007, 21). Michelle Alexander (2010) provides a scathing critique of racist policies and practices in U.S. drug enforcement. According to Bruce Western and Becky Pettit (2005), almost half of the jobless young black men in 1999 were in prison or jail, versus just 10 percent of whites.

8. Identified as just over 9 percent of the entire panel in table 6.2, but that is an undercount. A small number of those with GEDs continued their

schooling at the postsecondary level, almost all by way of vocational-technical certificate programs.

9. This group cannot be identified in table 6.2. In an earlier study (Entwisle, Alexander, and Olson 2004), we examine dropout recovery in the sample.

10. Nationally in 2010, 12 percent of GED recipients were age thirty or older (American Council on Education 2011, 65).

11. The breakdown is 15.1 percent certificates, 14.0 percent bachelor's degrees, and the balance associate's degrees (suppressed in table 6.2 owing to the small number of completed associate's degrees overall).

12. The 16 percent includes 3.1 percent who went on to complete graduate and professional degrees, including seven PhDs.

13. This is referred to in the literature as *right censoring.* The eventual fate of those still enrolled is unknown.

14. Some research combines completed degrees with current enrollment as a measure of persistence (for example, Horn and Berger 2005). Our interest centers on accomplishment, with enrollees treated as degreeless. In the sample, a fifth of those who pursued certificates were enrolled at the time of the MAS; at the associate's and bachelor's levels, a fourth were enrolled.

15. In the fall of 2010, for example, 44.8 percent of African American under-graduates were enrolled in two year colleges; of whites, 39.7 percent were (U.S. Department of Education 2011, table A-36-1). Of 2004 high school graduates who continued into college, 39.0 percent of African Americans began at two-year institutions versus 34.3 percent of whites (U.S. Department of Education 2006, table E-34-2). In 2003–2004, 25 percent of beginning postsecondary students came from families with annual incomes below $32,000. They made up 20 percent of students starting at four-year colleges, 28 percent of those starting at two-year colleges, and 65 percent of those starting at less than two-year institutions (Berkner, Choy, and Hunt-White 2008, vi–vii).

16. Many community colleges award certificates as well as the associate's degree. We monitor certificates and degrees; in the case of certificates, the institutional type where they are undertaken is incidental.

17. The others are two-year and four-year for profit degree programs, which enrolled 1.7 million students in the fall of 2009. Some of the better-known ones include the Apollo Group (University of Phoenix), Strayer University, and Kaplan Higher Education (Hendry 2009).

18. Much of this attention has been critical—early examples include Burton Clark 1960, Jerome Karabel 1972, Steven Brint and Jerome Karabel 1989, and Kevin Dougherty 1994.

19. We have already called attention to the frailty of such retrospective accounts.

20. Table 6.2 does not include graduate enrollments, but they deserve mention. Thirty-two of the sample pursued master's or doctoral studies.

Thirteen had master's degrees and seven had either doctorates or professional degrees. Seven of the remaining twelve were enrolled when interviewed. These thirty-two are counted as bachelor's degree completers in table 6.2.

21. "Time is the Enemy" is a pervasive problem throughout higher education, according to a recent report by Complete College America by that name (2011). The figures are shocking: just 27.8 percent of full-time students in one-year certificate programs complete them within two years; 18.8 percent of those in two-year associate's programs within four years; and 60.6 percent of those in four-year bachelor's programs within eight years. For those attending part-time, the corresponding figures are half or less. But time per se in not the problem; it is a holding place for the conditions that distinguish privileged fast-track students from those on the slow, round-about track.

22. *Occupation* and *job* have different meaning in the literature, but for convenience we use the terms interchangeably. *Job* is workplace specific—for example, the physician's job is chief of surgery at hospital X.

23. This gender advantage is peculiar to women of higher-SES background. The midrange SES group (also 25 percent of the panel) is not reported in table 6.3, but in this instance their experience is instructive: just 10.7 percent of these white women and 5.9 percent of African American women were employed in the professions. Hardly any completed college and, now we see, hardly any break through to high-level employment (for executive-managerial positions, the respective figures are 3.6 percent and zero).

24. Excluded are fifty who worked at part-time jobs exclusively during these two years and 120 others with no qualifying work experience. The data on spouse-partners are addressed below. See appendix B for measurement details.

25. We should say "living in and around the city." Nearly half of those interviewed for the MAS were living outside Baltimore at the time. Implications of this are taken up at the end of chapter 7.

26. These totals are for earnings from work and are not limited to the full-time job used to classify occupation in table 6.4. The question asked was "How much did you earn last year from all jobs before taxes and other deductions?" Separately, we elicited earnings from the most recent full-time and part-time jobs (limited here to jobs held within twenty-four months of the MAS). Their sum is used when the first question was missing or seemed unreasonably low (for example, in a few instances, hourly salaries were coded as monthly salaries).

27. For example, with an SEI average of 58.8, professionals rank comfortably highest, but the Youth Panel includes an attorney at an SEI rank of 80.3; at the other end are housecleaners, at 13.9.

28. In 1970, 40 percent of the spouses of male college graduates in the thirty to forty-four age range were college graduates; in 2007, the figure was 70 percent (Autor and Wasserman 2013, 28).

29. Floor and ceiling constraints no doubt come into play here. For those in higher status jobs, the pool of prospects is larger below than above; at the lower end, it is the reverse.

30. As noted, we have not monitored other sources of financial and in-kind support from extended family and others, or government assistance. For those struggling to survive, these extra resources can mean a great deal (for example, Edin and Lein 1997). They also are unstable, and a poor substitute for the security afforded by a spouse-partner as a second earner in the household.

31. This level of accomplishment is hardly the sample norm: there are just sixteen higher-SES white women with no children and a partner, among African American women, just two.

32. Almost all say they expect to have children eventually.

33. Among African Americans of lower-SES background, 58 percent of those whose mothers were teen parents became teen parents; 49 percent of those whose mothers were not teen parents became teen parents. The corresponding percentages for lower-SES white women are close at 56 percent and 32 percent. Thus, although teen parentage is more common among those raised by a teen parent, teen parenting is hardly predestined—the inheritance is a tendency, not a certainty.

34. Twenty-eight percent of those lacking earnings and employment data are lower-SES black men; the next highest percentages are lower-SES women, African American and white, at 16 percent for earnings and 17 percent for employment.

35. Here we also are obliged to address missing data. The 20 percent of the sample not interviewed at age twenty-eight are excluded from this part of the exercise altogether because we have no destination data for them. Others are missing information selectively. In these situations, we either turn to another source (for example, if there is no qualifying full-time job, we use a part-time job if one is available). For the composite, coverage is reasonably good: 88 percent of those interviewed and 69 percent of their partners have data on all three items—education level, occupational status, and earnings. The corresponding figures with just one item available (almost always level of schooling) are 5.1 percent and 11 percent. For the 43 percent of the panel with no partner, the family composite and personal composite are the same. For the others, the family composite combines sample and partner data. Most partners are spouses: 62 percent overall, from 73 percent among white men to 50 percent among African American men.

36. For the personal SES scale composite, level of educational attainment (coded in years), occupational status, and personal earnings are averaged after standardizing (mean of 0 and standard deviation of 1). The family composite adds partner educational level and occupational status and substitutes family earnings for personal earnings. For detail, see appendix B. The table entries are means for educational level and occupational

status, medians for earnings. We use the median for earnings to damp the pull of cases with extremely high values. The mean earnings figure for the sample is $32,900, $4,000 above the median reported in table 6.7. The minor discrepancies with table 6.4 involve differences in case coverage: N = 503 there, N = 559 here.

37. The overall figures show small discrepancies because table 6.4 screens on occupational category, which is not known for some of those covered in table 6.7.

38. Occupations around that SEI level include cashier, server, laborer, receptionist, painter, teller, nursing assistant, sales clerk, and carpet layer.

39. There also are skews along lines of race and gender in the destination SES distribution. The percentage of lower SES ranges between 22.7 percent (white men) and 34.5 percent (white women). With status calculated at the family level, white women are just about at expectation at 30.4 percent. At the higher-SES end, the range is 17.7 percent (African American women) to 27.3 percent (white men).

40. The official poverty thresholds vary by family size. These mothers had between one and five children.

41. The subsample sizes are from the years of education column, which is known for everyone. Household earnings other than those of a spouse or partner are not considered. This no doubt overlooks some household earnings, but whether it distorts comparisons across social lines is hard to know.

Chapter 7

1. For one, they afford but a snapshot-in-time picture, so it cannot be said how typical they are. Also, as the researchers caution, their analysis of factors associated with mobility patterns are correlational comparisons, and so cannot establish causal priorities.

2. *Same* is correct in relative terms, but the SES distributions are not perfectly aligned across generations—for example, the modal level of schooling for parents is high school dropout; for the sample grown up, it is high school graduate.

3. The expectation is the allocation were mobility determined, effectively, by a coin flip, with family background immaterial. This random allocation pattern affords a frame of reference for judging the mobility experience of the sample. For each cell, the expected count is calculated as the product of the row and column totals divided by the overall table total. For the lower–lower personal mobility cell it is $(314 \times 177)/626 = 88.8$.

4. If the two distributions were perfectly aligned, the correlation would be 1.0. With no alignment, indicating no relationship at all between origin and destination statuses—essentially random allocation in relation to family SES—it would be zero.

5. The National Child Development Study, conducted by the National Children's Bureau of London, monitored the life progress from birth until age twenty-three of the entire population of babies (a total of 17,333) born in Great Britain in the first week of March 1958.

6. There are many definitions of social capital. For our purposes it is sufficient to think of social capital as resources that flow within and through social networks, with parents included in children's network of intimates.

7. Whether maternal employment in fact is harmful to children's development is unclear (for example, compare Milne et al. 1986; Heyns and Catsambis 1986; see also Ludwig and Mayer 2006).

8. The Kandel Depression Scale (Kandel and Davies 1982) is widely used, mainly with adolescents, and has excellent psychometric properties (see Compas, Ey, and Grant 1993; NIMH 1999). Questioning is straightforward, for example, "During the past year, how much have you been . . . feeling hopeless about the future," with response options "A lot" (scored 1), "A little" (scored 2), and "Not at All" (scored 3). Parents are classified as high risk or not based on a latent class trajectory analysis (see, for example, Vermunt and Magidson 2004) of annual KDS administrations from years six through eleven. The two-trajectory solution—high versus low elevated risk—has good discrimination, with predicted placement probabilities above 0.90. Twenty percent of higher-SES parents are deemed at high risk of depressive mood, 61 percent of lower-SES white parents, and 46 percent of lower-SES black parents.

9. The black-white difference among lower-SES families traces mainly to risk of depression, which, as noted, is higher among white parents.

10. Results are reported as standardized regression coefficients, and so are in standard deviation units. The value of 0.51 indicates that a one standard deviation difference in family SES origins is, on average, associated with a 0.51 standard deviation difference in personal SES destinations, after adjustment for other factors included in the equation. See appendix B for additional detail.

11. The entries are interpretable as the average difference against white men, adjusted for the other predictors in the equation at issue.

12. These analyses exclude cases for which any data source is lacking across all the measures used in a given analysis. That includes the 20 percent of the panel without MAS interviews, so the maximum sample size effectively is 628 rather than 790. Across items, coverage is fairly good. For table 7.2, it averages N = 614. However, missing data are substantially independent across items, so screening for complete data excludes almost half the original sample. The sample size for table 7.2 is 445; the lowest figure for tables 7.3 through 7.7 is 390 for occupational status, half the size of the panel at the outset. However, as best we can determine, the consequences of this attrition are minor. For one thing, sample attrition in the Youth Panel over the years is not highly selective along social or academic lines. Evidence on the point is presented in appendix B. Additionally,

analyses with missing data imputed (Allison 2002) using the *ice* (imputation by chained equations) multiple imputation procedure in STATA
differ hardly at all from those reported. The samples used in the imputed
regressions are larger than those we report and so have somewhat greater
statistical power (the percentage of imputed values averages 3.1 percent
across all independent variables; the largest values are 14 percent for the
grade 6 through 8 resource composite and 15 percent for the ninth grade
resource composite), but there is no difference in substantive import of
the imputed regressions and those we report. Because we favor real data
over even high-quality made-up data, unimputed results are reported
throughout.

13.   For the individual components of the SES composite, the reduction ranges
from 100 percent (for personal and family earnings) to 76 percent for occupational status.

14.   The first two are explained where those issue arises.

15.   Excessively high correlations among variables in a predictor set can trigger a technical problem in multiple regression analysis known as multi-
collinearity. This often happens when the number of predictors is large
and the sample size is small, and it is magnified in the present instance:
for school and neighborhood context, all children in the same neighborhood or school are assigned that neighborhood's and school's context
values, which means there are just 20 discrete data points for those
measures. Additionally, contextual measures are typically more highly
correlated in single-city studies than over larger geographic areas, where
the contextual variability will be greater (Duncan and Raudenbush 1999,
36). In the presence of excessive collinearity, estimates become unreliable
and there were clear indications of that in preliminary analyses: when
evaluated separately, measures of neighborhood SES level, neighborhood
level of violent crime, schoolwide percentage low-income enrollment, and
schoolwide average achievement level all were significant in the analyses
performed for column 3 of table 7.2, but with any set of two, three or four of
them in the analysis at the same time, none retained its significance. On that
basis we elected to combine them into a single composite, *Neighborhood and
School Context*. Alternatively, we might have omitted some of the collinear
measures, but that would have been unfaithful to the lived experience of
the sample because measures from both contexts were highly relevant in
preliminary screening.

16.   These calculations indicate the percentage of children who would have to
move or change schools for the racial composition of every neighborhood
and school to mirror the racial makeup citywide.

17.   It also is significant predicting personal SES standing, occupational status,
and personal earnings.

18.   These measures are described in appendix B.

19.   We see much the same for the family SES composite and the composite's
separate components.

20. This high correlation is both substantive—that is, time invested in school after high school pays off in certificates and degrees—but also partly dictated by how years of education is measured: it is keyed to degrees, but in order to credit "some college," also quarters of postsecondary enrollment (appendix B). This detail of measurement could exaggerate the importance of investments in schooling for socioeconomic attainment and detract from the importance of other predictors. However, with *Months Enrolled* omitted from the analysis, coefficients associated with *Months Employed* are virtually unchanged (although explained variance does drop a bit in column 8, from 0.53 to 0.51). The exclusion of *Months Enrolled* does trigger other changes though: the coefficient for *SES Origins on Destinations* increases from 0.09 to 0.18 in column 8, as do those for several early experience predictors. What this means is a matter of judgment. We believe these newly revealed effects, including that for SES origins, are routed through investments in postsecondary schooling and show up because those investments have been omitted. However, if the changes occur because we have corrected for a methods confound, then the results in table 7.2 understate somewhat unmediated SES origins effects on SES outcomes, as well as influence grounded in early family, neighborhood and school experiences.

21. This holds for the sample's early vocational development also: lower-SES men, especially African Americans, are less likely to be employed at "regular" jobs while in middle school and high school, depriving them of potentially valuable on the job training and useful contacts, not only among the sample (Entwisle, Alexander, and Olson 2000) but also nationally (Morisi 2008, 58).

22. In these comparisons, sons' earnings are averaged over two years throughout.

23. The two left out are low prevalence (*Chew Tobacco*, at 5.0 percent of the sample) or substantially redundant with those displayed (*Ever Smoke*, at 51 percent). These data come from the age twenty-eight survey, supplanted by the age twenty-two survey for those not interviewed at age twenty-eight.

24. In preliminary analysis with the ten problem behaviors kept discrete, smoking and arrests-convictions were significant for five of six status outcomes, drug use for four of six, and teen parenting three of six; their sum, as in table 7.2, is significant in all six estimations. The relevance of problem behaviors thus appears to be pervasive, although alpha reliability for the scale is low, just 0.67. This is a sign that the scale lacks unitary character, but the alternative of keeping the ten items discrete was deemed too unwieldy to be practical.

25. We tested this by reestimating the column 8 equation omitting investments in school and work and the transition to adulthood milestones. These analyses saw no reduction in the SES origins coefficient from column 7, an exception to the otherwise consistent pattern of steady decline.

26. Dummy variable contrast codings are used, with values of 1 assigned to the pattern followed and 0 to the other two. The positive sequences

are: home-job-union, home-job, and job; the negative sequences are parent-job-union, parent-home-job, parent-home-union, and the seven low prevalence sequences not examined in chapter 5. These also were associated with more negative SES outcomes than the Done All sequence.

27.   Note the confound between the *Number of Transitions* tally and the *Transition Sequence* constructions in that the Done Alls, approximately half of the sample, all fall at the top of the milestone tally with scores of four. We have experimented with alternative formulations (evaluating the three predictors individually and in various combinations of two) and the results are fairly robust. The exception is the positive effect for the *Positive Transition Sequence* measure in table 7.2, which drops to nonsignificance when either of the other two is excluded. Because of this, we are reluctant to conclude that postponing or forgoing parenthood (the common circumstance across the positive transition paths) is distinctively advantageous as a resource for moving up the status ladder.

28.   This changes some at the model's interior stages, where women (African American and white) begin to lag behind white men, but only for status as personal accomplishment. For white women at the family level, there is no status shortfall. Coefficients usually decrease in size as intermediate stage predictors are added, but they also can increase, as here. Such changes are said to reflect suppressor effects. Here it is that women's status disadvantage relative to men is underestimated, or suppressed, because the analyses to that point do not take account of women's successes at school. Controlling for them statistically reveals that, compared with men of similar academic accomplishment, women's status as young adults lags behind. Women do not lag behind in column 1 because those estimations do not adjust for their academic advantages, which instead are credited to gender.

29.   Sixty-one percent of higher-SES children left Baltimore's public schools against 29 percent of the urban disadvantaged. For moving out of Baltimore, the respective figures are 72 percent and 37 percent.

30.   As a second test for relevance, we added the two exiting measures to the first equation, with family-SES origins, race, and gender. This is the most generous estimate of their importance, and in no instance does the coefficient for SES origins drop by as much as 10 percent.

Chapter 8

1.   That is not to say Wilson thinks poor blacks and poor whites on equal terms. His point, rather, is that the foremost barrier to African American progress in the modern era is economic marginality—family poverty overlaid on debilitating concentrated neighborhood poverty.

2.   The analyses are the same as in the previous chapter, but here only coefficients for race, sex, and SES background are reported because they are our focus.

3.   These figures are metric coefficients in the original units of measurement—here, dollars. That the earnings difference increases with controls for the

intermediate stage predictors signifies a suppressor relationship: white men's earnings advantage increases when white women's schooling advantages are separated out in later stages of the analysis. Until then, the comparison, in effect, is white women with higher levels of schooling against white men with lower levels of schooling, which suppresses, or moderates, white men's earnings advantage.

4. This is not the case for personal earnings. It seems the two-earner benefit for family earnings is sufficient in the case of African American men to offset their personal earnings deficit.

5. These figures are the unstandardized regression coefficients that correspond to the standardized table entries.

6. Our focus is the implications of a spouse or partner in the household as a second earner. This is far from an exhaustive account of economic conditions among poor single parents, as often these women receive help from other sources—their parents, other relatives, or the nonresident parent or parents of their children. And too, for getting by, many resort to illicit means (see Edin and Lein 1997). These other sources of support are unreliable though, and families reliant on them typically struggle.

7. Other large issues uncovered by Royster include the reluctance of employers to take on black students in the school's work-study program and the perceived coolness of instructors toward students of color.

8. The percentages sum to more than 100 percent because we allowed for multiple responses, coding up to four sources of help finding work.

9. From a local newspaper article on that neighborhood's future (Carrie Wells and Jean Marbella, "Little Italy Facing Big Challenges," *Baltimore Sun*, August 18, 2013, 24).

10. Timothy Smeeding, Irwin Garfinkel, and Ronald Mincy (2011) also implicate multiple-partner fertility and social policies that do little to mitigate the challenges associated with economic privation and single parenting.

Chapter 9

1. The 20 percent of the panel not interviewed at age twenty-eight no doubt would add to the total. For most of the known deceased, their passing came to light when we tried to arrange an interview. Appendix B gives a bit more detail.

2. The panel-wide standard deviation for this item is 0.91, so these average differences are large.

3. These setbacks partly trace to the recent deep recession, but as of this writing, prospects for a robust recovery remain highly uncertain.

4. Anthony Bryk and colleagues (2010) make the important point that smallness is advantageous because it affords opportunities to foster professional collegiality and cooperation and for school personnel to engage effectively

with their students and the surrounding community. If those opportunities are not exploited, the advantages of smallness will not be realized.

5. We mean work other than the informal pickup jobs of late childhood and adolescence—for example, babysitting and yard work.

6. A good source on programs and their evaluation is the National Healthy Marriage Resource Center, available at: http://www.acf.hhs.gov/pro grams/opre/research/project/supporting-healthy-marriages-2003-2013 (accessed December 3, 2012).

Appendix B

1. Spring of year 12 (1994) was the panel's expected high school graduation, but owing to prior retentions, many did not graduate on time. Known dropouts and those still in school were interviewed in year 13.

2. Seventy-one percent of the original panel are covered by both interviews.

3. This substitution is used in 9 percent of cases. Single-year earnings can be unreliable: a transition between school and work or stepping out for parenting, for example, will reduce yearly earnings. Because the intention was to get as good an estimate of earnings as possible, when low earnings were reported for the current year, we used the higher of the two.

4. The parental psychological support items in the first grade resource composite and the measures of within-family functional social capital in the "backdrop to schooling" stage overlap, in that they use the same data on parents' mark expectations and expectation for children's eventual level of schooling. They are handled differently, though: for the backdrop stage, they are dichotomized and coded as risk factors, and low expectations are scored high; for the resource composites, the full metrics are used, high expectations are coded high, and the other resources with which they are combined are different. They thus are both different and similar, but because they are so similar conceptually, a like pattern of results would be expected even if there were no measurement overlap.

5. Regression analyses often report metric coefficients instead of, or in addition to, standardized coefficients. These are calculated in terms of the original units of measurement—for example, a unit change in X is associated with so much of a unit change in Y, on average. We have several reasons for reporting standardized coefficients: one, our composite measures are scaled in standard deviation units, so for them metric and standardized coefficients are the same; two, the units of analysis for most variables have no real world representation (earnings in dollars is an exception), so what might follow from a unit change holds little intrinsic interest; and, three, we wish to gauge the relative importance of various measures and the common scaling of standardized coefficients is better suited to that.

6. It also makes strong assumptions about the behavior of potentially relevant variables not included in the analysis.

References

Abell Foundation. 1989. *A Growing Inequality: A Report on the Financial Condition of the Baltimore City Public Schools.* Baltimore, Md.: The Abell Foundation.

Adelman, Clifford. 2004. *Principal Indicators of Student Academic Histories in Postsecondary Education.* Washington: U.S. Department of Education, Institute of Education Science.

Ahituv, Avner, Marta Tienda, Lixin Xu, and V. Joseph Hotz. 1994. "Initial Labor Market Experiences of Black, Hispanic, and White Men." Chicago: University of Chicago, Population Research Center.

Alexander, Karl L. 1997. "Public Schools and the Public Good." *Social Forces* 76(1): 1–30.

Alexander, Karl L., and Doris R. Entwisle. 1996. "Educational Tracking During the Early Years: First Grade Placement and Middle School Constraints." In *Generating Social Stratification: Toward a New Research Agenda,* edited by Alan C. Kerckhoff. Boulder, CO: Greenwood Press.

Alexander, Karl L., Doris R. Entwisle, and Susan L. Dauber. 1996. "Children in Motion: School Transfers and Elementary School Performance." *Journal of Educational Research* 90(1): 3–12.

———. 2003. *On the Success of Failure: A Reassessment of the Effects of Retention in the Primary Grades,* 2nd ed. New York: Cambridge University Press.

Alexander, Karl L., Doris R. Entwisle, and Carrie Horsey. 1997. "From First Grade Forward: Early Foundations of High School Dropout." *Sociology of Education* 70(2): 87–107.

Alexander, Karl L., Doris R. Entwisle, and Nader Kabbani. 2001. "The Dropout Process in Life Course Perspective: Early Risk Factors at Home and School." *Teachers College Record* 103(5): 760–822.

Alexander, Karl L., Doris R. Entwisle, and Maxine S. Thompson. 1987. "School Performance, Status Relations and the Structure of Sentiment: Bringing the Teacher Back in." *American Sociological Review* 52(5): 665–82.

Alexander, Michelle. 2010. *The New Jim Crow, Mass Incarceration in the Age of Colorblindness.* New York: The New Press.

Allison, Paul D. 2002. *Missing Data.* Thousand Oaks, Calif.: Sage Publications.

American Civil Liberties Union. 2013. *The War on Marijuana in Black and White: Billions of Dollars Wasted on Racially Biased Arrests.* New York: ACLU.

American Council on Education. 2006. "Working Their Way Through College: Student Employment and Its Impact on the College Experience." *ACE* Issue Brief. Washington, D.C.: American Council on Education.

————. 2011. *2010 GED Testing Program Statistical Report.* Washington, D.C.: American Council on Education.

Anderson, Elijah. 2000. *Code of the Street: Decency, Violence, and the Moral Life of the Inner City.* New York: W. W. Norton.

————. 2008. *Against the Wall: Poor, Young, Black, and Male.* Philadelphia: University of Pennsylvania Press.

Annie E. Casey Foundation. 1997. *City Kids Count: Data on the Well-Being on Children in Large Cities.* Technical report no. ED431854. Baltimore, Md.: Annie E. Casey Foundation.

————. 2001. "Taking the Initiative on Jobs & Race: Innovations in Workforce Development for Minority Jobs Seekers and Employers." Baltimore, Md.: Annie E. Casey Foundation. Available at: http://www.aecf.org/upload/publicationfiles/taking%20initiatives%20on%20jobs.pdf (accessed November 19, 2013).

————. 2010. *The East Baltimore Revitalization Initiative: A Case Study of Responsible Redevelopment.* Baltimore, Md.: Annie E. Casey Foundation.

Apling, Richard N. 1993. "Proprietary Schools and Their Students." *Journal of Higher Education* 64(4): 379–416.

Arnett, Jeffrey Jensen. 2004. *Emerging Adulthood.* New York: Oxford University Press.

Arroyo, Carmen G. 2008. *The Funding Gap.* Washington, D.C.: The Education Trust.

Arroyo, Julia, Krista K. Payne, Susan L. Brown, and Wendy D. Manning. 2013. "Crossover in Median Age at First Marriage and First Birth: Thirty Years of Change." *NCFMR* Family Profiles FP-12–03. Bowling Green, Oh.: National Center for Family & Marriage Research. Available at: http://ncfmr.bgsu.edu/pdf/family_profiles/file107893.pdf (accessed November 18, 2013).

The Atlantic. 2011. "The 10 Most Dangerous Cities in America." *The Atlantic*, May 26. Available at: http://www.theatlantic.com/national/archive/2011/05/the-10-most-dangerous-cities-in-america/239513 (accessed November 18, 2013).

Attewell, Paul, and David Lavin. 2007. *Passing the Torch.* New York: Russell Sage Foundation.

Attewell, Paul, David Lavin, Thurston Domina, and Tania Levey. 2004. "The Black Middle Class: Progress, Prospects, and Puzzles." *Journal of African American Studies* 8(1): 6–19.

————. 2006. "New Evidence on College Remediation." *The Journal of Higher Education* 77(5): 886–924.

Autor, David H., and Melanie Wasserman. 2013. "Wayward Sons: The Emerging Gender Gap in Labor Markets and Education." *Third Way* economic report no. 662. Washington, D.C.: Third Way. Available at: http://www.thirdway.org/publications/662 (accessed November 18, 2013).

Ayscue, Jennifer B., Greg Flaxman, John Kucsera, and Genevieve Siegel-Hawley. 2013. "Settle for Segregation or Strive for Diversity: A Defining Moment for Maryland's Public Schools." Los Angeles: University of California, The Civil Rights Project.

Badger, Emily. 2013. "The Best Thing We Could Do About Inequality Is Universal Preschool." *The Atlantic Cities*, June 17. Available at: http://www.

theatlanticcities.com/jobs-and-economy/2013/06/best-thing-we-could-do-about-inequality-universal-preschool/5919 (accessed November 18, 2013).

Bailey, Martha J., and Susan M. Dynarski. 2011. "Inequality in Postsecondary Education." In *Whither Opportunity? Rising Inequality, Schools, and Children's Life Chances*, edited by Greg J. Duncan and Richard J. Murnane. New York: Russell Sage Foundation.

Baker, Bruce D., David G. Sciarra, and Danielle Farrie. 2010. "Is School Funding Fair? A National Report Card." Newark, N.J.: Education Law Center. Available at: http://www.schoolfundingfairness.org/National_Report_Card_2012.pdf (accessed November 18, 2013).

Baker, David P., and David L. Stevenson. 1986. "Mothers' Strategies for Children's School Achievement: Managing the Transition to High School." *Sociology of Education* 59(3): 156–66.

Baldwin, James. 1963. "Three Perspectives: Kenneth Clark's 1963 Interview with James Baldwin." *American Experience*. Available at: http://www.pbs.org/wgbh/amex/mlk/sfeature/sf_video.html (accessed November 18, 2013).

Baltimore City Department of Planning. 1983. *Neighborhood Statistics Program.* Baltimore, Md.: Baltimore City Department of Planning.

Baltimore City Public Schools. 1988. "School Profiles: School Year 1987–88." Baltimore, Md.: Office of the Superintendent of Public Instruction.

Bard, Harry. 1958. "Observations on Desegregation in Baltimore: Three Years Later." *Teacher's College Record* 59(5): 268–81.

Barnes, Sandra. 2005. *The Cost of Being Poor: A Comparative Study of Life in Poor Urban Neighborhoods in Gary, Indiana.* Albany: State University of New York Press.

Barnett, W. Steven. 2008. *Preschool Education and Its Lasting Effects: Research and Policy Implications.* Phoenix: Arizona State University Education Policy Research Unit.

Barnett, W. Steven, and Clive R. Belfield. 2006. "Early Childhood Development and Social Mobility." *The Future of Children: Opportunity in America* 16(2): 73–98.

Barton, Paul E. 2005. *One-Third of a Nation.* Princeton, N.J.: Educational Testing Service, Policy Information Center.

Bendick, Marc, Jr., Charles W. Jackson, and Victor A. Reinoso. 1994. "Measuring Employment Discrimination Through Controlled Experiments." *Review of Black Political Economy* 23(1): 25–48.

Bentley, Amy. 1993. "Wages of War: The Shifting Landscape of Race and Gender in World War II Baltimore." *Maryland Historical Magazine* 88(Winter): 420–43.

Bergquist, Erick. 2001. "Acorn: Racial Lending Gap Widened in 2000." *American Banker* 167(190): 9. Available at: http://www.acorn.org/campaigns (accessed June 11, 2002).

Berkner, Lutz, Susan Choy, and Tracy Hunt-White. 2008. "Descriptive Summary of 2003–04 Beginning Postsecondary Students: Three Years Later." *NCES* technical report no. 2008–174. Washington: U.S. Department of Education, Institute of Education Science.

Berktold, Jennifer, Sonya Geis, and Phillip Kaufman. 1998. "Subsequent Educational Attainment of High School Dropouts." *NCES* report no. 98–085. Washington: U.S. Department of Education, National Center for Education Statistics.

Berlin, Gordon, Frank F. Furstenberg Jr., and Mary C. Waters. 2010. "Introducing the Issue." *The Future of Children* 20(1): 3–18.

Bianchi, Suzanne M., John P. Robinson, and Melissa A. Milkie. 2006. *Changing Rhythms of American Family Life.* New York: Russell Sage Foundation.

Bishop, John H. 1989. "Why the Apathy in American High Schools?" *Educational Researcher* 18(1): 6–10.

Blake, Judith. 1989. *Family Size and Achievement.* Berkeley: University of California Press.

Blank, Rebecca M. 2009. "Economic Change and the Structure of Opportunity for Less-Skilled Workers." *Focus* 26(2): 14–20.

Blau, Peter M., and Otis D. Duncan. 1967. *The American Occupational Structure.* New York: John Wiley & Sons.

Blossfeld, Hans-Peter. 2009. "Educational Assortative Marriage in Comparative Perspective." *Annual Review of Sociology* 35(1): 513–30.

Bobo, Lawrence, James R. Kluegel, and Ryan A. Smith. 1997. "Laissez-Faire Racism: The Crystallization of a Kinder, Gentler, Antiblack Ideology." In *Racial Attitudes in the 1990s: Continuity and Change,* edited by Steven A. Tuch and Jack K. Martin. Westport, Conn.: Praeger Publishers.

Bonilla-Silva, Eduardo. 1996. "Rethinking Racism: Toward a Structural Interpretation." *American Sociological Review* 62(3): 465–80.

Borman, Geoffrey D., and Matthew Boulay. 2004. *Summer Learning: Research, Policies, and Programs.* Mahwah, N.J.: Lawrence Erlbaum Associates.

Borman, Geoffrey D., and Maritza Dowling. 2010. "Schools and Inequality: A Multilevel Analysis of Coleman's Equality of Educational Opportunity Data." *Teachers College Record* 112(May): 1201–46.

Bourdieu, Pierre. 1990. *The Logic of Practice.* Stanford, Calif.: Stanford University Press.

Bowler, Mike. 1991. "The Lessons of Change: Baltimore Schools in the Modern Era." Baltimore, Md.: The Fund for Educational Excellence.

Bowles, Samuel, Herbert Gintis, and Melissa Osborne Groves. 2005. *Unequal Chances.* New York: Russell Sage Foundation.

Boykin, A. Wade. 1986. "The Triple Quandary and the School of Afro-American Children." In *The School Achievement of Minority Children: New Perspectives,* edited by U. Neisser. Hillsdale, N.J.: Lawrence Erlbaum Associates.

Bozick, Robert. 2007. "Making It Through the First Year of College: The Role of Students' Economic Resources, Employment, and Living Arrangements." *Sociology of Education* 80(3): 261–85.

Bozick, Robert, Karl L. Alexander, Doris R. Entwisle, Susan L. Dauber, and Kerri A. Kerr. 2010. "Framing the Future: Revisiting the Place of Educational Expectations in Status Attainment." *Social Forces* 88(5): 2027–52.

Bozick, Robert, and Stefanie DeLuca. 2005. "Better Late Than Never? Delayed Enrollment in the High School to College Transition." *Social Forces* 84(1): 529–50.

Bradley, Robert H., and Robert F. Corwyn. 2002. "Socioeconomic Status and Child Development." *Annual Review of Psychology* 53: 371–99.

Brand, Jennie E., and Yu Xie. 2010. "Who Benefits Most from College? Evidence for Negative Selection in Heterogeneous Economic Returns to Higher Education." *American Sociological Review* 75(2): 273–302.

Brint, Steven, and Jerome Karabel. 1989. *The Diverted Dream: Community Colleges and the Promise of Educational Opportunity in America, 1900–1985.* New York: Oxford University Press.

Brock, Thomas. 2010. "Young Adults and Higher Education: Barriers and Breakthroughs to Success." *The Future of Children* 20(1): 109–32.

Browne, Irene, and Joya Misra. 2003. "The Intersection of Gender and Race in the Labor Market." *Annual Review of Sociology* 29: 487–513.

Bryk, Anthony S., Valerie E. Lee, and Peter Blakeley Holland. 1993. *Catholic Schools and the Common Good.* Cambridge, Mass.: Harvard University Press.

Bryk, Anthony S., Penny Bender Sebring, Elaine Allensworth, Stuart Luppescu, and John Q. Easton. 2010. *Organizing Schools for Improvement: Lessons from Chicago.* Chicago: University of Chicago Press.

Burdick-Will, Julia, Jens Ludwig, Stephen W. Raudenbush, Robert J. Sampson, Lisa Sanbonmatsu, and Patrick Sharkey. 2011. "Converging Evidence for Neighborhood Effects on Children's Test Scores: An Experimental, Quasi-Experimental, and Observational Comparison." In *Whither Opportunity? Rising Inequality, Schools, and Children's Life Chances,* edited by Greg J. Duncan and Richard J. Murnane. New York: Russell Sage Foundation.

Bureau of Labor Statistics. 2010. "Number of Jobs Held, Labor Market Activity, and Earnings Growth Among the Youngest Baby Boomers: Results from a Longitudinal Survey." Technical report no. USDL-10–1243. Washington: U.S. Department of Labor.

———. 2012. *Education Pays.* Washington: U.S. Department of Labor.

California Achievement Test. 1979. *California Achievement Tests: Norms Tables, Level 18, Forms C and D.* Monterey, Calif.: CTB/McGraw-Hill.

Cameron, Stephen V., and James J. Heckman. 1993. "The Nonequivalence of High School Equivalents." *Journal of Labor Economics* 11(1): 1–47.

Carnevale, Anthony P., and Jeff Strohl. 2010. "How Increasing College Access Is Increasing Inequality, and What to Do About It." In *Rewarding Strivers: Helping Low-Income Students Succeed in College,* edited by R. D. Kahlenberg. New York: Century Foundation Press.

Carter, Samuel Casey. 2000. *No Excuses: Lessons from 21 High-Performing, High-Poverty Schools.* Washington, D.C.: Heritage Foundation.

Casserly, Michael. 1983. "Statistical Profiles of the Great City Schools 1970–1982." Washington, D.C.: Council of the Great City Schools.

Cellini, Stephanie, R. 2008. "Vocational College Research: Case Studies of the United States." In *Handbook of Vocational Education Research,* edited by Felix Rauner and Rupert Maclean. New York: Springer.

Charles, Kerwin Kofi, and Ming Ching Luoh. 2010. "Male Incarceration, the Marriage Market, and Female Outcomes." *Review of Economics and Statistics* 92(3): 614–27.

Cherlin, Andrew J. 2005. "American Marriage in the Early Twenty-First Century." *The Future of Children* 15(2): 33–55.

————. 2009. *The Marriage-Go-Round: The State of Marriage and the Family in America Today.* New York: Alfred A. Knopf.

Cherlin, Andrew J., Caitlin Cross-Barnet, Linda M. Burton, and Raymond Garrett-Peters. 2008. "Promises They Can Keep: Low-Income Women's Attitudes Towards Motherhood, Marriage, and Divorce." *Journal of Marriage and Family* 70(4): 919–33.

Chetty, Raj, Nathaniel Hendren, Patrick Kline, and Emmanuel Saez. 2013. "The Economic Impacts of Tax Expenditures: Evidence from Spatial Variation Across the U.S." Cambridge, Mass.: Equality of Opportunity Project. Available at: http://scholar.harvard.edu/files/hendren/files/whitepaper_taxexpenditures_july13r6.pdf (accessed November 19, 2013).

Citizens Planning and Housing Association. 1990. *Take This School and Love It! Every Citizen Can. A Reference Manual on the Baltimore City Public School System.* Baltimore, Md.: Citizens Planning and Housing Association.

Clark, Burton R. 1960. "The 'Cooling Out' Function in Higher Education." *American Journal of Sociology* 65(6): 569–76.

Clogg, Clifford C., Scott R. Eliason, and Robert Wahl. 1990. "Labor Market Experience and Labor Force Outcomes." *American Journal of Sociology* 95(6): 1536–76.

Cohany, Sharon R., and Emy Sok. 2007. "Trends in Labor Force Participation of Married Mothers of Infants." *Monthly Labor Review* 130(2): 9–16.

Cohen, James R. 2001. "Abandoned Housing: Exploring Lessons from Baltimore." *Housing Policy Debate* 12(3): 415–48.

Coleman, James S., Ernest Q. Campbell, Charles J. Hobson, James McPartland, Alexander Mood, Frederic D. Weinfeld, and Robert L. York. 1966. *Equality of Educational Opportunity.* Washington: U.S. Government Printing Office.

Coleman, James S., and Thomas Hoffer. 1987. *Public and Private Schools: The Impact of Communities.* New York: Basic Books.

Compas, Bruce E., Sydney Ey, and Kathryn E. Grant. 1993. "Taxonomy, Assessment, and Diagnosis of Depression During Adolescence." *Psychological Bulletin* 114(2): 323–44.

Complete College America. 2011. *Time Is the Enemy: The Surprising Truth About Why Today's College Students Aren't Graduating and What Needs to Change.* Washington, D.C.: Complete College America.

Connolly, Helen, and Peter Gottschalk. 2006. "Differences in Wage Growth by Education Level: Do Less-Educated Workers Gain Less from Work Experience?" *IZA* discussion paper no. 2331. Berlin: Institute for the Study of Labor.

Danziger, Sheldon. 2004. "Earnings by Education for Young Workers, 1975 & 2002." Technical report no. 17. Philadelphia, Pa.: MacArthur Foundation Research Network on Transitions to Adulthood and Public Policy.

Danziger, Sheldon, and David Ratner. 2010. "Labor Market Outcomes and the Transition to Adulthood." *The Future of Children* 20(1): 133–58.

Darling-Hammond, Linda. 2010. *The Flat World and Education: How America's Commitment to Equity Will Determine Our Future.* New York: Teachers College.

David, Eric M. 1994. "Blurring the Color Line: The Desegregation of the Baltimore City Public Schools, 1954–1994." *The Urban Review* 26(4): 243–55.

Deil-Amen, Regina. 2006. "'Warming Up' the Aspirations of Community College Students." In *After Admission: From College Access to College Success*, edited by James E. Rosenbaum, Regina Deil-Amen, and Ann E. Preston. New York: Russell Sage Foundation.

DeLuca, Stefanie, Peter Rosenblatt, and Holly Wood. 2012. "Why Poor People Move (and Where They Go): Residential Mobility, Selection, and Stratification." Unpublished manuscript. The Johns Hopkins University, Baltimore, Md.

DeNavas-Walt, Carmen, Bernadette D. Proctor, and Jessica C. Smith. 2012. "Income, Poverty, and Health Insurance Coverage in the United States 2011." Report no. P60–243. Washington: U.S. Census Bureau. Available at: http://www.census.gov/prod/2011pubs/p60-239.pdf (accessed November 18, 2013).

Dickler, Jessica. 2010. "Boomerang Kids: 85% of College Grads Move Home." *CNN Money.* Available at: http://money.cnn.com/2010/10/14/pf/boomerang_kids_move_home/index.htm (accessed November 18, 2013).

Dionne, E. J., Jr. 2013. "Can Same-Sex Couples Help Save Marriage?" *The Washington Post,* July 31. Available at: http://articles.washingtonpost.com/2013-07-31/opinions/40912817_1_gay-couples-gay-marriage-61-percent (accessed November 18, 2013).

Dohan, Daniel. 2003. *The Price of Poverty: Money, Work, and Culture in the Mexican-American Barrio.* Berkeley: University of California Press.

Dohrenwend, Bruce P. 2006. "Inventorying Stressful Life Events as Risk Factors for Psychopathology." *Psychological Bulletin* 132(3): 477–95.

Dougherty, Kevin J. 1994. *The Contradictory College: The Conflicting Origins, Impacts, and Futures of the Community College.* Albany: State University of New York Press.

Downey, Douglas B., and Shana Pribesh. 2004. "When Race Matters: Teachers' Evaluations of Students' Classroom Behavior." *Sociology of Education* 77(4): 267–82.

Downey, Douglas B., Paul T. von Hippel, and Beckett Broh. 2004. "Are Schools the Great Equalizer? Cognitive Inequality During the Summer Months and the School Year." *American Sociological Review* 69(5): 613–35.

Duncan, Greg J., and Jeanne Brooks-Gunn. 1997. *Consequences of Growing Up Poor.* New York: Russell Sage Foundation.

Duncan, Greg J., and Katherine Magnuson. 2004. "Individual and Parent-Based Intervention Strategies for Promoting Human Capital and Positive Behavior." In *Human Development Across Lives and Generations: The Potential for Change,* edited by P. Lindsay Chase-Lansdale, Kathleen Kiernan, and Ruth J. Friedman. New York: Cambridge University Press.

———. 2011. "The Nature and Impact of Early Achievement Skills." In *Whither Opportunity? Rising Inequality, Schools, and Children's Life Chances,* edited by Greg J. Duncan and Richard J. Murnane. New York: Russell Sage Foundation.

Duncan, Greg J., and Richard J. Murnane. 2011. "Introduction: The American Dream, Then and Now." In *Whither Opportunity? Rising Inequality, Schools, and Children's Life Chances,* edited by Greg J. Duncan and Richard J. Murnane. New York: Russell Sage Foundation.

Duncan, Greg J., and Stephen W. Raudenbush. 1999. "Assessing the Effects of Context in Studies of Child and Youth Development." *Educational Psychologist* 34(1): 29–41.

Durr, Kenneth D. 2003. *Behind the Backlash: White Working-Class Politics in Baltimore, 1940–1980.* Chapel Hill: University of North Carolina Press.

Economic Mobility Project. 2009. *Renewing the American Dream: A Road Map to Enhancing Economic Mobility in America.* Washington, D.C.: Economic Mobility Project.

Edelman, Peter, Harry J. Holzer, and Paul Offner. 2006. *Reconnecting Disadvantaged Young Men.* Washington, D.C.: Urban Institute Press.

Edin, Kathryn, and Maria Kefalas. 2005. *Promises I Can Keep: Why Poor Women Put Motherhood Before Marriage.* Los Angeles: University of California Press.

Edin, Kathryn, and Laura Lein. 1997. *Making Ends Meet: How Single Mothers Survive Welfare and Low-Wage Work.* New York: Russell Sage Foundation.

Edin, Kathryn, and Timothy J. Nelson. 2013. *Doing the Best I Can: Fatherhood in the Inner City.* Berkeley: University of California Press.

Edin, Kathryn, and Joanna M. Reed. 2005. "Why Don't They Just Get Married? Barrier to Marriage Among the Disadvantaged." *The Future of Children* 15(2): 117–37.

Eggebeen, David J., and Daniel T. Lichter. 1991. "Race, Family Structure, and Changing Poverty Among American Children." *American Sociological Review* 56(6): 801–17.

Elder, Glen H., Jr. 1974. *Children of the Great Depression: Social Change in Life Experience.* Chicago: University of Chicago Press.

Elder, Glen H., Jr., Jacquelynne S. Eccles, Monika Ardelt, and Sarah Lord. 1995. "Inner-City Parents Under Economic Pressure: Perspectives on the Strategies of Parenting." *Journal of Marriage and the Family* 57(3): 771–84.

Ellwood, David T., and Christopher Jencks. 2004. "The Spread of Single-Parent Families in the United States Since 1960." In *The Future of the Family,* edited by Daniel P. Moynihan, Timothy M. Smeeding, and Lee Rainwater. New York: Russell Sage Foundation.

Entwisle, Doris R., and Karl L. Alexander. 1989. "Early Schooling as a 'Critical Period' Phenomenon." In *Sociology of Education and Socialization,* edited by Krishnan Namboodiri and Ronald G. Corwin. Greenwich, Conn.: JAI Press.

———. 1993. "Entry into Schools: The Beginning School Transition and Educational Stratification in the United States." *Annual Review of Sociology* 19: 401–23.

———. 2000. "Diversity in Family Structure: Effects on Schooling." In *Handbook on Family Diversity,* edited by D. Demo, K. Allen and M. Fine. New York: Oxford University Press.

Entwisle, Doris R., Karl L. Alexander, and Linda S. Olson. 1997. *Children, Schools, and Inequality.* Boulder, Colo.: Westview Press.

———. 2000. "Early Work Histories of Urban Youth." *American Sociological Review* 65(2): 279–97.

———. 2003. "The First-Grade Transition in Life Course Perspective." In *Handbook of the Life Course,* edited by Jeylan T. Mortimer and Michael J. Shanahan. New York: Kluwer Academic/Plenum Publishers.

———. 2004. "Temporary as Compared to Permanent High School Dropout." *Social Forces* 82(3): 1181–205.

———. 2005. "First Grade and Educational Attainment by Age 22: A New Story." *American Journal of Sociology* 110(5): 1458–502.

———. 2006. "Educational Tracking Within and Between Schools: From First Grade Through Middle School and Beyond." In *Middle Childhood: Contexts of Development*, edited by Aletha C. Huston and Marika N. Ripke. New York: Cambridge University Press.

———. 2010a. "The Long Reach of SES in Education." In *Handbook of Research in Schools, Schooling, and Human Development*, edited by Jacquelynne S. Eccles and Judith L. Meece. New York: Routledge.

———. 2010b. "Joblessness of Young African American Men: A Riddle Solved." Unpublished manuscript. The Johns Hopkins University, Baltimore.

Farkas, George, and Kurt Beron. 2004. "The Detailed Age Trajectory of Oral Vocabulary Knowledge: Differences by Class and Race." *Social Science Research* 33(3): 464–97.

Featherman, David L., and Gillian Stevens. 1982. "A Revised Socioeconomic Index of Occupational Status: Application in Analysis of Sex Differences in Attainment." In *Social Structure and Behavior: Essays in Honor of William Hamilton Sewell*, edited by Robert M. Hauser, David Mechanic, Archibald O. Haller, and Taissa S. Hauser. New York: Academic Press.

Federal Interagency Forum on Child and Family Statistics. 2009. *America's Children: Key National Indicators of Well-Being, 2009*. Washington: U.S. Government Printing Office. Available at: http://www.childstats.gov/pdf/ac2009/ac_09.pdf (accessed November 19, 2013).

Ferguson, Ronald F. 1998. "Teachers' Preceptions and Expectations and the Black-White Test Score Gap." In *The Black-White Test Score Gap*, edited by Christopher S. Jencks and Meredith Phillips. Washington, D.C.: Brookings Institution Press.

Flanagan, William G. 1999. *Urban Sociology: Images and Structure*. Lanham, Md.: Rowman and Littlefield Publishers, Inc.

Frank-Ruta, Garance. 2012. "Robert Putnam: Class Now Trumps Race as the Great Divide in America." *The Atlantic*, June 30. Available at: http://www.theatlantic.com/politics/archive/2012/06/robert-putnam-class-now-trumps-race-as-the-great-divide-in-america/259256 (accessed November 18, 2013).

Furchtgott-Roth, Diana, Louis Jacobson, and Christine Mokher. 2009. *Strengthening Community Colleges' Influence on Economic Mobility*. Washington, D.C.: Economic Mobility Project.

Furstenberg, Frank F., Jr. 1976. *Unplanned Parenthood: The Social Consequences of Teenage Childbearing*. New York: Free Press.

Furstenberg, Frank F., Jr., Jeanne Brooks-Gunn, and S. Philip Morgan. 1987. *Adolescent Mothers in Later Life*. New York: Cambridge University Press.

Furstenberg, Frank F., Jr., Thomas D. Cook, Jacquelynne Eccles, Glen H. Elder Jr., and Arnold Sameroff. 1999. *Managing to Make It: Urban Families and Adolescent Success*. Chicago: University of Chicago Press.

Giguere, Andrew M. 2009. "'And Never the Twain Shall Meet': Baltimore's East-West Expressway and the Construction of the 'Highway to Nowhere.'" M.A. Thesis, Ohio University.

Goldin, Claudia, and Lawrence F. Katz. 2008. *The Race Between Education and Technology*. Cambridge, Mass.: Belknap Press.

Goldrick-Rab, Sara. 2006. "Following Their Every Move: How Social Class Shapes Postsecondary Pathways." *Sociology of Education* 79(1): 61–79.

Goldrick-Rab, Sara, and Josipa Roksa. 2008. *A Federal Agenda for Promoting Student Success and Degree Completion*. Washington, D.C.: Center for American Progress.

Goldscheider, Frances, and Calvin Goldscheider. 2000. *The Changing Transition to Adulthood: Leaving and Returning Home*. Thousand Oaks, Calif.: Sage Publications.

Gosa, Travis L. and Karl L. Alexander. 2007. "Family (Dis)Advantage and the Educational Prospects of Better Off African American Youth: How Race Still Matters." *Teachers College Record* 109(2): 285–321.

Governor's Office of Crime Control and Prevention. 2013. "Maryland Statistical Analysis Center." Baltimore, Md.: State of Maryland. Available at: http://www.goccp.maryland.gov/msac.php (accessed December 3, 2013).

Granovetter, Mark S. 1974. *Getting a Job: A Study of Contacts and Careers*. Cambridge, Mass.: Harvard University Press.

———. 1983. "The Strength of Weak Ties: A Network Theory Revisited." *Sociological Theory* 1: 201–33.

———. 1995. *Getting a Job: A Study of Contacts and Careers*, 2nd ed. Chicago: University of Chicago Press.

Gregory, James N. 1995. "The Southern Diaspora and the Urban Dispossessed: Demonstrating the Census Public Use Microdata Samples." *Journal of American History* 82(June): 111–34.

———. 2005. *The Southern Diaspora: How the Great Migrations of Black and White Southerners Transformed America*. Chapel Hill: University of North Carolina Press.

Hacker, Andrew. 1995. *Two Nations: Black and White, Separate, Hostile, Unequal*. New York: Ballantine Books.

Haggerty, Robert J., Lonnie R. Sherrod, Norman Garmezy, and Michael Rutter. 1996. *Stress, Risk, and Resilience in Children and Adolescents*. New York: Cambridge University Press.

Hampden-Thompson, Gillian, and Suet-ling Pong. 2005. "Does Family Policy Environment Moderate the Effect of Single-Parenthood on Children's Academic Achievement? A Study of 14 European Countries." *Journal of Comparative Family Studies* 36(2): 227–48.

Hanushek, Eric A. 2004. "Teacher Quality." In *Talented Teachers: The Essential Force for Improving Student Achievement*, edited by Lewis C. Solmon and Tamara W. Schiff. Greenwich, Conn.: Information Age Publishing.

Hart, Betty, and Todd R. Risley. 1995. *Meaningful Differences in the Everyday Experience of Young American Children*. Baltimore, Md.: Paul H. Brookes Publishing Co.

Harter, Susan. 1982. "The Perceived Competence Scale for Children." *Child Development* 53(1): 87–97.

Haskins, Ron, and Cecilia E. Rouse. 2005. "Closing Achievement Gaps." *The Future of Children* 15(1): 1–7.

Hauser, Robert M., and John R. Warren. 1997. "Socioeconomic Indexes for Occupations: A Review, Update, and Critique." *Sociological Methodology* 27(1): 177–298.

Heckman, James J. 2008. "Role of Income and Family Influence on Child Outcomes." *Annals of the New York Academy of Sciences* 1136(1): 307–23.

Hendry, Erica R. 2009. "For-Profit Colleges See Large Increases in Enrollment and Revenue." *Chronicle of Higher Education*, August 25. Available at: http://chronicle.com/article/For-Profit-Colleges-See-Lar/48173 (accessed November 18, 2013).

Heyns, Barbara. 1978. *Summer Learning and the Effects of Schooling.* New York: Academic.

Heyns, Barbara, and Sophia Catsambis. 1986. "Mother's Employment and Children's Achievement: A Critique." *Sociology of Education* 59(July): 140–51.

Hill, Herbert. 1961. "Racism Within Organized Labor: A Report of Five Years of the AFL-CIO, 1955–1960." *Journal of Negro Education* 30(2): 109–18.

———. 1965. "Racial Inequality in Employment: The Patterns of Discrimination." *Annals of the American Academy of Political and Social Science* 357(1): 30–47.

Hoffman, Saul D. 1998. "Teenage Childbearing Is Not So Bad After All . . . Or Is It? A Review of the New Literature." *Family Planning Perspectives* 30(5): 236–43.

Holloway, Steven R., and Elvin K. Wyly. 2001. "'The Color of Money' Expanded: Geographically Contingent Mortgage Lending in Atlanta." *Journal of Housing Research* 12(1): 55–90.

Holt, Alex. 2013. "Last Year the "Worst in a Decade" for High-Quality Pre-K, Annual Report Finds." Education Policy Program. New York: New America Foundation. Available at: http://earlyed.newamerica.net/blogposts/2013/last_year_the_worst_in_a_decade_for_high_quality_pre_k_annual_report_finds-83105 (accessed November 19, 2013).

Holzer, Harry J. 2009. "The Labor Market and Young Black Men: Updating Moynihan's Perspective." *Annals of the American Academy of Political and Social Science* 621(January): 47–69.

———. 2010. "Is the Middle of the U.S. Job Market Really Disappearing: A Comment on the 'Polarization' Hypothesis." Washington, D.C.: Center for American Progress. Available at: http://www.americanprogress.org/issues/labor/report/2010/05/13/7843/is-the-middle-of-the-u-s-job-market-really-disappearing/ (accessed November 19, 2013).

Holzer, Harry J., and Robert J. LaLonde. 1999. "Job Change and Job Stability Among Less-Skilled Young Workers." JCPR Working Paper 80, Northwestern University/University of Chicago Joint Center for Poverty Research.

Holzer, Harry J., Steven Raphael, and Michael A. Stoll. 2004. "Will Employers Hire Former Offenders? Employer Preferences, Background Checks, and Their Determinants." In *Imprisoning America: The Social Effects of Mass Incarceration,* edited by Mary Pattillo, David Weiman, and Bruce Western. New York: Russell Sage Foundation.

Horn, Laura, and Rachel Berger. 2005. *College Persistence on the Rise? Changes in 5-Year Degree Completion and Postsecondary Persistence Rates Between 1994 and 2000.* Washington: U.S. Department of Education, National Center for Educational Statistics.

Hotz, V. Joseph, Susan Williams McElroy, and Seth G. Sanders. 1996. "The Costs and Consequences of Teenage Childbearing for the Mothers and the Government." *Chicago Policy Review* 1(1): 55–94.

Hout, Michael. 2012. "Social and Economic Returns to College Education in the United States." *Annual Review of Sociology* 38(April): 379–400.

Huston, Aletha C., and Alison C. Bentley. 2010. "Human Development in Social Context." *Annual Review of Psychology* 61(2): 411–37.

Hymowitz, Kay, Jason S. Carroll, W. Bradford Wilcox, and Kelleen Kaye. 2013. "Knot Yet: The Benefits and Costs of Delayed Marriage in America." The National Marriage Project. Charlottesville: University of Virginia.

Isaacs, Julia B. 2008. "International Comparisons of Economic Mobility." In *Getting Ahead or Losing Ground: Economic Mobility in America*, edited by Isaacs, Julia B., Isabel V. Sawhill, and Ron Haskins. Washington, D.C.: Brookings Institution Press.

Isaacs, Julia B., Katherine Toran, Heather Hahn, Karina Fortuny, and Eugene C. Steuerle. 2012. *Kids' Share. Report on Federal Expenditures on Children Through 2011.* Washington, D.C.: Urban Institute Press.

Jargowsky, Paul A. 2003. "Stunning Progress, Hidden Problems: The Dramatic Decline of Concentrated Poverty in the 1990s." *Living Cities Census Series.* Washington, D.C.: Brookings Institution Press.

Jargowsky, Paul A., and Isabel V. Sawhill. 2006. "The Decline of the Underclass." *CCF Brief* no. 36. Washington, D.C.: Brookings Institution Press.

Jarrett, Robin L. 1997. "African American Family and Parenting Strategies in Impoverished Neighborhoods." *Human Sciences Press* 20(2): 275–88.

———. 1999. "Successful Parenting in High-Risk Neighborhoods." *The Future of Children* 9(2): 45–50.

Jencks, Christopher S. 1991. "Is the American Underclass Growing?" In *The Urban Underclass*, edited by Christopher S. Jencks and Paul E. Peterson. Washington, D.C.: Brookings Institution Press.

Jessor, Richard. 1993. "Successful Adolescent Development Among Youth in High-Risk Settings." *American Psychologist* 48(2): 117–26.

Job Opportunities Task Force. 2003. "Baltimore's Choice: Workers and Jobs for a Thriving Economy." Baltimore, Md.: Job Opportunities Task Force. Available at: http://www.ubalt.edu/jfi/jfi/reports/jotf2.pdf (accessed November 18, 2013).

Kahlenberg, Richard D. 2001. *All Together Now: Creating Middle-Class Schools Through Public School Choice.* Washington, D.C.: Brookings Institution Press.

———. 2012. *The Future of School Integration: Socioeconomic Diversity as an Education Reform Strategy.* New York: Century Foundation Press.

Kalleberg, Arne L., and Aage B. Sorensen. 1979. "The Sociology of Labor Markets." *Annual Review of Sociology* 5: 351–79.

Kalmijn, Matthijs. 1998. "Intermarriage and Homogamy: Causes, Patterns, Trends." *Annual Review of Sociology* 24(December): 395–421.

Kandel, Denise, and Mark Davies. 1982 "Epidemiology of Depressive Mood in Adolescents: An Empirical Study." *Archives of General Psychiatry* 39(10); 1205–12.

Karabel, Jerome. 1972. "Community Colleges and Social Stratification." *Harvard Educational Review* 42(4): 521–62.

Kasarda, John D. 1990. "Structural Factors Affecting the Location and Timing of Urban Underclass Growth." *Urban Geography* 11(3): 234–64.

———. 1993. "Inner-City Concentrated Poverty and Neighborhood Distress: 1970 to 1990." *Housing Policy Debate* 4(3): 253–302.

Kasinitz, Philip, and Jan Rosenberg. 1996. "Missing the Connection: Social Isolation and Employment on the Brooklyn Waterfront." *Social Problems* 43(2): 180–96.

Kaushal, Neeraj, Katherine Magnuson, and Jane Waldfogel. 2011. "How Is Family Income Related to Investments in Children's Learning?" In *Whither Opportunity? Rising Inequality, Schools, and Children's Life Chances,* edited by Greg J. Duncan and Richard J. Murnane. New York: Russell Sage Foundation.

Kellam, Sheppard G., Jeanette D. Branch, Khazan C. Agrawal, and Margaret E. Ensminger. 1975. *Mental Health and Going to School: The Woodlawn Program of Assessment, Early Intervention, and Evaluation.* Chicago: University of Chicago Press.

Kemple, James J., and Judith Scott-Clayton. 2004. "Career Academies: Impact on the Labor Market Outcomes and Educational Attainment." New York: MDRC. Available at: http://www.mdrc.org/publication/career-academies-impacts-work-and-educational-attainment (November 19, 2013).

Kerckhoff, Alan C. 1993. *Diverging Pathways: Social Structure and Career Deflections.* New York: Cambridge University Press.

———. 2003. "From Student to Worker." In *Handbook of the Life Course,* edited by Jeylan T. Mortimer and Michael J. Shanahan. New York: Kluwer Academic/Plenum Publishers.

Kerckhoff, Alan C., and Elizabeth Glennie. 1999. "The Matthew Effect in American Education." *Research in Sociology of Education and Socialization* 12(1): 35–66.

Kerr, Kerri A. 2002. "An Examination of Approaches to Promote Ninth Grade Success in Maryland Public High Schools." *ERS Spectrum* 20(3): 4–13.

Kirschenman, Joleen, and Kathryn M. Neckerman. 1991. "'We'd Love to Hire Them, But . . .': The Meaning of Race for Employers." In *The Urban Underclass,* edited by Christopher Jencks and Paul E. Peterson. Washington, D.C.: Brookings Institution Press.

Knapp, Laura G., Janice E. Kelly-Reid, and Scott A. Ginder. 2011. *Enrollment in Postsecondary Institutions, Fall 2009; Graduation Rates, 2003 & 2006 Cohorts; and Financial Statistics, Fiscal Year 2009. NCES* report no. 2011–230. Washington: U.S. Department of Education, National Center for Educational Statistics.

Kneebone, Elizabeth, Carey Nadeau, and Alan Berube. 2011. "The Re-emergence of Concentrated Poverty: Metropolitan Trends in the 2000s." *Metropolitan Opportunity Series* no. 25. Washington, D.C.: Brookings Institution Press. Available at: http://www.brookings.edu/research/papers/2011/11/03-poverty-kneebone-nadeau-berube (accessed November 18, 2013).

Kolodner, Ferne K. 1962. "The Unaccepted Baltimoreans: A Report of the White Southern Rural Migrants." Baltimore, Md.: National Council of Jewish Women.

Krueger, Alan B., and Diane M. Whitmore. 2002. "Would Smaller Classes Help Close the Black-White Achievement Gap?" In *Bridging the Achievement Gap,* edited by John E. Chubb and Tom Loveless. Washington, D.C.: Brookings Institution Press.

Lareau, Annette. 2003. *Unequal Childhoods: Class, Race, and Family Life.* Berkeley: University of California Press.

Lee, Valerie E., and David T. Burkam. 2002. *Inequality at the Starting Gate: Social Background Differences in Achievement as Children Begin School.* Washington, D.C.: Economic Policy Institute.

Lee, Valerie E., and Susanna Loeb. 1995. "Where Do Head Start Attendees End up? One Reason Why Preschool Effects Fade Out." *Educational Evaluation and Policy Analysis* 17(1): 62–82.

Lenski, Gerhard E. 1966. *Power and Privilege: A Theory of Social Stratification.* New York: McGraw-Hill.

Levenson, Bernard, and Mary S. McDill. 1966. "Vocational Graduates in Auto Mechanics: A Follow-up of Negro and White Youth." *Phylon* 27(4): 347–57.

Leventhal, Tama, and Jeanne Brooks-Gunn. 1998. *The Neighborhoods They Live in: The Effects of Neighborhood Residence on Child and Adolescent Outcomes.* New York: Center for Children and Families, Teachers College, Columbia University.

————. 2000. "The Neighborhoods They Live in: The Effects of Neighborhood Residence on Child and Adolescent Outcomes." *Psychological Bulletin* 126(2): 309–37.

Levine, Marc V. 1987. "Downtown Redevelopment as an Urban Growth Strategy: A Critical Appraisal of the Baltimore Renaissance." *Journal of Urban Affairs* 9(2): 103–23.

————. 2000. "A Third-World City in the First World: Social Exclusion, Racial Inequality, and Sustainable Development in Baltimore, Maryland." In *The Social Sustainability of Cities: Diversity and the Management of Change,* edited by Mario Polese and Richard Stren. Toronto: University of Toronto Press.

Levitt, Steven D., and Stephen J. Dubner. 2005. *Freakonomics: A Rogue Economist Explores the Hidden Side of Everything.* New York: HarperCollins.

Levitt, Steven D., and Sudhir Alladi Venkatesh. 2000. "An Economic Analysis of a Drug-Selling Gang's Finances." *Quarterly Journal of Economics* 115(3): 755–89.

Lindsey, Duncan. 2009. *Child Poverty and Inequality: Securing a Better Future for America's Children.* New York: Oxford University Press.

Lipset, Seymour, and Reinhard Bendix. 1959. *Social Mobility in Industrial Society.* New Brunswick, N.J.: Transaction Publishers.

Logan, John R. 2002. "Choosing Segregation: Racial Imbalance in American Public Schools, 1990–2000." Albany, N.Y.: University at Albany, Lewis Mumford Center for Comparative Urban and Regional Research.

Ludwig, Jens, Greg J. Duncan, Lisa A. Gennetian, Lawrence F. Katz, Ronald C. Kessler, Jeffrey R. Kling, and Lisa Sanbonmatsu. 2012. "Neighborhood Effects on the Long-Term Well-Being of Low-Income Adults." *Science* 337(6101): 1505–10.

Ludwig, Jens, and Susan Mayer. 2006. "'Culture' and the Intergenerational Transmission of Poverty: The Prevention Paradox." *The Future of Children* 16(2): 175–96.

Lyall, Katherine. 1993. "The Nation's Cities: Is History About to Be Repeated?" In *Urban Finance Under Siege,* edited by Thomas R. Swartz and Frank J. Bonello. New York: M. E. Sharpe.

MacLeod, Jay. 2008. *Ain't No Makin' It: Aspirations and Attainment in a Low-Income Neighborhood,* 3rd ed. Boulder, Colo.: Westview Press.

Magnet, Myron. 1987. "America's Underclass: What to Do?" *Fortune Magazine,* May 11.

Magnuson, Katherine, and Elizabeth Votruba-Drzal. 2009. "Enduring Influences of Childhood Poverty." *Focus* 26(Fall): 32–37.

Marcotte, David E., Thomas Bailey, Carey Borkoski, and Gregory S. Kienzl. 2005. "The Returns of a Community College Education: Evidence from the National Education Longitudinal Survey." *Education Evaluation and Policy Analysis* 27(2): 157–75.

Martin, Joyce A., Brady E. Hamilton, Paul D. Sutton, Stephanie J. Ventura, Fay Menacker, Sharon Kirmeyer, and T. J. Mathews. 2009. *Births: Final Data for 2006*. National Vital Statistics Reports, vol. 57, no. 7. Hyattsville, Md.: National Center for Health Statistics.

Martin, Joyce A., Brady E. Hamilton, Stephanie J. Ventura, Michelle J. K. Osterman, Elizabeth C. Wilson, and T. J. Mathews. 2012. *Births: Final Data for 2010*. National Vital Statistics Reports, vol. 61, no. 1. Hyattsville, Md.: National Center for Health Statistics.

Maryland Department of Education. 1983. *The Fact Book: 1982–1983*. Baltimore: Maryland State Department of Education.

———. 2012. *The Fact Book: 2011–2012*. Baltimore: Maryland State Department of Education.

Massey, Douglas S., Gretchen A. Condran, and Nancy A. Denton. 1987. "The Effect of Residential Segregation on Black Social and Economic Well-Being." *Social Forces* 66(1): 29–56.

Massey, Douglas S., and Nancy A. Denton. 1993. *American Apartheid: Segregation and the Making of the Underclass*. Cambridge, Mass.: Harvard University Press.

Masten, Ann S., Karin M. Best, and Norman Garmezy. 1991. "Resilience and Development: Contributions from the Study of Children Who Overcome Adversity." *Development and Psychopathology* 2(4): 425–44.

Mayer, Susan E. 1997. *What Money Can't Buy: Family Income and Children's Life Chances*. Cambridge, Mass.: Harvard University Press.

———. 2010. "Revisiting an Old Question: How Much Does Parental Income Affect Child Outcomes." *Focus* 27(2): 21–26.

Maynard, Rebecca A., ed. 1997. *Kids Having Kids: Economic Costs and Social Consequences of Teen Pregnancy*. Washington, D.C.: Urban Institute Press.

Mazumder, Bhashkar. 2005. "The Apple Falls Even Closer to the Tree Than We Thought: New and Revised Estimates of the Intergenerational Inheritance of Earnings." In *Unequal Chances: Family Background and Economic Success*, edited by Samuel Bowles, Herbert Gintis, and Melissa O. Groves. Princeton, N.J.: Princeton University Press and Russell Sage Foundation.

———. 2008. *Upward Intergenerational Economic Mobility in the United States*. Washington, D.C.: Economic Mobility Project.

McLanahan, Sara S. 2004. "Diverging Destinies: How Children Are Faring Under the Second Demographic Transition." *Demography* 41(4): 607–27.

McLanahan, Sara S., and Christine Percheski. 2008. "Family Structure and the Reproduction of Inequalities." *Annual Review of Sociology* 34: 257–76.

McLanahan, Sara S., and Gary Sandefur. 1994. *Growing up with a Single Parent: What Hurts, What Helps*. Cambridge, Mass.: Harvard University Press.

McLoyd, Vonnie C. 1990. "The Impact of Economic Hardship on Black Families and Children: Psychological Distress Parenting, and Socioemotional Development." *Child Development* 61(2): 311–46.

McLoyd, Vonnie C., Ana M. Cauce, David T. Takeuchi, and Leon Wilson. 2000. "Marital Processes and Parental Socialization in Families of Color: A Decade Review of Research." *Journal of Marriage and Family* 62(November): 1070–93.

Michael, Robert T., and Colm O'Muircheartaigh. 2008. "Design Priorities and Disciplinary Perspectives: The Case of the U.S. National Children's Study." *Journal of the Royal Statistical Society* A171(2): 465–80.

Mickelson, Roslyn A. 2005. "How Tracking Undermines Race Equity in Desegregated Schools." In *Bringing Equity Back: Research for a New Era in American Educational Policy*, edited by Janice L. Petrovich and Amy Stuart Wells. New York: Teachers College Press.

Milne, Ann M., David E. Myers, Alvin Rosenthal, S., and Alan Ginsburg. 1986. "Single Parents, Working Mothers, and the Educational Achievement of School Children." *Sociology of Education* 59(July): 125–39.

Morisi, Teresa L. 2008. "Youth Enrollment and Employment During the School Year." *Monthly Labor Review* 131(2): 51–53.

Morris, Aldon. 1996. "What's Race Got to Do with It?" *Contemporary Sociology* 25(3): 309–13.

Moss, Philip, and Chris Tilly. 2001. *Stories Employers Tell: Race, Skill, and Hiring in America*. New York: Russell Sage Foundation.

Mullainathan, Sendhil, and Marianne Bertrand. 2004. "Are Emily and Greg More Employable than Lakisha and Jamal? A Field Experiment on Labor Market Discrimination." *American Economic Review* 94(4); 991–1013.

Murray, Charles. 2012. *Coming Apart: The State of White America, 1960–2010*. New York: Crown.

Nathan, Richard P., and Charles F. Adams. 1989. "Four Perspectives on Urban Hardship." *Political Science Quarterly* 104(3): 483–508.

National Center for Education Statistics. 1999. "Early Childhood Longitudinal Study, Kindergarten Class of 1998–99 (ECLS-K: 1999)." Washington: U.S. Department of Education, Institute of Education Sciences. Available at: http://nces.ed.gov/eds.kindergarten.asp (accessed December 4, 2013).

———. 2011. "Early Childhood Longitudinal Study, Kindergarten Class of 2010–11 (ECLS-K: 2011)." Washington: U.S. Department of Education, Institute of Education Sciences. Available at: http://nces.ed.gov/eds.kinder garten2011.asp (accessed December 4, 2013).

National Institute of Mental Health (NIMH). 1999. *Mental Health: A Report of the Surgeon General—Executive Summary*. Bethesda, Md.: National Institute of Mental Health.

Neild, Ruth Curran. 2009. "Falling Off Track During the Transition to High School: What We Know and What Can Be Done." *The Future of Children* 19(1): 53–76.

Newman, Katherine S. 2000. *No Shame in My Game: The Working Poor in the Inner City*. New York: Russell Sage Foundation.

———. 2012. *The Accordion Family: Boomerang Kids, Anxious Parents, and the Private Toll of Global Competition*. Boston, Mass.: Beacon Press.

Newman, Katherine S., and Rebekah Peeples Massengill. 2006. "The Texture of Hardship: Qualitative Sociology of Poverty, 1995–2005." *Annual Review of Sociology* 32: 423–46.

Olson, Karen. 2005. *Wives of Steel: Voices of Women from the Sparrows Point Steelmaking Communities.* University Park: Pennsylvania State University Press.

Olson, Sherry H. 1976. *Baltimore.* Cambridge, Mass.: Ballinger Publishing.

———. 1997. *Baltimore: The Building of an American City.* Baltimore, Md.: The Johns Hopkins University Press.

Orfield, Gary, and Chungmei Lee. 2005. *Why Segregation Matters: Poverty and Educational Inequality.* Cambridge, Mass.: Harvard University Press.

Orr, Marion, Clarence N. Stone, and Circe Stumbo. 2002. "Concentrated Poverty and Educational Achievement: Politics and Possibility in the Baltimore Region." Draft manuscript. University of Maryland, College Park.

Ou, Suh-Ruu, and Arthur J. Reynolds. 2006. "Early Childhood Intervention and Educational Attainment: Age 22 Findings from the Chicago Longitudinal Study." *Journal of Education for Students Placed at Risk* 11(2): 175–98.

Pager, Devah. 2007. *Marked: Race, Crime, and Finding Work in an Era of Mass Incarceration.* Chicago: University of Chicago Press.

Pager, Devah, and Diana Karafin. 2009. "Bayesian Bigot? Statistical Discrimination, Stereotypes, and Employer Decision Making." *Annals of the American Academy of Political and Social Science* 621(1): 70–93.

Pager, Devah, and Hana Shepherd. 2008. "The Sociology of Discrimination: Racial Discrimination in Employment, Housing, Credit, and Consumer Markets." *Annual Review of Sociology* 34: 181–209.

Pager, Devah, Bruce Western, and Bart Bonikowski. 2009. "Discrimination in a Low-Wage Labor Market: A Field Experiment." *American Sociological Review* 74(5): 777–99.

Pallas, Aaron M. 1993. "Schooling in the Course of Human Lives: The Social Context of Education and the Transition to Adulthood in Industrial Society." *Review of Educational Research* 63(4): 409–47.

Parker, Kim. 2012. "The Boomerang Generation: Feeling OK About Living with Mom and Dad." Social & Demographic Trends. Washington, D.C.: Pew Research Center. Available at: http://www.pewsocialtrends.org/files/2012/03/PewSocialTrends-2012-BoomerangGeneration.pdf (accessed November 18, 2013).

Pattillo, Mary. 2005. "Black Middle-Class Neighborhoods." *Annual Review of Sociology* 31: 305–29.

Pattillo-McCoy, Mary. 2000. *Black Picket Fences: Privilege and Peril Among the Black Middle Class.* Chicago: University of Chicago Press.

Pearce, Diane. 1978. "The Feminization of Poverty: Women, Work, and Welfare." *Urban and Social Change Review* 11(1): 28–36.

Pew Charitable Trusts. 2010. "Collateral Costs: Incarceration's Effect on Economic Mobility." Washington, D.C.: The Pew Charitable Trusts.

Phelps, Erin, Frank F. Furstenberg, and Anne Colby. 2002. *Looking at Lives: American Longitudinal Studies in the Twentieth Century.* New York: Russell Sage Foundation.

Phillips, Meredith. 2011. "Parenting, Time Use, and Disparities in Academic Outcomes." In *Whither Opportunity? Rising Inequality, Schools, and Children's Life Chances,* edited by Greg J. Duncan and Richard J. Murnane. New York: Russell Sage Foundation.

Phipps, Ronald A., Katheryn V. Harrison, and Jamie P. Merisotis. 1999. "Students at Private, For-Profit Institutions." *NCES* report no. 2000-175. Washington: U.S. Department of Education, National Center for Education Statistics.

Pong, Suet-ling, Jaap Dronkers, and Gillian Hampden-Thompson. 2003. "Family Policies and Children's School Achievement in Single-Versus Two-Parent Families." *Journal of Marriage and the Family* 65(3): 681–99.

Quane, James M., and William Julius Wilson. 2011. "All Together Now, One by One: Building Capacity for Urban Education Reform in Promise Neighborhoods." *Pathways Magazine* (Summer 2011): 9–13.

Rainwater, Lee, and Timothy M. Smeeding. 2004. "Lone Parent Poverty, Inequality, and the Welfare State." In *The Future of the Family*, edited by Daniel P. Moynihan, Timothy M. Smeeding, and Lee Rainwater. New York: Russell Sage Foundation.

Ravitch, Diane. 2010. *The Death and Life of the Great American School System: How Testing and Choice Are Undermining Education.* New York: Basic Books.

Reardon, Sean F., and Kendra Bischoff. 2011. "Growth in the Residential Segregation of Family by Income, 1970–2009." US2010 Project. Providence, R.I.: Russell Sage Foundation.

Reardon, Sean F., Chad R. Farrell, Stephen A. Matthews, David O'Sullivan, and Kendra Bischoff. 2009. "Race and Space in the 1990s: Changes in the Geographic Scale of Racial Residential Segregation, 1990–2000." *Social Science Research* 38(1): 55–70.

Rector, Robert. 2010. "Marriage: America's Greatest Weapon Against Child Poverty." Backgrounder no. 2465. Washington, D.C.: The Heritage Foundation.

Rector, Robert, and Melissa G. Pardue. 2004. "Understanding the President's Healthy Marriage Initiative." Backgrounder no. 1741. Washington, D.C.: The Heritage Foundation.

Ricketts, Erol R., and Isabel V. Sawhill. 1988. "Defining and Measuring the Underclass." *Journal of Policy Analysis and Management* 7(2): 316–25.

Rindfuss, Ronald. 1991. "The Young Adult Years: Diversity, Structural Change, and Fertility." *Population Association of America* 28(4): 493–512.

Rindfuss, Ronald R., C. Gray Swicegood, and Rachel A. Rosenfeld. 1987. "Disorder in the Life Course: How Common and Does It Matter?" *American Sociological Review* 52(6): 785–801.

Roberts, Brandon, Deborah Povich, and Mark Mather. 2012. "Low-Income Working Families: The Growing Economic Gap." *WPFP* policy brief. Washington, D.C.: Urban Institute Press. Available at: http://www.working poorfamilies.org/wp-content/uploads/2013/01/Winter-2012_2013-WPFP-Data-Brief.pdf (accessed November 18, 2013).

Roderick, Melissa, and Eric Camburn. 1999. "Risk and Recovery from Course Failure in the Early Years of High School." *American Educational Research Journal* 36(2): 303–43.

Rosenbaum, James E. 2001. *Beyond College for All: Career Paths for the Forgotten Half.* New York: Russell Sage Foundation.

Rosenblatt, Peter, and Stefanie DeLuca. 2012. "We Don't Live Outside, We Live in Here: Neighborhoods and Residential Mobility Decisions Among Low-Income Families." *City and Community* 11(3): 254–84.

Royster, Deirdre A. 2003. *Race and the Invisible Hand: How White Networks Exclude Black Men from Blue-Collar Jobs.* Berkeley: University of California Press.

Rudacille, Deborah. 2010. "In the Shadow of Steel." *Urbanite Magazine,* April 1.

Ruggles, Steven, Matthew Sobek, Trent Alexander, Catherine A. Fitch, Ronald Goeken, Patricia Kelly Hall, Miriam King, and Chad Ronnander. 2008. *Integrated Public Use Microdata Series.* Version 4.0 [machine-readable database]. Minneapolis: Minnesota Population Center.

Rumberger, Russell W., and Gregory J. Palardy. 2005. "Does Segregation Still Matter? The Impact of Student Composition on Academic Achievement in High School." *Teachers College Record* 107(9): 1999–2045.

Sampson, Robert J. 2000. "The Neighborhood Context of Investing in Children: Facilitating Mechanisms and Undermining Risks." In *Securing the Future: Investing in Children from Birth to College,* edited by Sheldon Danziger and Jane Waldfogel. New York: Russell Sage Foundation.

———. 2012. *Great American City: Chicago and the Enduring Neighborhood Effect.* Chicago: University of Chicago Press.

Sampson, Robert J., Jeffrey D. Morenoff, and Thomas Gannon-Rowley. 2002. "Assessing 'Neighborhood Effects': Social Processes and New Directions in Research." *Annual Review of Sociology* 28: 443–78.

Sampson, Robert J., and Stephen Raudenbush. 1999. "Systematic Social Observation of Public Spaces: A New Look at Disorder in Urban Neighborhoods." *American Journal of Sociology* 105(3): 603–51.

Schmitt, John, Kris Warner, and Sarika Gupta. 2010. *The High Budgetary Cost of Incarceration.* Washington, D.C.: Center for Economic and Policy Research.

Schwartz, Heather. 2010. "Housing Policy Is School Policy: Economically Integrative Housing Promotes Academic Success in Montgomery County, Maryland." New York: The Century Foundation.

Schweinhart, Lawrence J., and David P. Weikart. 1997. "The High/Scope Preschool Curriculum Comparison Study Through Age 23." *Early Childhood Research Quarterly* 12(2): 117–43.

Service Employees International Union. 2004. "Putting Baltimore's People First: Keys to Responsible Economic Development of Our City." Baltimore, Md. SEIU. Available at: http://www.nathanielturner.com/robertmooreand 1199union3.htm (accessed November 18, 2013).

Settersten, Richard A., Jr., and Barbara Ray. 2010. "What's Going On with Young People Today? The Long and Twisting Path to Adulthood." *The Future of Children* 1(Spring): 19–41.

Sewell, William H., Archibald O. Haller, and G. W. Ohlendorf. 1970. "The Educational and Early Occupational Attainment Process: Replications and Revisions." *American Sociological Review* 35(6): 1014–27.

Sewell, William H., Archibald O. Haller, and Alejandro Portes. 1969. "The Educational and Early Occupational Attainment Process." *American Sociological Review* 34(1): 82–92.

Sewell, William H., and Robert M. Hauser. 1980. "The Wisconsin Longitudinal Study of Social and Psychological Factors in Aspirations and Achievements." In *Research in Sociology of Education and Socialization,* vol. 1, edited by A. C. Kerckhoff. Greenwich, Conn.: JAI Press.

Sharkey, Patrick. 2008. "The Intergenerational Transmission of Context." *American Journal of Sociology* 113(4): 931–69.

———. 2010. "The Acute Effect of Local Homicides on Children's Cognitive Performance." *Social Sciences* 107(26): 11733–38.

Sharkey, Patrick, and Felix Elwert. 2011. "The Legacy of Disadvantage: Multigenerational Neighborhood Effects on Cognitive Ability." *American Journal of Sociology* 116(6): 1934–81.

Shen, Fern. 2010. "Highway to Nowhere Coming Down? Not Really." *Baltimore Brew,* September 24. Available at: http://www.baltimorebrew.com/2010/09/24/highway-to-nowhere-coming-down-not-really (accessed November 18, 2013).

Shierholz, Heidi. 2013. "Wages of Young College Graduates Have Failed to Grow Over the Last Decade." *Economic Policy Institute,* April 4. Available at: http://www.epi.org/publication/snapshot-wages-young-college-graduates-failed-grow (accessed November 18, 2013).

Siegelman, Peter. 1999. "Racial Discrimination in 'Everyday' Commercial Transactions: What Do We Know, What Do We Need to Know, and How Can We Find Out?" In *A National Report Card on Discrimination in America: The Role of Testing,* edited by Michael E. Fix and Margery A. Turner. Washington, D.C.: Urban Institute Press.

Silver, Christopher. 1997. "The Racial Origins of Zoning in American Cities." In *Urban Planning and the African American Community: In the Shadows,* edited by June M. Thomas and Marsha Ritzdorf. Thousand Oaks, Calif.: Sage Publications.

Simon, David, and Edward Burns. 1997. *The Corner: A Year in the Life of an Inner-City Neighborhood.* New York: Broadway Books.

Smeeding, Timothy M., Irwin Garfinkel, and Ronald B. Mincy. 2011. "Young Disadvantaged Men: Fathers, Families, Poverty, and Policy." *Annals of American Academy of Political and Social Sciences* 635(May): 6–21.

Smith, Sandra Susan. 2010. *Lone Pursuit: Distrust and Defensive Individualism Among the Black Poor.* New York: Russell Sage Foundation.

Stack, Carol B. 1974. *All Our Kin.* New York: Harper & Row.

Stinchcombe, Arthur L. 1987. *Constructing Social Theories.* Chicago: University of Chicago.

Sugrue, Thomas J. 2004. "Affirmative Action from Below: Civil Rights, the Building Trades, and the Politics of Racial Equality in the Urban North, 1945–1969." *Journal of American History* 91(1): 145–73.

Sum, Andrew M., Ishwar Khatiwada, Joseph McLaughlin, and Paulo Tobar. 2007. "The Educational Attainment of the Nation's Young Black Men and Their Recent Labor Market Experiences: What Can Be Done to Improve Their Future Labor Market and Educational Prospects?" Unpublished manuscript. Northeastern University, Boston. Available at: http://www.northeastern.edu/clms/wp-content/uploads/Ed_Attainment_of_Black_Males.pdf (accessed November 18, 2013).

Sum, Andrew M., Ishwar Khatiwada, Frimpomaa Ampaw, Paulo Tobar, and Sheila Palma. 2004. "Trends in Black Male Joblessness and Year-Round Idleness: An Employment Crisis Ignored." Boston, Mass.: Northeastern University, Center for Labor Market Studies.

Swartz, David. 1977. "Pierre Bourdieu: The Cultural Transmission of Social Inequality." *Harvard Educational Review* 47(4): 545–64.

Swartz, Teresa Toguchi. 2009. "Intergenerational Family Relations in Adulthood: Patterns, Variations, and Implications in the Contemporary United States." *Annual Review of Sociology* 35: 191–212.

Szanton, Peter L. 1986. *Baltimore 2000: A Choice of Futures.* Baltimore, Md.: Morris Goldseker Foundation.

Taylor, Ralph B. 1999. *Crime Changes in Baltimore, 1970–1994.* ICPSR 2352. Baltimore, Md.: Battelle/Survey Research Associates. Distributed by Inter-university Consortium for Political and Social Research, Ann Arbor, Mich. Available at: http://www.icpsr.umich.edu/icpsrweb/ICPSR/studies/2352 (accessed November 18, 2013).

———. 2001. *Breaking Away from Broken Windows: Baltimore Neighborhoods and the Nationwide Fight Against Crime, Grime, Fear, and Decline.* Boulder, Colo.: Westview Press.

Thibos, Megan, Danielle Lavin-Loucks, and Marcus Martin. May 2007. "The Feminization of Poverty." Dallas, Tx.: J. McDonald Williams Institute.

Tienda, Marta, and Haya Stier. 1991. "Joblessness and Shiftlessness: Labor Force Activity in Chicago's Inner City." In *The Urban Underclass,* edited by Christopher Jencks and Paul E. Peterson. Washington, D.C.: Brookings Institution Press.

———. 1996. "Generating Labor Market Inequality: Employment Opportunities and the Accumulation of Disadvantage." *Social Problems* 43(2): 147–65.

Timberlake, Jeffrey M. 2007. "Racial and Ethnic Inequality in the Duration of Children's Exposure to Neighborhood Poverty and Affluence." *Social Problems* 54(3): 319–42.

Tinto, Vincent. 1994. *Leaving College: Rethinking the Causes and Cures of Student Attrition.* Chicago: University of Chicago Press.

Toch, Thomas. 2010. "Small Is Still Beautiful: Breaking Up Big, Dysfunctional High Schools into Smaller Units Looked Like a Reform That Failed. Look Again." *Washington Monthly,* July/August. Available at: http://www.washington monthly.com/features/2010/1007.toch.html (accessed November 18, 2013).

Tomaskovic-Devey, Donald, Melvin Thomas, and Kecia Johnson. 2005. "Race and the Accumulation of Human Capital Across the Career." *American Journal of Sociology* 111(1): 58–89.

Turner, Margery Austin, Stephen L. Ross, George C. Galster, and John Yinger. 2002. "Discrimination in Metropolitan Housing Markets: National Results from Phase 1 of the Housing Discrimination Study." Washington: U.S. Department of Housing and Urban Development. Available at: http://www. huduser.org/publications/hsgfin/phase1.html (accessed February 12, 2003).

Tyson, Karolyn. 2011. *Integration Interrupted: Tracking, Black Students, and Acting White After Brown.* New York: Oxford University Press.

U.S. Bureau of the Census. 1983. *Census of Population: 1980,* vol. 1. *Characteristics of the Population.* Washington: U.S. Government Printing Office. Available at: http://www2.census.gov/prod2/decennial/documents/1980/1980census ofpopu8011u_bw.pdf (accessed November 18, 2013).

———. 1992. "Census of Population and Housing, 1990: 5% Public Use Microdata Samples." Washington: U.S. Government Printing Office. Available at: http://www.census.gov/main/www/pums.html (accessed November 18, 2013).

———. 2000. "Population Division, Special Tabulation STP #121, Baltimore Neighborhoods 2004." Washington: U.S. Government Printing Office. Available at: http://webapps.jhu.edu/census/2knhoods/2kaboutdata.html (accessed November 18, 2013).

U.S. Census Bureau. 2005. *2005 American Community Survey Data, Baltimore City*. Washington: U.S. Government Printing Office.

U.S. Department of Education. 2006. *The Educational Longitudinal Study of 2002 (ELS: 2002), Second Follow-up*. Washington: National Center for Education Statistics.

———. 2011. *Integrated Postsecondary Education Data System (IPEDS)*. Washington: National Center for Education Statistics.

U.S. Government Accountability Office. 2009. *Proprietary Schools: Stronger Department of Education Oversight Needed to Help Ensure Only Eligible Students Receive Federal Student Aid*. Technical report no. GAO-09–600. Washington: U.S. Government Printing Office. 40.

Ventura, Stephanie J., and Christine A. Bachrach. 2000. "Nonmarital Childbearing in the United States, 1940–99." *National Vital Statistics Reports* 48(6): 1–39. Hyattsville, Md.: Center for Disease Control and Prevention, National Center for Health Statistics. Available at: http://www.cdc.gov/nchs/data/nvsr/nvsr48/nvs48_16.pdf (accessed November 18, 2013).

Vermunt, Jeroen K., and Jay Magidson. 2004. "Latent Class Analysis." In *The Sage Encyclopedia of Social Sciences Research Methods*, edited by Michael S. Lewis-Beck, Alan E. Bryman, and Tim Futing Liao. Thousand Oaks, Calif.: Sage Publications.

Walters, Stephen J. K., and Louis Miserendino. 2008. "Baltimore's Flawed Renaissance: The Failure of Plan-Control-Subsidize Redevelopment." *Perspectives on Eminent Domain Abuse* no. 3. Arlington, Va.: Institute for Justice.

Warikoo, Natasha, and Prudence Carter. 2009. "Cultural Explanations for Racial and Ethnic Stratification in Academic Achievement: A Call for a New and Improved Theory." *Review of Educational Research* 79(1): 366–94.

Wellman, Jane V. 2008. "The Higher Education Funding Disconnect: Spending More, Getting Less." *Change: The Magazine of Higher Learning* 40(6): 18–25.

Western, Bruce. 2006. *Punishment and Inequality in America*. New York: Russell Sage Foundation.

Western, Bruce, and Becky Pettit. 2005. "Black-White Wage Inequality, Employment Rates, and Incarceration." *American Journal of Sociology* 111(2): 553–78.

White, Karl R. 1982. "The Relation Between Socioeconomic Status and Academic Achievement." *Psychological Bulletin* 91(3): 461–81.

Wickrama, Kandauda, and Diana L. Baltimore. 2010. "Adolescent Precocious Development and Young Adult Health Outcomes." *Advances in Life Course Research* 15(4): 121–31.

Willie, Charles V. 1978. "The Inclining Significance of Race." *Society* 15(5): 10–15.

Wilson, Franklin D., Marta Tienda, and Lawrence Wu. 1995. "Race and Un-employment: Labor Market Experiences of Black and White Men 1968–1988." *Work and Occupations* 22(3): 245–70.

Wilson, William Julius. 1978. *The Declining Significance of Race: Blacks and Changing American Institutions.* Chicago: University of Chicago Press.

———. 1987. *The Truly Disadvantaged: The Inner City, the Underclass, and Public Policy.* Chicago: University of Chicago Press.

———. 1997. *When Work Disappears: The World of the New Urban Poor.* New York: Alfred A. Knopf.

———. 2006. "Social Theory and the Concept 'Underclass.'" In *Poverty and Inequality,* edited by David Grusky and S. M. Ravi Kanbur. Stanford, Calif.: Stanford University Press.

———. 2008. "The Economic Plight of Inner-City Black Males." In *Against the Wall: Poor, Young, Black, and Male,* edited by Elijah Anderson. Philadelphia: University of Pennsylvania Press.

———. 2010. "Why Both Social Structure and Culture Matter in a Holistic Analysis of Inner-City Poverty." *The Annals of the American Academy of Political and Social Science* 629(1): 200–19.

Wilson, William Julius, and Robert Aponte. 1985. "Urban Poverty." *Annual Review of Sociology* 11: 231–58.

Wirt, John, Susan Choy, Patrick Rooney, Stephen Provasnik, Anindita Sen, and Richard Tobin. 2004. *The Condition of Education 2004. NCES* report no. 2004–077. Washington: U.S. Department of Education. Available at: http://nces.ed.gov/pubs2004/2004077.pdf (accessed November 18, 2013).

Woodhead, Martin. 1988. "When Psychology Informs Public Policy: The Case of Early Childhood Intervention." *American Psychologist* 43(6): 443–54.

Yamamoto, Yoko, and Susan D. Holloway. 2010. "Parental Expectations and Children's Academic Performance in Sociocultural Context." *Educational Psychology Review* 22(3): 189–214.

Zumbrum, Alvin J. T., ed. 1968. "Maryland Crime Report." No. 68-2, July. Baltimore, Md.: Maryland Crime Investigating Commission. Available at: http://archives.ubalt.edu/bsr/archival-resources/documents/maryland-crime-report.pdf (accessed November 18, 2013).

Index

Boldface numbers refer to figures and tables.

absentee fathers, 81
academic achievement. *See* school performance
accelerated role transitions, 75–76
Adelman, Clifford, 100, 102
adulthood, transition to. *See* transition to adulthood
African American men: blue-collar employment opportunities, 183–85; college degree completion, 103; earnings, **117, 159,** 160–61; employment, 92–94; employment history and marital-partnership status, **115**; incarceration, 94, 95, 164–65, 171; intergenerational mobility, 136, **137–41**; occupational status, **105,** 106, **117**; problem behaviors, **151**; schooling, **117**; unemployment, 171, 182
African Americans: in Baltimore City Public Schools, 29–30, **66,** 67; in Baltimore County Public Schools, 30; Baltimore neighborhoods, 42; Baltimore population, 28; earnings, 12, 24, **180**; employment history and marital-partnership status, **115**; female-headed households, 213n8; jobs after WWII, 23–24; marriage, 45, 77, 170–71; occupational status, **105,** 106, **117, 180**; out-of-wedlock childbearing, 13; poverty, 8–9, 39, 218n3; schooling, **117**; status attainment through school, xvii; teen childbearing, 45
African American women: earnings, 112–14, **117,** 118, 119, **159,** 160–61; employment history and marital-partnership status, **115**; intergenerational mobility, 125, 136, **137–41**; marriage, 170–71; occupational status, **105,** 106, **117**; problem behaviors, **151**; schooling, **117**
Alexander, Michelle, 221n7
American Apartheid (Massey and Denton), 30
American Community Survey, 109
American Dream, 14
Anderson, Elijah, 4
Annie E. Casey Foundation, 28
Aponte, Robert, 45–46
Appalachian migrants, 22–23
apprenticeships, 23–24
Armisted Gardens, Baltimore, 42
arrests, 6–7, 29, 84, 94–95, 152
Arroyo, Carmen, 220n21
assault, **57**
associate's degrees, 99–100, 127, 175, 179, **180**
attendance, school, **70,** 71
auto mechanics, 161
auto theft, **57**
Ayscue, Jennifer, 30

257

baby boomers, 21
bachelor's degree, 102–4, 127, 175, 179, **180**
Bailey, Martha, 180
Baker, David, 177–78
Baldwin, James, 62
Baltimore, Md., 21–31; demographic changes, 28; economic decline (1980s–present day), 1–2, 26–29; industrial boom years and bust, 21–26; intergenerational mobility, 122; neighborhood conditions, 29, 167–68; population, 28
Baltimore City Public Schools, 14, 29–31, 39–40, 65–67, 155–56
Baltimore County Public Schools, 30
banking, 168–69
Barnes, Sandra, 8–9
Beginning School Study Youth Panel (BSSYP, or Youth Panel): advantages of, 16–17; description of, xv, xvi, 14–15; interviews, 15–16; neighborhood data, 52; participants, 189–94; research design, 14, 32, 195–97; transition to adulthood data, 76–77
Bentley, Alison, 33
Bentley, Amy, 22
best practice reforms, schools, 73
Bethlehem Steel, 21–22, 25, 166–67
Bianchi, Suzanne, 216n10
birth, average age of first, 220n1
Black Picket Fences (Pattillo-McCoy), 4
blacks. *See* African Americans
Blank, Rebecca, 215n5
Blau, Peter, 126
blue-collar work and workers: African Americans, 106, 161; occupational inheritance from father to son, 123; occupations, 36; skilled trade positions, 23–24, 109–10, 166–67; social network advantage, 163, 166; status attainment, 19; white advantage, 183–85
Bobo, Lawrence, 114
Bonilla-Silva, Eduardo, 168
boomerang children, 82, 83–85

B&O railroad yards, white poverty in neighborhoods surrounding, 40
Boston, Mass., gang members in public housing project study, 214n23
Bourdieu, Pierre, 145
Bowles, Samuel, 150
Bradley, Robert, 34
Brint, Steven, 222n18
broken window theory, 51
Brooklyn, Baltimore, 41
Brooks-Gunn, Jeanne, 33, 147, 216n3
Bryk, Anthony, 71, 230–31n4
BSSYP (Beginning School Study Youth Panel). *See* Beginning School Study Youth Panel (BSSYP, or Youth Panel)
burglary, **57**

California Achievement Test (CAT), 69, 197, 207
car dealerships, racial discrimination by, 168
career academies, 182
Carnevale, Anthony, 101–2
census data, 4–6, 51–56, 104
certificate programs, 99–100, **180**
Charles, Kerwin, 171
Cherlin, Andrew, 43, 86
Cherry Hill, Baltimore, 42
Chetty, Raj, 121
Chicago, Ill.: *Black Picket Fences* setting, 4; employer stereotypes, 165; school reform (1990s), 71; Woodlawn project, xv–xvi
child care, 44, 64, 181
child development, 127
child poverty rate, 28
cities, intergenerational mobility differences, 121–22
Citizens Planning and Housing Association, 65
Clark, Burton, 222n18
class size, 179
clerical jobs, **105, 107, 108**
Code of the Street (Anderson), 4
cohabitation, 76–77, 114–16
Coleman, James, 37, 130, 166

Coleman report, 69, 147
college education: associate's degree
  programs, 99–100, 127, 175, 179,
  180; bachelor's degree programs,
  102–4, 127, 175, 179, **180**; Baltimore
  City Public School parents, 39;
  BSSYP participants, 96, 98–104;
  certificate programs, 99–100, **180**;
  community colleges, 99–102; completion rates, 96, 98–99, 102, 103–4;
  for-profit colleges, 222*n*17; and
  intergenerational mobility, 149–50,
  179–81; and motherhood, 86; and
  occupational status, **180**; part-time
  students, 96; policy considerations,
  181; tuition subsidies, 176; value of,
  213*n*10
college graduates: black-white
  employment gap, 12; earnings,
  12, 127, **180**; marriage, 223*n*28;
  unemployment, 127–28
*Coming Apart: The State of White
  America, 1960–2010* (Murray), 43
community attachment, 59, **60**
community colleges, 99–102
community disadvantage. *See* neighborhood disadvantage
community identity, 40–42
Complete College America, 223*n*21
construction, 23–24, 109–10, 162
Corwyn, Robert, 34
cosmetology, 100
cost per pupil, 30, **72, 73**
Council of Great City Schools, 31
craft jobs, **105, 107, 108,** 109–10, 162
crime: academic effects of children's
  exposure to, 52; in Baltimore neighborhoods, 56–58; broken window
  theory, 51; perceptions of, 59, **60**;
  and weak social cohesion, 51, 61
Crime Changes project, 58
criminal record, difficulties for those
  with, 94–95, 165, 169
Curtis Bay, Baltimore, 41

Danziger, Sheldon, 221*n*4
data collection, xix, 14, 32, 195–97

deindustrialization, 24–26, 109–10
Denton, Nancy, 30, 68
desegregation, 29–30
Dionne, E. J., 172
disorder, 89
Diverging Pathways (Kerckhoff),
  127–28
diversity, 89
Domino Sugar, 109
Done All path to adulthood, 79,
  80–81, 88–89, 152–53, 157
drugs and drug use: dealers, 84;
  marijuana, 94–95; racial dif-
  ferences, 84, 151–52; of West
  Baltimore residents, 3–4, 6–7, 10
Dubner, Stephen, 84
Duncan, Greg, 33, 216*n*3
Duncan, Otis, 126
Durr, Kenneth, 24
Dynarski, Susan, 180

early schooling, xv–xvi, 32–34
earnings: gender differences, 111–14,
  117, 158–61; intergenerational
  mobility, 150; marriage timing
  impact, 75; in mature adulthood,
  116–19; measurement of, 204–5;
  and occupational status, 106–10;
  racial differences, 12, 24, **117,**
  118, 158–61, **180**; and schooling,
  12, 127, **180**; of West Baltimore
  residents, 7, 10. *See also* income,
  household
Ebony magazine, 23–24
Economic Mobility Project, 125
Edin, Kathryn, 86, 215*n*23
education: aspirations for, 145–46,
  176–77; BSSYP participants, 91,
  93, 96–104; class size, 179; cost per
  pupil, 30, **72, 73;** funding, 73, 176;
  in Great Britain, 127–28; lifelong
  learning, 76; policy considerations,
  178–79; reforms, 71, 73; school
  attendance, **70,** 71; special education, 30, 73, 126, 219*n*18; student-
  teacher ratio, **72;** subsidized school
  breakfast and lunch programs, 37,

202; tracking, 126, 127–28, 207–8. *See also* college education
educational attainment. *See* schooling
Eggebean, David, 42
Elder, Glen, xv
elementary schools, 32–33, 39–40, 65–67, **129,** 147–48
employment: black-white gap, 12, 161, 165, 166; BSSYP participants, 91–94, 104–11; gender differences and issues, 37–38, 169–70; hiring process, 162–66, 169; intergenerational mobility, 149–50; manufacturing jobs, 22–24; and marital-partnership status, 114–16; SES differences, 36–40; teens, 181–82; transition to adulthood patterns, 80–88; of West Baltimore residents, 5–6, 7, 10
employment discrimination, 165, 169
Equality of Opportunity Project, 121
equal opportunity, 1
executive and managerial jobs, 104, **105, 107, 108,** 109, 111
expenditures per pupil, 30, **72,** 73
extended family, 44, 46–48, 60–61

Fair Employment Council, 169
family, socioeconomic standing defined around, 114, 119
family circumstances and resources: connections and support systems, 44, 46–48, 60–61, 161, 166–67; and intergenerational mobility, 121, 145–46, 153, 154, 177–78; and school performance, 32–34, 130–32, 166
family disadvantage, 32–49; across socioeconomic gradient, 36–38; during early elementary school years, 32–34; and extended family support, 44, 46–48; and household composition, 42–46; and neighborhoods, 50–64; racial differences, 39; and school disadvantage, 64–73, 177–78; white Baltimore City Public School students, 39–42

family instability, 43–44, 46–48, 172
family size, 46
family structure, 42–46, 130
Fayetteville, N.C., intergenerational mobility, 122
female-headed households. *See* single-parent families
financial aid, 181
first grade transition, xvi, 147–48
for-profit colleges, 222*n*17
Franke-Ruta, Garance, 158
Franklin Square (FS), 4–9
Freakonomics (Levitt and Dubner), 84
funding, school, 73, 176
Furstenberg, Frank, 130

Garfinkel, Irwin, 230*n*10
GED, 98, **180**
gender differences and issues: earnings, 111, **117,** 158–61; employment, 37–38, 169–70; intergenerational mobility, 154–55; occupational status, 104–6, **117;** parenting, 170–71; schooling, 106, **117**
Giguere, Andrew, 63
Gintis, Herbert, 150
Goldin, Claudia, 214*n*11
grade retention, 33, 69, 126, 175
graduate students, 37
grandparents, 44, 47–48
Granovetter, Mark, 162
Great Britain, educational tracking study, 127–28
Great Depression, xv
Groves, Melissa, 150

Hampden, Baltimore, 41
happiness, 173
Harlem Park, Baltimore, 62
Haskins, Ron, 45, 114
health care, 44
Heckman, James, 33, 216*n*2
higher education. *See* college education
high school dropouts: Baltimore City Public School parents, 39; Baltimore statistics, 29; black-white

employment gap, 12, 165, 166; BSSYP participants, 98; earnings, 12, 127, **180**; labor force participation of women, 38; motherhood, 86; occupational status, **180**; unemployment, 127

high school graduates: black-white employment gap, 12; BSSYP participants, 98; earnings, 127, **180**; occupational status, **180**; unemployment, 127

high school guidance counselors, 183–84

high schools, 40, 73, **129**, 148

hiring process, 162–66, 169

Hispanics: earnings of high school dropouts, 12; out-of-wedlock childbearing, 13

Hoffer, Thomas, 37, 130, 166

Holzer, Harry, 100

homicides, 52, **57**, 58, 173

household composition, 42–46, 130

household income. *See* income, household

housing discrimination, 168–69

housing vouchers, 52

human capital investments, 91–96

Huston, Aletha, 33

hypersegregation, 30, 40, 65, 67

idleness, 92, 94, 182

incarceration, 94, 95, 152, 164–65, 171

income, household: of Baltimore City Public School students, 65–68; of Baltimore residents, 28; median neighborhood and percentage of African American residents, 51; single-parent households, 112–14; of West Baltimore residents, 6. *See also* earnings

industrialization, 21–24

integration, school, 179

intergenerational mobility, 121–56; and college education, 149–50, 179–81; conclusions, 154; and employment, 149–50; family circumstances and resources impact-

ing, 121, 145–46, 154, 177–78; framework for, 122–29; gender differences, 154–55; and marriage, 170; methodology, 210–12; neighborhood effects, 132–33, 146–47, 154; pathways, 136–42; and place, 121–22; racial differences, 136, **137–41,** 154–55; and schooling, 126–33, 146–49, 154, 175–79; through out-migration, 155–56; and transition to adulthood, 133–35, 149–53, 154; in U.S. vs. other countries, 121

International Brotherhood of Electrical Workers, 166

Isaacs, Julia, 114

Jessor, Richard, 135

job loss. *See* unemployment and job loss

jobs. *See* employment

job searches, 94, 161–66, 169

Kandel Depression Scale, 226n8

Karabel, Jerome, 222n18

Kasinitz, Philip, 165, 166

Katz, Lawrence, 214n11

Kefalas, Timothy, 86

Kellam, Sheppard, xv–xvi

Kerckhoff, Alan, 127–28, 148

Kiehl, Stephen, 219n15

kin relationships, 44, 46–48, 60–61

Kirschenman, Joleen, 165

Kluegel, James, 114

laborers, **105, 107, 108,** 109, 110

labor force participation, 37–38, 95. *See also* employment

labor unions, 80–83, 166

language skills, 131

larceny, **57**

Lareau, Annette, 130

Lenski, Gerhard, 214n22

Levenson, Bernard, 24, 161

Leventhal, Tama, 147

Levitt, Steven, 84

Lichter, Daniel, 42

life-course approach, 127–35, 142–53, 173–88
life satisfaction, 173–75
Little Italy, Baltimore, 167
living without parents, 80–83, 85–88
Logan, John, 146
low birth rate, 28
low-wage work, 2, 25–26, 169–70, 221n2
Luoh, Ming Ching, 171

MacLeod, Jay, 214n23
Magnet, Myron, 3
manufacturing, 2, 21–28
marijuana, 94–95
marriage: by age twenty-eight, 76–77; average age of first, 220n1; college-educated women, 75; policies promoting, 184; racial differences in rates of, 45, 77, 170–71, 172; same-sex couples, 172; of similar individuals, 110–11; and socio-economic status, 114–16
Massey, Douglas, 30, 68
maternal employment, 37–38
math, 69, **70**
Mature Adult Survey (MAS), 16, 17, 91, 110, 197–200
Mazumder, Bhashkar, 150
McDill, Mary, 24, 161
medical assistants, 100
Memphis, Tenn., intergenerational mobility, 122
men: earnings, 111, **117,** 158–61; employment, 37–38, 169–70; inter-generational mobility, 154–55; occupational status, 104–6, **117;** parenting, 170–71; schooling, 106, **117.** *See also* African American men; white men
mentoring, 182
middle school, 40, 128, **129,** 148
migrant workers, 22–23
Mikulski, Barbara, 219n13
Milkie, Melissa, 216n10
Mincy, Ronald, 230n10
mobility, residential, 68

mobility, social. *See* intergenerational mobility
mobility table analysis, 123–25
moms: employment, 37–38; median age of, 220–21n1; school enrich-ment activities, 216n10. *See also* single-parent families
Montgomery County Public Schools, 30
Morrell Park, Baltimore, 41–42
multiple-partner fertility, 230n10
Murray, Charles, 43

National Child Development Study, 226n5
National Children's Bureau of London, 226n5
Neckerman, Kathryn, 165
neighborhood disadvantage, 50–64; child development effects, 33–34, 51–52; crime rates, 51, 52, 56–58; data sources, 52; and intergenera-tional mobility, 132–33, 146–47, 154; neighborhood conditions using census data, 50–56; neighbor-hood quality perceptions using surveys, 58–64; racial differences, 51, 53–54, 167–68
neighborhoods: of Baltimore, 40–42, 53; social cohesion in, **60,** 61–64, 171
networks. *See* social capital
New York Times Opinionator, 121
nonmarital childbearing. *See* out-of-wedlock childbearing

occupational inheritance, 110–11, 123
occupational status: and earnings, 106–10; family influences, 110–11, 123; gender differences, 104–6, 118; measurement of, 204; of parents, **35,** 36–37; racial differences, 118; by schooling, **180;** by socioeconomic status, 104, **105,** 116–19
occupational type, 104–11, 204
Olson, Karen, 166–68
Olson, Sherry, 26, 40
operator jobs, **105, 107, 108,** 109, 110

out-migration, 155–56
out-of-wedlock childbearing:
growth of, 13, 170; low-SES
women, 85–88; and poverty,
42–43; racial differences in, 13,
45; teens, 45, 75–76, 152. *See also*
single-parent families

Pager, Devah, 169
Paquin School, 217*n*19
parent attitudes, 208
parenting, 61, 170–71. *See also* family
circumstances and resources
Pattillo-McCoy, Mary, 4
Pearce, Diane, 13
Penrose–Fayette Street Outreach
(PF), 4–6
personal resources, **129,** 208–10
Pettit, Becky, 221*n*7
Pew Charitable Trusts, 95
Philadelphia, Pa.: *Code of the Street*
setting, 4; residential mobility, 68
Phillips, Meredith, 131
playgrounds, 3
population statistics, 28
postsecondary education. *See* college
education
poverty: in Baltimore, 2, 14–15, 146;
of children, 28; feminization of,
13, 112; neighborhood differences,
54, 55–56; policy considerations,
45; racial differences, 8–9, 39; of
single-parent families, 13, 42, 86;
trends, 216*n*11; of West Baltimore
residents, 6, 8–9
preschools, 64, 176, 178, 179
prestige, 106–11
principals, **72**
probability sampling, 14, 32
problem behaviors, 135, 150–53, 183
professionals: earnings, **108,** 109, 111;
marriage, 111; occupational status,
108, 110; occupations, **107;** schooling, **108;** socioeconomic background, 104, **105;** women, 106
property crimes, **57**
protective jobs, **105, 107, 108**

public schools, 29–31, 216–17*n*12
Putnam, Robert, 158

quality of life, 59, **60**

racial conflict, 11
racial differences and issues:
Baltimore City Public School
students, 65–68; blue-collar
employment opportunities, 183–85;
earnings, **117,** 118, 158–61; family disadvantage, 39; industrial
and construction employment,
110; intergenerational mobility,
136, **137–41,** 154–55; job searches,
161–66, 169; labor force participation, 95; marriage, 45, 77, 170–71,
172; neighborhood conditions, 51,
53–54, 167–68; occupational status, **117,** 118; poverty, 8–9, 39; and
school disadvantage, 65–68; schooling, **117;** single-parent families,
213*n*8; socioeconomic profiles, 39;
well-being measures, 8–10
racial discrimination, 168–69
racial identity, 8
racism, 168–69
rape, **57,** 58
Ratner, David, 221*n*4
reading, 69, **70,** 71
Reardon, Sean, 176
remedial courses, 101
resilience, 13–14
retail, 28
Rindfuss, Ronald, 77, 89
riots, 63
robbery, **57**
Robinson, John, 216*n*10
Rosenbaum, James, 100–101, 102
Rosenberg, Jan, 165, 166
Royster, Deirdre, 161, 214–15*n*23,
215*n*3, 230*n*7
Rudacille, Deborah, 166

sales jobs, **105, 107, 108,** 163
Salt Lake City, Utah, intergenerational mobility, 122

same-sex marriage, 172
sampling, 14, 32, 212
Sampson, Robert, 51
Sawhill, Isabel, 45, 114
school-based interventions, 33
school choice, 220*n*22
school disadvantage, 64–73; in academic achievement, 68–71; data sources, 64–65; and racial and socioeconomic composition, 65–68; in school resources, 71–73
school enrichment activities, 130–31, 177–78
schooling: aspirations for, 145–46, 176–77; BSSYP participants, **93**, 96–104; earnings by, **180**; gender differences, 106, **117**; and intergenerational mobility, 126–33, 146–49, 154, 175–79; marriage partners' similarity, 110–11; in mature adulthood, 116–19; measurement of, 203–4; occupational status by, **180**; racial differences, **117**; resources in support of children's, 206–7; of West Baltimore residents, 5, 7, 10
school performance: of Baltimore City Public School students, 69–71; of children from single-parent families, 43; family circumstances and resources impacting, 32–34, 130–32, 166; measurement of, 207; neighborhood effects, 132–33, 146–47
"School Profiles: School Year 1987–1988" (Baltimore City Public Schools), 65
school quality, 73, 122, 147
Scranton, Pa., intergenerational mobility, 122
segregation: residential, 4, 23, 31, 51, 146, 167, 179; schools, 29–30, 67–68, 146
service jobs, **105, 107, 108,** 110, 111
Sewell, William, xvi
Sharkey, Patrick, 52
Silver, Christopher, 40
single-parent families: earnings, 112–14, 118; growth of, 42–43, 170;

low-SES women, 85–88; neighborhood differences, 55; number of children living in, 28; poverty of, 13, 42, 86; racial differences, 213*n*8; residential moving frequency, 61; social problems associated with, 43–45
skilled trade, 23–24, 109–10, 166–67
Smeeding, Timothy, 230*n*10
Smith, Ryan, 114
social capital: job searches, 24, 161–67, 183–84, 185; loss of in poor black communities, 64; schooling, 130–32, 145–46, 185
social class, 11
social cohesion, **60**, 61–64, 171
social mobility. *See* intergenerational mobility
social safety net, 184–85
Social Security Administration, 24, 150
social status, 106–11
socioeconomic destinations, 91–120; earnings, 111–14; employment, 104–11; human capital investments, 91–96; intergenerational mobility, 121–56; life-course perspective, 173–88; in mature adulthood, 114–19; measurement of, 203–6; schooling undertaken and completed, 96–104; and white privilege, 157–72
Socioeconomic Index (SEI), 36–37
socioeconomic origins: of Baltimore City Public School families, 39–42, 65–68; family disadvantage, 32–49; measurement of, 34–36, 200–203; neighborhood disadvantage, 50–64; school disadvantage, 64–73
Sparrows Point, Bethlehem Steel plant, 21–22, 25
special education, 30, 73, 126, 219*n*18
special programs, school, 71, **72**
spouse-partner earnings, **108, 117,** 118, 119, 205
spouse-partner education, **108, 117,** 205

spouse-partner occupation, **108, 117,** 205

staffing, school, 71–73

standardized testing, 33, 69–71

standards, academic, 179

status attainment framework, to intergenerational mobility, 126–28, 136, 142–53

Steir, Haya, 221*n*5

stereotypes, 94, 112–14, 165

Stevenson, David, 177–78

Stiglitz, Joseph, 1, 121

stressful life events, 131–32

Strohl, Jeff, 101–2

student-teacher ratio, **72**

subsided school meals, 37, 202

suburbs, white flight to, 29–30

success, 7–8, 173

Sum, Andrew, 46

Take This School and Love It: A Reference Manual on the Baltimore City Elementary Schools (Citizens Planning and Housing Association), 65

taxi drivers, racial discrimination by, 168

Taylor, Ralph, 215*n*6

teachers, 179

technical jobs, **105, 107, 108,** 111

teens: jobs, 181–82; pregnancy, 45, 75–76, 152

The Corner: A Year in the Life of an Inner-City Neighborhood (Simon and Burns), 3–12

Tienda, Marta, 221*n*5

Timberlake, Jeffrey, 218*n*3

tracking, educational, 126, 127–28, 207–8

transition to adulthood, 75–90; diversity vs. disorder in, 89–90; and intergenerational mobility, 133–35, 149–53, 179–83; milestones, 76–77, **78**; patterns, 77–88; role transitions during, 75–76; and socioeconomic attainment, 88–89

transport jobs, **105, 107, 108**

two-income households: economic benefits, 37–38, 112, 114, 118, 170; racial differences, 160, 172

two-parent households, **35,** 43, 46

underclass, 3

unemployment and job loss: in Baltimore, 28; in Great Britain vs. U.S., 127–28; in low-SES neighborhoods, 54; racial differences, 92, 94, 171

unions, 80–83, 166

universal health care, 44

unmarried childbearing. *See* out-of-wedlock childbearing

urban disadvantaged, definition of, 2–12. *See also specific index headings*

urban renewal, 62

U.S. Census Bureau, 4–6, 51–56, 104

U.S. Department of Housing and Urban Development, 168

violent crime, **57,** 58

vocational training, 99–100, 161

wages. *See* earnings

Wall Street Journal, 43

wealth per pupil, 30–31

well-being, measurement of, xv

well-being–family conditions relationship, introduction to, 1–14

West Baltimore, 2, 3–12

Western, Bruce, 221*n*7

White, Karl, 130

white flight, 29–30

white men: earnings, **117,** 158–61; employment, 92; employment history and marital-partnership status, **115;** incarceration, 94; intergenerational mobility, 136, **137–41;** occupational status, **105,** 106, **117;** problem behaviors, **151;** schooling, **117**

white privilege, 157–72; earnings, 158–62; introduction, 157–58; neighborhoods, 167–68; and racism, 168–69; social capital, 162–67; of women, 169–72

whites: in Baltimore City Public Schools, 39–42, **66,** 67; Baltimore population, 28; earnings, 12, 24, **180;** employment history and marital-partnership status, **115;** female-headed households, 213n8; migrant workers after WWII, 22–23; occupational status, **105,** 106, **117, 180;** out-of-wedlock childbearing, 43; poverty, 8–9, 39; schooling, **117;** status attainment through school, xvii; teen childbearing, 45

white women: earnings, 112–14, **117,** 118, 119, **159;** employment history and marital-partnership status, **115;** intergenerational mobility, 136, **137–41;** occupational status, **117;** occupations, **105,** 106; problem behaviors, **151;** schooling, 106, **117**

Wilson, William Julius, 3, 38, 45–46, 50–51, 63, 158, 171

women: college degree completion, 103; earnings, 111–14, **117,** 118, 119, 158–61, **159;** employment, 37–38, 169–70; intergenerational mobility, 125, 154–55; occupational status, 104–6, **117;** parenting, 170–71; priorities across social class, 86–88; school enrollment, 92; schooling, 106, **117.** *See also* African American women; white women

work. *See* employment

Young Adult Survey (YAS), 16, 197–200

Youth Panel. *See* Beginning School Study Youth Panel (BSSYP, or Youth Panel)